pg 13-19
94-99

A History of the H

A History of the Holocaust
From Ideology to Annihilation

Fourth Edition

Rita Steinhardt Botwinick
Florida Atlantic University

Prentice Hall
Boston Columbus Indianapolis New York San Francisco
Upper Saddle River Amsterdam Cape Town Dubai London Madrid
Milan Munich Paris Montreal Toronto Delhi Mexico City
Sao Paulo Sydney Hong Kong Seoul Singapore Taipei Tokyo

Vice President, Editorial Director, Liberal Arts: Leah Jewell
Executive Editor: Charles Cavaliere
Editorial Project Manager: Rob DeGeorge
Editorial Assistant: Lauren Aylward
Director of Marketing: Brandy Dawson
Director of Assistant: Ashley Fallon
Project Manager: Renata Butera
Creative Art Director: Jayne Conte
Cover Designer: Margaret Kenselaar
Manager, Visual Research: Beth Brenzel
Manager, Rights and Permissions: Zina Arabia
Image Permission Coordinator: Debbie Hewitson
Manager, Cover Visual Research & Permissions: Karen Sanatar
Cover Art: Candle: Dorling Kindersley Media Library; Newspaper montage: Courtesy Leonard Botwinick
Full-Service Project Management: Shiny Rajesh, Integra Software Services, Ltd.
Composition: Integra Software Services, Ltd.
Printer/Binder: R.R. Donnelley/Harrisonburg
Cover Printer: R.R. Donnelley/Harrisonburg
Text Font: 10/12 Times

Credits and acknowledgments borrowed from other sources and reproduced, with permission, in this textbook appear on appropriate page within the text.

Library of Congress Cataloging-in-Publication Data

Botwinick, Rita S.
A history of the Holocaust/Rita Steinhardt Botwinick.—4th ed.
p. cm.
Includes bibliographical references and index.
ISBN-13: 978-0-205-65414-7 (alk. paper)
ISBN-10: 0-205-65414-2 (alk. paper)
1. Holocaust, Jewish (1939–1945) I. Title.
D804.3.B68 2010
940.53'18—dc22

2009019286

10 9 8 7 6 5 4 3 2 1

Prentice Hall
is an imprint of

PEARSON

www.pearsonhighered.com

ISBN 10: 0-205-65414-2
ISBN 13: 978-0-205-65414-7

In loving memory of my brothers:
Walter who was Wally in England,
Josef who was Jup in Holland, and
Siegfried who was Freddy in the USA.

Contents

Preface

This fourth edition of *A History of the Holocaust* is offered in response to the continuing need to understand the Nazi genocide of European Jewry. The question of how it was possible to translate ideology into annihilation in modern Germany, a nation much admired for its cultural and technological achievements, has confounded every generation since 1945. The Holocaust itself is an event of historic magnitude, but beyond that, it remains a prime example of the speed and extent with which a civil society can return to barbarism. Clearly, the lesson of the ashes around Auschwitz has not been learned as pictures of mass graves of innocents appear on our television screens with appalling regularity. Evil men continue to commit evil deeds, while the majority of people remain silent. Only when each bystander recognizes that his inaction makes him an accomplice can we hope to end the cycle of mass killings. So the work of teaching and learning must continue.

Generally, revisions of a text are prompted by new research, by the critiques of valued experts in the field of study, by the need to correct mistakes and, certainly, by suggestions from students using this book. The second edition of the *History* added material on the fate of the survivors of Nazi concentration and slave labor camps as well as information on Jews who survived by hiding or being hidden by Gentiles. The third edition reported on the relationship between the contemporary German governments and the increasing number of Jews living in Germany as well as on Israeli–German ties. With the fourth edition, the narrative has been enhanced, some chapters condensed, others updated, and errors corrected. It should be noted that instead of the previous 10 chapters, the fourth edition has 12 chapters. The erstwhile Chapter 10, titled "Resistance and Rescue," has been divided into two chapters (Chapters 10 and 11) for better organization. The Epilogue and Postscript have been merged for the same reason and now constitute the last chapter of the text (Chapter 12). Lastly, we introduce a new feature: VOICES. They are the recollections of people willing to share their experiences with the author and with you, the reader. These help put a human face on the history of the Holocaust. Their testimonies, written by them, have not been previously published. It was necessary to edit some of their descriptions, but each contributor has approved the version printed in the text.

It bears repeating that this book does not claim to be a record of Nazi inhumanity to man; it does not include the important history of the five million non-Jewish civilians murdered during Hitler's regime. Some among them sacrificed their lives by aiding Jews, other were killed to implement Hitler and Himmler's plans of a new Aryan world, and many died simply because they were in the wrong place at the wrong time. They too must be remembered and mourned as victims of the Nazi Holocaust.

A textbook is never complete; as long as it is in print, it remains a work in progress, and new editions reflect the need for modification. This author is particularly indebted to Maarten Pereboom of Salisbury University and to others for reviewing the third edition of the book and offering helpful suggestions and criticisms. Many of their recommendations are incorporated into this revision. I also wish to extend my gratitude to the publisher, Pearson Prentice Hall, and specifically to Charles Cavaliere, executive editor, and to Rob DeGeorge, project manager, whose patience and guidance were invaluable.

Introduction

Education remains our best defense against repetitions of the Shoah, the Holocaust. Only when the role of the uninvolved bystander is discredited, when "I did nothing" and "I minded my own business" become unacceptable alibis, and no rationalization is allowed to justify genocide, only then will teaching the History of the Holocaust become nonessential. To bring about such profound changes in attitudes continues to call for patience and commitment. At the end of World War II, pictures of liberated concentration camps horrified hundreds of millions of people, and it seemed reasonable to expect that the very magnitude of the disaster would make further genocides unthinkable. But events throughout the world have frustrated that hope. Governments continue to initiate mass murder of the innocents, and so the lessons must be repeated again and again until they are learned.

The Holocaust was more than a Jewish tragedy. It was a human disaster of unprecedented proportion in the modern world. It represents a turning point that reversed the flow of Western humanism. The ideal of Western Enlightenment to seek the greatest good for the greatest number was abandoned by a nation much admired for its culture. The use of modern technology and organizational skills enabled relatively few men to destroy millions of lives, not in combat, not in the heat of battle, but in deliberate, cold-blooded carnage. The Shoah was much more than the prime example of man's inhumanity to man—it overturned some of the foundations of civilized society. The ancient Greeks had taught us concepts of man as a rational being who is capable of improvement; the Old Testament admonished the Hebrews to act justly and love mercy; Christ's ministry granted special love to the weak and the poor; and Western law was founded to protect citizens and their possessions. All these principles were turned on their head by the Nazi government of Germany. When the SS men defended their acts by claiming "we only followed orders," they were quite correct; the atrocities they committed had indeed been ordered by a government whose legitimacy was never in doubt.

The terrible waste of life and property during World War I had raised the question whether man was a rational being. In the wake of the Holocaust, such doubts intensified, and much of the optimism of the nineteenth century was swept away. The earlier promise that the future would be based on reason and progress was overthrown by the Nazi *Weltanschauung* of might makes right. Even the notion of enlightened self-interest was challenged when the Nazis enacted policies that hastened Germany's self-destruction. A case in point: Millions of Jews were killed, although they were desperately needed to work in fields and factories and as highly skilled professionals.

The Shoah raised profound problems for religious communities. The oft-repeated article of faith that his ways are mysterious and unknowable rings hollow in the presence of Auschwitz. It is not within the scope of this book to examine the theological dilemma of faith in the presence of death camps, but it is proper to consider the actions of religious institutions. Churches, supposedly committed to bring the teachings of Christ into the lives of their members, failed to meet the Nazis' challenge. Even after the disclosure of the death camps, the major denominations carried on their "business as usual." Few ministers and priests anywhere in the Christian world preached sermons on the evils of the Holocaust. The most common response to the question, "Am I my brother's keeper?" was silence.

The Holocaust stands as a tragedy exemplifying both uniqueness and universality. The annals of history are replete with massacres and even genocides, yet the Holocaust is singular in its utter senselessness. When governments have waged war against their own citizens, they did so in order to achieve some desired political or economic end. The destruction of the Jews, however, was itself the sought-after end. The factories of death did not promote national or religious unity nor did they enrich the state or advance its borders. This genocide did not promote public security or the economy. Instead, the Holocaust deprived Germany of hands and minds desperately needed in the conduct of the war. The justification offered by the Nazis, that the elimination of Jews from Germany would result in the desirable Aryan racial purity for the master race, is utterly without scientific foundation. As a matter of fact, the vast majority of the victims never lived in Germany. We cannot know how many of the killers actually believed the myth of German Aryan superiority, but we do know that every German schoolchild was taught the *Voelkerwanderung,* the centuries-long trek of tribes such as Goths, Vandals, and Huns across the center of Europe. The preservation of ethnic purity on the crossroads of such vast population movements is clearly illusory.

The scale of Holocaust killings within the brief period of four years is another unique aspect of the Holocaust. Concentration camp commanders reported with pride to their superiors that they fulfilled or exceeded their death quotas. The chilling cruelty and efficiency of the mass murders have often been characterized as a return to savagery. But the man in the SS uniform who wanted to impress his chief, Heinrich Himmler, with his effectiveness was not a savage; he was an official of an established, legal authority. He did not run amok with a knife between his teeth; he sat in his office and issued orders. He may, or may not, have felt any emotion concerning his task. Certainly, he did not view himself as a criminal. The murders committed within his sight and hearing were carried out by complex procedures involving many government agencies, requiring the cooperation of important representatives from German industry and technology, and with the acquiescence of a considerable number of Germans. The postwar claims of nearly the entire German population that they never supported the Nazi regime is self-serving. In 1945, the American occupation authority ordered the German population in their zone to fill out long questionnaires about their past affiliations. The effort served no practical purpose; only those who held official positions were unable to deny their Nazi past; the rest judged themselves blameless of any wrongdoing.

The number of civilians murdered by the Nazis—six million Jews and five million Gentiles—staggers the imagination. The human mind cannot envision so many corpses. The unlimited power of a twentieth-century dictatorship was unleashed to expedite the killings. Considerable organizational skill was required to keep the flow of victims coming into the killing centers, and the expertise of engineers and scientists was required to execute them. Disposing of so many thousands of bodies every day was a task that caused some camp commanders moments of despair. Medical and legal professionals, among the most highly educated segment of German society, were accessories in the Shoah. They perverted their sworn duty to uphold justice and heal the sick by participating in the destruction of innocent men, women, and children.

From the Nazi point of view, the annihilation of the Jews was a success. Indeed, a few hundred thousand Jews remained alive in the lands they controlled, but they would have been disposed of easily if Hitler had won the war. Such a victory would have created a *Judenrein* (cleansed of Jews) Europe. When Allied armies closed in on Berlin, when the great cities of the Reich lay in rubble, and the German people endured the suffering of total defeat, Hitler consoled himself that at least he had won his struggle against the Jews. That was the essence of his last will and testament.

Great historical events are generally subject to divergent points of view. Few issues are clear-cut; differences of interpretation are elucidated, defended, and attacked. But one cannot be pro- or anti-Holocaust. There is no justification, no defense, and no rejoinder. There is only sorrow and guilt. Except for a small lunatic fringe that refuses to deal with facts, the world acknowledges that the Holocaust happened and that it stands as a landmark of man's faculty for evil. The amount of evidence is staggering. This would be true even if only German sources were available to historians. The most extensive depository of Holocaust documents is open for inspection in Berlin. The intent and execution of the "Final Solution of the Jewish question" simply cannot be disputed. German governments since the fall of the Third Reich have acknowledged the culpability of their predecessors and have attempted to indemnify Holocaust survivors for their suffering.

Although there can be no question concerning the reality of the Holocaust, a number of specific issues have given rise to conflicting points of view. Several of these questions are treated in this text. The author offers few conclusions, but it is hoped that differing assessments will stimulate discussion and research. Among the controversial topics are the following:

1. Was the Holocaust the inevitable final step of centuries of anti-Semitism, basically a pogrom of unprecedented magnitude, or was Hitler's persecution a distinctly different assault?
2. The Intentionalists and the Functionalists debate whether the destruction of the Jews had been Hitler's plan from the inception of his ideology or whether the death camps evolved from events originally not foreseen by the Nazis.

3. Did the victims go to their deaths like the proverbial sheep to the slaughter or was there significant Jewish resistance to the implementation of the Final Solution?
4. Under the Nazi regime, was Germany a goose-stepping, Hitler-hailing monolith of obedience, or was this a government riddled with rivalries and ineptitude?
5. Why did Hitler hate Jews?
6. What and when did the world learn of the Holocaust? Could earlier intervention have lessened the magnitude of the disaster?
7. How should the performance of the *Judenraete* (councils of Jewish elders in the ghettos) be evaluated? Did their work as administrators of the day-by-day administration of the ghettos help or hinder the SS in the commission of their assignments?
8. Why did some individuals, usually designated as the Righteous Gentiles, remain true to their ethical standards? What inner forces compelled them to risk their own lives to save others?

This book is a history text. It is a narrative that delineates what happened, where, how, when, to whom, and by whom. Holocaust study is humbling; so many of the moral and philosophical questions remain unanswered. We are reminded that civilization is but a thin veneer, that political apathy is very dangerous, and that prejudice is a cancer that can infect and destroy an entire national body. The Third Reich teaches us that the power of persuasion and personal charisma are no substitute for character, that there are no quick fixes for serious problems, and finally, perhaps most importantly, that to stand aloof while others are oppressed is to participate in the commission of that crime.

CHAPTER 1

The Nature and Roots of Prejudice

Most of us can recall a situation where we felt the sting of prejudice. Perhaps the job interview had gone well until you revealed something of your family background, your political affiliation, or your religious beliefs. Suddenly the opportunity for employment vanished. Do you recall a promising social encounter that never developed because the potential friend harbored some long-standing bias against your ethnicity? Was it not painful to be prejudged by someone who did not know you? You may believe that such a minor incident has no relationship to the events of the Holocaust. But you would be wrong. Just think back on a time when *you* were the person who demeaned another because of your bias. Did you find that moment of superiority pleasant? Now imagine that your government applauds, even rewards such behavior. In addition, the authorities that you have been taught to respect tell you over and over that all your problems are caused by "them" and that no failure is yours—"they" are responsible. Could you resist the pressure to believe such soothing lies? The best answer to that question is, "I don't know."

The Shoah was the poisoned fruit of centuries of prejudice. It was possible because hatred for Jews was translated from attitude, to language, to murder. An estimated two-thirds of the nine million Jews living in Europe in the first half of the twentieth century were killed by the Nazi regime in Germany. The exact number of victims will never be known, but, among others, the renowned scholar Martin Gilbert, in his *Macmillan Atlas of the Holocaust* (Macmillan, 1982, p. 244), estimated that Polish Jewry suffered losses of three million, the Soviet Union one million and the Balkan countries and Austria account for well over one and a half million deaths. When Germany, the Benelux nations, France, and the Baltic States are added, a total of over six million is reached. These figures are not of deaths resulting from military action but represent mass killing of civilians carried out at the direction of a legally constituted German government. Hitler had achieved power lawfully, and his party platform had clearly expressed hatred for the Jewish people. It was, however, beyond the imagination of ordinary people that an Auschwitz lay at the end of Hitler's dictatorship.

SOME DYNAMICS OF PREJUDICE

Prejudice may be defined as a stereotyped negative attitude toward a person or group, an attitude that is unrelated to any factual information. Sociologists and psychologists agree that it is a learned reaction, not an instinct. Most often it is acquired at such a young age that the adult cannot recall its onset. Dislike, even hatred, of a particular group generally predates school age. Thus, prejudice is instilled even before the child is capable of independent reasoning. The human capacity to make critical judgments usually begins at age eight. Younger children accept without question the values and mores of those in authority, usually their mothers and fathers. It is not necessary for parents to verbalize their own intolerance; children will absorb their judgments indirectly. Obviously, parental praise for conforming to acceptable attitudes or punishment for opposing them will reinforce prejudice, but the tone of voice or the dismissing gesture of the hand has a language that children understand.

The bias instilled during early childhood is difficult to change even in the face of contrary information. We tend to cling to our early constructs even when they are harmful to others and ourselves. To deny what mother taught you seems disloyal to her or her memory. It is not true that prejudices result from a disagreeable or frightening personal experience, although such an experience may confirm an existing negative disposition. If all unpleasant encounters were to create prejudice, surely each of us would be ill-disposed toward everyone else.

PERSONALITY AND PREJUDICE

The environment is not the only determining factor in the formation of a prejudiced person. Individual personality differences play an important role in the willingness to accept or reject the social inheritance of one's culture. It is quite possible for siblings reared in the same environment to exhibit widely differing attitudes. The question that arises is this: What factors or influences shape personality? Researchers are placing ever-greater emphasis on genetic predisposition. A growing number of characteristics, formerly ascribed to environmental factors, may well be of genetic origin. To the student interested in the causes of prejudice, the development of authoritarian personalities is particularly important. Such individuals exhibit a strong need to conform to conventional values. Their thinking is marked by inflexibility, and they are often preoccupied with concerns regarding status. Authoritarian personalities tend to be obedient to a fault and admire those who appear strong and powerful. The connection between the men who implemented the Holocaust and their claim that they were only carrying out orders seems clear. Blind obedience and the authoritarian personality appear to be threads from the same fabric. Such rigid individuals rank the need for law and order as a prime priority. The theory has been advanced that such personalities harbor secret or overt frustration, anger, and jealousy against the powerful. These emotions may become evident by acts of brutality against the powerless. Ethnic minorities have always served as a convenient target for antagonism. When prejudice is elevated to patriotism, to doing one's duty for the Fatherland, such behavioral excesses are not only possible, they are probable.

Bigots look for the company of other bigots. They are followers rather than leaders and seek the approval of their peers. Fellow bigots, expressing similar views, will legitimize their prejudices; in fact, when intolerance takes on the aura of communal acceptance, it provides comfort and cohesion to the group. Thus, it is possible to speak of institutionalized prejudice, that is, hostility by consensus: "Everybody hates . . . ." The bond of hatred is as strong as the bond of love. As we will see in later chapters, the organizations that executed the Nazi orders to commit mass murders were bonded into an arcane coalition of common objectives and guilt.

Prejudiced people avoid facing the irrationality of their intolerance by stereotyping. Their victims are invested with deficiencies that have little or no relationship to reality. For example, if their bias is directed against Jews, the single characteristic often used to taint all Jews may be their supposed avarice. Any positive traits of the Jews are ignored or denied. Charitable Jews are merely the "exception to the rule" as are the sober Irishman, the law-abiding Italian, the intelligent Pole, and the enterprising African American . . . .

Prejudice is not a static phenomenon, it has high and low tides that are usually pushed and pulled by economic condition. One is tempted to compare such fluctuations with those of the stock market. When the economy is strong and expectations high, minorities experience little bias. But as economic hardships return, so do prejudice and its kin, using a scapegoat for whatever is wrong. Authoritarian personalities find it almost impossible to accept any blame for their own failures or reverses. They alleviate their disappointments, no matter what the cause, by placing the guilt on someone else. The greater the frustration, the more intense the culpability of the hated group. During periods of severe economic suffering, plunder and bloodshed may result, particularly when fomented by irresponsible leaders. Pogroms, that is, government-sponsored or government-tolerated riots against Jews, were suffered by generations of Russian Jews. They illustrate how mob action can result in arson, plunder, and murder. Criminal acts seem acceptable when committed by a crowd. Even after the excitement of terrorizing defenseless victims has worn off, there is no sense of guilt, only justification. The outrages committed by the Ku Klux Klan after the Civil War are a familiar example of criminality by consent. Far from viewing themselves as arsonists and murderers, Klan members wrapped themselves in the flag of Southern patriotism.

The persecution of the Jews nearly always had an economic component. Medieval Crusaders looted Jewish properties along the road to Jerusalem; Ferdinand and Isabella expelled the Jews from Spain but forbade them to take their goods, and when the Nazis rounded up the Jews, all their assets were confiscated.

THE COSTS

Social scientists have studied the reactions of both the victim and the victimizer of negative stereotyping. Both pay a dear price. The oppressor does not remain untainted by his power. In order to hate blindly, it is necessary to become blind. The act of prejudging another person on the basis of misinformation demands the suspension of independent thought and action. Bigots must stifle the impulses of compassion for those who suffer at their hands. In order to affirm and reaffirm the illusion of their superiority, they must play elaborate games of self-deception. The greater the injustice of their conduct, the greater the amount of psychic energy required to maintain the facade of their superiority.

The victims of prejudice are, of course, deeply affected. They may lose more than personal freedom; they may lose their sense of wholeness, the self-respect that is so vital to well-being. Whether actually or seemingly powerless, they may accept society's rejection as justified. The resulting self-depreciation will exacerbate their doubts. A sense of worthlessness, coupled with hopelessness, will weaken any efforts to bring about change. The need to fit in, to be identified with the majority, seems an almost universal human trait. This herd instinct, especially strong during teenage years, exerts a lifelong influence. When the dominant element in society excludes a minority, individuals often react by questioning, even denying, the values of their own culture. For example, lightness of skin may be valued higher than darkness; aquiline noses are straightened and personal names changed to echo those of the majority; Jews may convert to Christianity for nonreligious reasons; traditions are abandoned as ill-suited to the main currents in society. In the process, pride in one's heritage, so essential in a well-adjusted personality, is traded for the plastic image of conformity.

It requires no imagination to recognize that a common response to prejudice is prejudice. Hate begets hate, and misunderstandings deepen. Generalized accusations further poison the atmosphere. "All white people are racist," "All Christians believe that Jews killed their Lord," "All men want to dominate women," "All Arabs are double-dealing," and so on. Stereotyping and scapegoating are handed down from one generation to the next like valued gifts.

ORIGINS OF ANTI-SEMITISM

Anti-Semitism, hostility toward the Jewish people, is a nineteenth-century word for an ancient malignancy. One can begin to trace its history at various points. When the rebellious ancient Hebrews exhausted the patience of their Roman masters, they lost their national home in 70 C.E. and were scattered throughout the Mediterranean lands. Thus began the Diaspora, their dispersion. Unlike other nationalities who lost their homelands, they remained faithful to their monotheism, language, and heritage. Their history and their religious observances honor the martyrs who died for their faith. Theirs was a jealous God who could not become part of any pagan pantheon. The moral demands of that nameless, invisible, all-powerful, all-knowing God were exacting indeed. He commanded His people to adhere to ethical standards no other god required. Sacrifices and festivals in His honor did not suffice; this deity invaded the daily life, the very thoughts of His worshipers. Yet, Jewish rituals, such as circumcision and food taboos, although burdensome and isolating, did not diminish, but perhaps increased, the zealous attachment of the Jews for their God and His law.

After the fall of the Roman Empire, Arab peoples dominated the Middle East. The establishment of Islam by Muhammad in 622 was followed by great conquests as his followers swept across the Arabian Peninsula, fusing warring tribes into a theocratic nation. The wave of victories encompassed the eastern regions, previously part of the now-disintegrated Roman Empire. In view of the present Arab–Israeli conflict, it is noteworthy to recall that Islam did not force the subjugated peoples into conversion. The Jews of the Middle East prospered under their Islamic masters. In fact, when the Moslems advanced into Iberia in the eighth century, large numbers of Jews settled in Spain. The Golden Age of Jewish culture was celebrated during the Moslem domination of Spain, and great achievements in the areas of literature, science, philosophy, and religion speak of a bygone spirit of Islamic tolerance.

CHRISTIANITY AND THE JEWS

The development of Christianity as the primary faith of Europe marks the most important cultural revolution of the West. For the Jews, it was a disaster. As U.S. citizens, we accept the fact that it is possible for people of different faiths to live side by side in harmony. This concept, however, is a recent and wonderful New World innovation. The European record reveals an appalling history of mankind's inhumanity to the men and women who prayed in different houses of worship. In the name of the Prince of Peace, religious persecutions among differing branches of Christianity and wars of atrocious cruelty lasted for hundreds of years. All major Christian denominations, however, were united on one issue: their animosity toward Jews.

For nearly 2,000 years, Jews were kept outside the Christian world. They were outcasts because they denied that Jesus was the messianic son of God. The accusation that Jews had killed Christ was reiterated by generations of theologians, and a reenactment of the crucifixion in which Jews are the deicides was common practice during the Easter pageants throughout Europe. Jewish devotion to the faith of their ancestors was construed as both a challenge and an insult to Christianity. Their conversion was an abiding missionary objective. In the nineteenth century, a racial component was added. This will be discussed in connection with the rise of Hitler. At present, we are concerned with the religious origins because these have the deepest roots that have sustained the entire framework of anti-Semitic prejudice.

The historic Jesus, as opposed to Jesus—the object of religious veneration, is shrouded in mystery. He wrote nothing at all. Later descriptions of his life were more concerned with his message than with his biography. We know that he was born in the year 7 B.C.E. during the reign of King Herod. The meager material available acknowledges the fact that Jesus was born a Jew and that he was baptized in a public ceremony by an Essene preacher named John. The Dead Sea Scrolls, found in a cave near the Dead Sea in 1947, gave researchers a more detailed picture of the life and times of John and Jesus. The Essenes were one of several Jewish sects that arose in response to the challenges of Greco-Roman civilization. They lived ascetic, pious lives in communities isolated from the world. John exhorted all who would listen that the coming of the Messiah was imminent. God's promise of a heavenly kingdom on earth, prophesied earlier by Isaiah, would soon be fulfilled. In preparation for that day, all sinners must repent. The contrite and penitent congregation then took part in a ritual of washing away past transgressions in the river Jordan. Among those thus baptized was Jesus.

Jesus began his work as a teacher at the age of 30 years. The best summary of his ministry is contained in his Sermon on the Mount: God's blessing has nothing to do with earthly wealth and power; the meek, the children, and the peacemakers, those who live in purity and act justly, will receive mercy from the heavenly father. He stressed God's love and spoke of the power of faith. His teachings urged men and women to obey God's law and to share their worldly goods. The empty rituals that had replaced the core of Jewish ethics were an abomination to Jesus who preached that spiritual, not material values, secured eternal life. He lived during a contentious time in Jewish history, when zealots, moderates, and conservative factions bickered endlessly with each other and with their Roman overlords. According to Jesus, the promise of salvation, that is, life after death, was open to all who lived righteously. His insistence that neither social standing nor worldly success won any merit before the throne of God offended both Jews and Romans.

Jesus' ministry probably lasted only one year, three at most. The influence he exerted during that brief time leaves us in awe. Because Jesus referred to himself as the Son of Man, as the Son of God, and as King, it is impossible to reconstruct how he viewed his role. The fact that he urged his followers to observe certain practices, now called sacraments, might imply that perhaps Jesus wanted more than to merely reform the Jewish faith. However, the institution of Christianity was not his work. The church was founded by his disciples after his death. Jesus lived and died a Jew. In his own words, he had come to fulfill the law, not to destroy it.

The crucifixion of Jesus plays an important role in the history of anti-Semitism. Few events have caused as much controversy and misrepresentation as Jesus' crucifixion. It is generally accepted that Jesus was arrested on the night of the Last Supper, the Seder meal he shared with his closest disciples. It is also believed that Judas of Kerioth betrayed him and that the Sanhedrin, the Jewish court, indicted him and turned him over to the Romans for punishment. Accounts of the trial describe that, when questioned, Jesus replied that he was the Messiah. Thus he confirmed the threat he allegedly posed to the tranquility of the city. Because the Sanhedrin had no jurisdiction over capital offenses, such as blasphemy and messianic claims, the prisoner was turned over to the Roman procurator, Pontius Pilate. The biblical account of Pilate's reluctance to condemn Jesus was written almost a century later and may or may not be correct. We do know that the Romans used crucifixion routinely for political offenders.

The Romans governed dozens of diverse people and had much experience in dealing with revolts. There was no reason to assume that the death of this obscure carpenter would have any lasting effect. After all, these so-called Christians (translated "followers of the messiah") were a mere splinter group in the total body of Judaism. The early Christians were Jews, observant of the law but differing from the majority in their conviction that Jesus was indeed the Messiah. The teachers of this small sect, led by the apostle Peter, lived according to the principles of brotherly love and shared their possessions. The only rituals they observed that were not part of established Judaism were baptism and the Lord's Supper. The most revolutionary doctrine pertained to their certainty that Jesus had ascended to heaven after three days of being entombed and that he would return once again to earth to establish his kingdom.

THE NEW FAITH ESTABLISHED

The beginning of the amazing transformation of Christianity from a gentle brotherhood to a triumphant, worldwide church was largely the work of a Roman citizen named Saul of Tarsus, known as Paul in the New Testament. An observant Jew, until his maturity, he experienced a vision that changed his life. He became, in fact, the founder of the church by detaching the Christian sect from the parent Jewish faith. Paul made the far-reaching decision that the Gentiles, that is, the pagan world, should be converted to the faith of Jesus. The church would be *catholica,* or universal. No longer was Jesus the king of the Jews, but the king of the entire spiritual cosmos. Paul's missionary zeal took him through much of the Roman world, and his success was extraordinary. In the process of that expansion, the simple faith of Jesus was elaborated and given doctrinal foundations.

According to Paul, the carpenter from Nazareth was neither an ordinary human being nor merely a great prophet. He was God's own beloved son. Paul ordained that circumcision was no longer required of converts. Dietary restrictions were removed. The concept of the Messiah of the Old Testament was revised. In the Jewish tradition, the coming of the redeemer would institute an earthly realm of peace and plenty. According to Paul the heavenly kingdom, not the earthly one, will reward the just. Clearly, the distance between Jews and Christians widened. And it became impossible for converts to be both Jews and Christians at the same time. The final rupture in the thread connecting the old and the new faiths took place when Paul, toward the end of his life, broke with Judaism completely. From the foundations he had constructed, other fathers of the church erected a mighty edifice, one that humanized many aspects of life, yet remained hostile to Jews for nearly 2,000 years.

THE MEDIEVAL CHURCH AND THE JEWS

As the Christian church spread across the Roman Empire and beyond, it evolved from the faith of a small band of persecuted martyrs to a position of supreme power. When Roman authority collapsed in the fifth century, the Christian church averted the complete breakdown of civilization. Influential Roman bishops assumed leadership on questions of orthodoxy, until ultimately popes assumed preeminence in all religious affairs and greatly influenced the legal, economic, and organizational affairs of Europe. In an age that forgot how to read and write, where Roman law nearly disappeared, the Christian church filled much of the void. The human need for beauty was realized by the building of magnificent cathedrals that often became focal points for the revival of towns. Monks, nuns, and priests provided hospitals, schools, and charity. The power of excommunication brought sinners to conformity, be they emperors or beggars. When challenged by heresies (doctrines that were declared unsound and unacceptable by the orthodox hierarchy), the church was implacable. Disobedience to a specific article of faith was (and is) a grievous sin. Tolerance, as we interpret that concept today, was not viewed as benign, not even acceptable, because diversity in religious thought was seen as destructive. Serious questions of faith were debated and usually settled by councils within the church. When it was not possible to reconcile the differing views and practices of eastern and western believers, the church split. The western Roman and Eastern Orthodox churches have been officially separated since 1054.

Medieval Christianity granted neither indulgence nor sufferance to Jews. During the Age of Faith, the nearly 1,000 years between the fifth and fifteenth centuries, the church controlled life on earth and beyond the grave. Political, economic, and social activity was judged by standards set by the church. Religion had hardened into the absolute conviction that Christianity, as interpreted by its hierarchy, was the truth—the only truth. No compromise was possible. Jews, who insisted on clinging to the error of their ways by refusing to convert, were condemned to live in degradation. Their very misery was then exploited as a sign of God's punishment for their rejection of Christ. Isolation, economic ruin, false accusations, extortion, expulsion, plunder, and murder were employed in the attempt to eradicate the faith that once had been practiced by Jesus. From the time of the Crusades, which began at the close of the eleventh century, until the Age of Enlightenment in the 1700s, hatred for Jews was a common denominator within the diversity of European culture. Although the waves of persecution varied in time and place, the threat of disaster was ever present.

The Crusades were a watershed in Jewish history. The cry "God wills it" commanded the faithful, from kings to commoners, to join the war against the nonbelievers. With the exception of the Iberian Peninsula, the convulsion swept across Western Europe. For nearly 200 years, wave upon wave of warriors for Christ trekked to the Holy Land. The original motivation was soon adulterated by the expectation of material benefits: wealth, land, trade, and freedom from serfdom. Self-appointed laymen and delegated churchmen crisscrossed Catholic Europe and roused the crowds to join the war against the infidel. Their appeal was hard to resist: a great adventure and the promise of worldly and otherworldly benefits.

But why wait to fight the enemy of Christ in faraway Jerusalem when there were nonbelievers, that is Jews, close at hand? Mobs razed Jewish houses of worship, schools, businesses, and homes. As the rioters fed each other's violence, the destruction of goods escalated into rape, plunder, and murder. The rabble that made up the Peoples' Crusade pillaged its way across Europe and attacked Jewish communities wherever they were found. Even church leaders were unable to restore order. The events in the German city of Worms are a case in point. About 800 Jews had been granted refuge in the Episcopal palace of Worms. Jews who had remained in their homes were butchered, stripped of their clothing, and left naked in the streets. Many corpses were mutilated. The bishop protested but, unable to exercise his authority, gave the Jews refuge. The rioters then attacked his palace. In two days they overcame its defenders and proceeded to murder nearly all the Jews they could find. Many had committed suicide before the killers could reach them; a handful were spared because they had consented to be baptized. The cities of Speyer, Mainz, and Cologne fell victim to similar mania.

Long after the impetus for the Crusades had been transformed from a religious mission to avarice and after the Moslems had retaken the Crusader states in the Middle East, the persecution of the "accursed race" persisted. From the eleventh to the eighteenth centuries, Jewish history in Christian lands was mostly one of affliction interspersed with periods of violence. The kings of France, England, and later Spain, as well as various German and Italian princes, ordered the expulsion of the

Jews. Always, they left as paupers. Sometimes they were permitted to return upon payment of a tax or duty. Some German princes contrived a new indignity—their Jews were designated as chattels or possessions of the ruler, who had the right to sell their services, even their future taxes. Only conversion granted release from the bitterness of Jewish life. It was offered again and again, a simple ceremony that would win acceptance and greater security. Against all reasonable persuasion, few Jews left their faith. The stronger the push toward the baptismal font, the greater the unwillingness of the Jews to accept Christianity.

What made the Jews so despicable to Christian eyes? One cannot understand anti-Judaism without its religious components. Jewish theology differs from Christianity in several major concepts. Foremost among these is the denial of Christ as the messiah and redeemer. But beyond the repudiation of the Godhood of Christ, Jews reject other critical articles of Christian faith. They do not accept such doctrines as original sin or predestination; they reject the sacraments, do not hold that priests act as intermediaries between man and God, and dispute the Christian visions of heaven, purgatory, and hell. The Five Books of Moses remained the bedrock of their faith.

The notion that the Jews must be in league with the devil took hold in the medieval mind, and Jews were held responsible for all sorts of natural and unnatural disasters. Added to Jews' guilt as Christ killers, even the most bizarre charges were believed: They were infidels (nonbelievers); they required Christian children's blood to prepare their Passover matzos; a mysterious death or disappearance of a Gentile child was "proof" of ritual murder; Jews desecrated the host (wafer used during mass) by piercing it with sharp instruments, supposedly reenacting the killing of Jesus; they owed allegiance to Satan and caused droughts, storms, floods, illnesses, miscarriages, and birth defects; they poisoned wells; and they caused a bubonic plague called the Black Death, which annihilated one-fourth to one-third of the population of Europe in the fourteenth century. Finally, they lived in a state of misery, which was an unmistakable sign that God hated them.

The certainty that Jews were an abomination in the eyes of man and God was translated into decrees designed to prevent contact between the Christian majority and the infectious Jewish minority. Church councils, popes, and temporal rulers enacted laws designed to disconnect Jews from Gentiles. Within their own communities, the Jews could do as they pleased, but commerce with the world beyond was severely restricted. In most European communities, the opportunities for Jews to make a decent living were few. This is a representative list:

Jews were prohibited from joining guilds, thus making it impossible for them to engage in nearly all business and manufacturing activities.

Jews could not practice medicine or law.

Jews could not own land.

Jews could not hold public office.

Jews could not leave their homes during Easter week.

Jews were forced to wear distinctive badges or hats in public to alert any unsuspecting Christians.

Jews could not intermarry with Christians.

The most restrictive laws concerned the separation of housing, giving rise to the ghetto. By forcing Jews to live in their own crowded and wretched quarters, their isolation was assured. Whether walled in or barricaded by fences, they had little contact with events outside their narrow world. Only a few were granted exception—these were usually Jews who achieved prominence in import-export trade, in banking, or as special "court Jews" in service of a ruler. Their unique circumstances did not diminish the general poverty of the ghetto dwellers. Despised and segregated, degraded and fearful, the once-proud people of the Bible reacted to their plight both negatively and positively. It must be remembered that until the modern era, separation between church and state did not exist. Christian rulers, even those who disputed the right of the papacy to interfere in their public administration, were unlikely to offend the church authorities and become defenders of Jews.

EARLY GHETTOS

Within the confines of their ghettos, the Jews created a life significantly different from that of Christian neighborhoods. In the ghetto, religious observance was not a matter of weekly prayer but was ingrained into the fabric of daily activity. In churches it was common for women to outnumber men at services; in synagogues men made up the majority of worshipers. The most highly esteemed member of the community was not the wealthiest man but the scholar, the rabbi. His congregation took great pride in his reputation and his Talmudic learning. Teachers and students pored over the holy texts and subjected each word to discussion as well as contention. The mysticism of Kabbalah found supporters who pursued the search for secret meaning within the holy books. Kabbahlists were not granted a magical shortcut to understand God; this study was open only to the most learned members of the community. The hardships of ghetto life, particularly its poverty and insecurity, also inspired the impulse to follow false messiahs, who promised that the time of deliverance was at hand.

With the passage of centuries, the isolation of ghetto dwellers from the world beyond increased. Many Jews forgot how to play, how to enjoy the beauty of nature, and how to take pleasure from physical activity. Children were taught to avoid confrontations, especially with non-Jews. Most of the Central European Jews, whose ancestors had migrated eastward when invited by several tolerant Polish kings, maintained a version of the German language, Yiddish. Thus, differing vernaculars widened the distance between the Jews and the life outside the ghetto walls. Any influence originating from the Gentile world was emphatically resisted. A child who married a Christian was mourned as dead; his or her name was erased from membership in the community. Tradition hardened into stifling regimentation that dictated even such matters as clothing and the shape of beards. Individuality or privacy had no place in the crowded houses of the Jewish ghetto.

Lest ghetto life be perceived as unremittingly dreary, it must be noted that it also produced some positive responses. Jewish life was marked by a deep sense of community, a bond forged by shared suffering and common values. The synagogue was more than a house of prayer, it was the focus of life. Religious, communal, and personal activity overlapped. In a world of illiteracy, most male Jews could read and write. The family was the source and center of joy and pride. The Sabbath meal, the celebration of the festivals, and the milestones in the lives of the children were occasions of collective joy. Sweet Yiddish melodies were sung by mothers to their babies, hospitality was gladly extended to visitors, and charity toward the poor was a religious as well as a public duty.

It is estimated that toward the close of the Middle Ages there were three million Jews in the world. Nearly all lived in Europe in designated quarters within villages, towns, and major cities such as Rome, Frankfurt, and Prague. This Jewish apartheid was supported and fostered by the church, which feared that exposure to Judaism might be harmful to Christian beliefs. In light of the fact that Jews do not proselytize, the basis for this fear is hard to fathom.

The greatest challenge for ghetto dwellers was earning a livelihood. In many regions of Europe, the economic restrictions were so severe that one marvels that Jews survived at all. Closed off from farming and many crafts, they were forced into such occupations as rag picking, peddling, moneylending, and innkeeping. Wherever such prohibitions were relaxed, Jews turned their skills to tailoring, shoemaking, distilling beer and whiskey, goldsmithing, and silversmithing. Of course, within the ghettos Jews provided for the needs of fellow Jews. As was common throughout Europe, skilled craftsmen handed down their expertise to their sons. Because of the ban against Jewish landowning, ghettos depended on Christian peasants for their food supply, although chickens, even a cow, might roam the ghetto's unpaved roads.

Whereas the scholar stood at the top of the Jewish hierarchy, in the Christian world the social order was fixed by birth. With the exception of the clergy, a person was born to be a serf, a free peasant or artisan, or a noble. Serfs made up the great majority; they were bound to the land, neither free nor slaves, burdened with long-established duties and few rights. Their labor provided the food and feed that maintained medieval society. In towns, the small middle class was organized into highly restrictive associations, or guilds, of craftsmen and traders. They imported or manufactured the necessities and luxuries desired mainly by the upper class. But Jews, physically isolated and socially scorned, did not fit into the established categories of serf, freeman, member of the Christian religious community, or the aristocracy. Their pariah status was justified as God's will, but, and an important but it is, they were permitted to survive. The church did not advocate their physical annihilation. According to the New Testament, the Second Coming of Christ will be preceded by the conversion of the Jews after their ingathering in the Holy Land.

General acceptance of that doctrine hung as a double-edged sword over the ghettos; the Jews must suffer so that their baptism would have the greatest possible appeal.

THE REFORMATION

The Middle Ages, a 900-year period from the fall of the Roman Empire to the fourteenth century, appears stagnant, but actually slow and uneven change was taking place. The eventual transition from the medieval to modern eras was marked by the Renaissance, that surge of renewed intellectual activity. Fueled by the spirit of inquiry, it questioned many long-accepted concepts and created the basis for the values of present-day Western society. But change creates tensions. In the waning Middle Ages, an obvious arena for conflict and confrontation was the conduct of the church. The uses and abuses of its temporal and spiritual power had long disturbed men of courage and vision. For centuries, their pleas and warnings went unheeded. The church labeled them heretics, excommunicated them, and condemned them to die at the stake. Not until Martin Luther did a reformer succeed in defying the Catholic Church. In the process, he, and the men who followed his path, left the mother church and thereby destroyed the unity of Western Christendom. The legacy of that revolt is pertinent to our commentary on Jewish life.

Martin Luther came from within the church. He was an Augustinian monk and professor of theology at the University of Wittenberg in the German state of Saxony. His personal crisis of conscience led him to protest the church's practice of raising money, known as indulgences. He opposed the practice because it led people to believe that donations could serve as a substitute for true penance and shorten or ease the suffering of the soul in purgatory. His first act of protest was modest enough; his 95 Theses detailed his objections to indulgences. The complaint was written in Latin, hardly a cry of revolt to incite the masses. He nailed the text on the church door at Wittenberg in 1517 and hoped it might lead to a theological debate. His aim was simply to stop the sale of indulgences because they made false promises to sinners. But economic and political abuses of the church had readied great numbers of the faithful to confront a wide range of religious abuses. Common folk and princes, the Elector of Saxony who was prominent among the latter, united in a spiritual opposition that had economic and political components as well. Rulers begrudged the great wealth flowing from their countries to Rome. A developing national consciousness resented papal interference in political issues. As pressure mounted for and against Luther, the rift between his doctrines and the established tradition widened. A man of great personal courage, Luther stood by his convictions. Unlike some of his predecessors who died at the stake, his excommunication was not the prolog to a fiery death. Instead, his supporters multiplied. The split in the church grew into a chasm that could not be bridged.

The establishment of the Lutheran churches in northern Germany was followed by other religious revolts. Once the principle was fixed that individuals, not the dictates of the popes, may interpret the Bible, a bewildering number of sects evolved. The meaning of every phrase and every word of the holy texts was weighed and measured. Differences in interpretations became the basis for the founding of many denominations, each claiming to be in sole possession of the truth.

In his relationship with Jews, there are two Luthers. The early idealist believed that the long-sought conversion of the Jews was imminent. The Renaissance, with its cosmopolitan, humanistic views, had ushered in a period of relief from the most severe oppression for some Jews. Protestant scholars, particularly the Calvinists, studied the Gospels with renewed vigor, often leaning upon the Jewish erudition of the Old Testament. Nonetheless, the pressure to convert the Jews intensified. Luther understood the Jewish origins of Christianity and had rebuked the Catholic hierarchy for its shameful treatment of the Jews. His pamphlet, *Jesus Was Born a Jew,* issued seven times in a single year, reminded Germans of the debt the Christian world owed to the Hebrew people. He fully expected that his antipapal position and his admonition that Jews be treated with kindness would result in extensive conversions. When it became clear that such an assumption was wrong, Luther became violently anti-Jewish. Some of his tirades are comparable to Nazi propaganda. His later pamphlet, *Concerning the Jews and their Lies*, repeated the worst stereotyped vilifications. He urged civil authorities to raze the synagogues, confiscate Jewish property, and drive those obstinate people from the land. Unhappily, it is the second message that took hold.

THE ERA OF ENLIGHTENMENT

The winds of change blew gingerly indeed over the Jewish communities during the late eighteenth century. Here and there doors had been cracked open and provided the opportunity to prosper. Poland had provided a haven, as did Holland and England under Oliver Cromwell. Although Jews were not treated on a basis of equality with Christians, they were granted greater legal and economic protection. Generally, their improved status was the result of the growing rationalism of the educated classes, coupled with the new materialism. Monarchs encouraged the pursuit of wealth by the middle class in order to collect increased taxes. Jews could be helpful in the accumulation of riches because they understood business, trade, and banking. No longer could the church persuade the faithful to shun possessions of this world in order to ensure a place in the next. The "just price" imposed by guilds, which had set limits on profits, was losing its hold. As the world of commerce and production expanded, Jews found new economic opportunities.

Social restrictions that had been in place for centuries also eased in many parts of Europe. Here and there voices were raised to declare the maltreatment of the Jews as a shameful injustice. Among these was the influential German dramatist Gotthold Ephraim Lessing. His play *Nathan der Weise* was an eloquent appeal for fraternity and tolerance. The Prussian counselor Christian Wilhelm von Dohm wrote extensively in support of political, economic, and educational equality. Several of the French philosophers, notably Baron de Montesquieu and Count Honore Mirabeau, vehemently decried the inhumanity of the archaic Christian posture concerning the Jews. Austria's emperor Joseph II, son of the anti-Jewish Maria Theresa, issued an Edict of Toleration in 1782. However, not all the philosophers of the Enlightenment shared an enlightened attitude toward the Jews. Voltaire's diatribes echoed the aversion for Jews held by his sometime friend, the Prussian king Fredrick the Great. The masses, as always, found attacks on their cherished prejudices intolerable. The light of reason hardly penetrated below the level of the salons frequented by the intellectuals. Even so, the forces impelling a reshaping of society could not be held back forever. The middle class became aware of its own importance and power and demanded its rightful place. A society organized by hereditary privilege was no longer accepted as immutable. In the great upheaval of the French Revolution, the vestiges of feudalism were eradicated, absolute monarchy was shattered, and outdated class distinctions were demolished. The storm sweeping away so many inequities of the past eventually also benefited the Jews.

THE FRENCH REVOLUTION

The changes wrought by the French Revolution stirred the entire continent. Despite the excesses of the Reign of Terror and the short-lived Republic, the principle of Égalité took root—not social equality, but equality before the law. For the first time in modern Western European history, the privilege of citizenship was granted regardless of religion. After a protracted debate, the Legislative Assembly voted in favor of Jewish citizenship, and Jews became Frenchmen in 1791. In the wars that followed the execution of Louis XVI, victorious French troops exported the ideals of the Declaration of the Rights of Man far beyond France. Holland was the second nation to tear down the restrictions on their comparatively prosperous Jews. The phenomenal career of Napoleon Bonaparte extended French influence across the German states. In his personal attitude toward the Jews, Napoleon vacillated between his desire to integrate them into French life and his acceptance of the well-worn allegation that Jews were incapable of patriotism. In the end, expediency motivated him to extend citizenship to Jews who might help to advance his grand designs. In total, his influence was salutary for the Jews. He went so far as to summon an assembly of Jewish notables in order to assure them of his willingness to lift them from their distress in return for their loyalty. Wherever French guns boomed during the Napoleonic Wars, ghetto walls fell; wherever members of Napoleon's family assumed the thrones vacated by fleeing rulers, Jews emerged from centuries of humiliation. There were instances of popular participation in the spirit of enlightenment. In the city of Bonn, for example, the Christian citizenry broke down the ghetto walls and jubilantly linked arms with the Jews. Sadly, after Waterloo many of the liberties were rescinded by the restored, so-called legitimate monarchies.

THE AGE OF REACTION

When Napoleon was exiled, so were many of the changes he had forced upon Europe. His foes met at Vienna in 1814 and tried to undo the novel concept that people are citizens, not subjects. The Age of Reaction attempted, and temporarily succeeded, in reversing many of the advances toward a more liberal society. Some of the old restrictions were revived by reactionary autocrats. Between 1815 and 1848, liberal ideas were anathema and Prince Metternich's Austrian firemen were quick to extinguish the flames of freedom wherever they might flare up. For most of the Jews, the Age of Reaction was at least a partial return to the medieval darkness of isolation and confinement in ghettos. But bayonets could not hold back the impetus for change. Fear of change by the conservatives muddied the atmosphere. Inequalities accepted for hundreds of years were no longer borne in silence. The French Revolution had spread the message that the present need not define the future. The revolutionary spirit, long simmering beneath the surface, broke through. The German and Italian people, denied an independent national existence by the powerful Austrian hegemony, exploded into revolutions. Wherever suppression had become intolerable, from Spain to Poland, revolts shook the old order as nationalism and liberalism combined, and hopes for liberal constitutional governments resulted in waves of revolutionary activity. Patriotism was molded into rebellion in 1830 and, on an even wider scale, in 1848. Only England was spared. British governments, through evolutionary legislation, had permitted power to shift from the aristocracy to the middle class. By 1850, the full rights of citizenship were inherent privileges of all Englishmen.

INDUSTRIALIZATION

The continental uprisings were largely confrontations between military and civilian forces, and arms won over ideas. But, even repressive rulers, such as the Prussian king and Austrian emperor, could not turn back the clock full circle to the old order. In part, this was due to another revolution, one that transformed lives beyond human imagination. The economic upheavals of the Industrial Revolution changed not only the methods of manufacturing but altered what people did, thought, and wanted. New opportunities opened up, which, in some part, the Jews could share. Europe's fledgling capitalist systems needed men of ability in the boardrooms and the factory. The religion of either the financial director or the operator of a new machine was irrelevant. Jews, so long on the economic fringes, were willing and able to promote industrial development. Had not certain privileged Jews, such as the patriarchs of the House of Rothschild, proven that they possessed great business acumen? Their admirers wove a new myth (based on the exception rather than the rule), namely that Jews were born with the ability to make money.

The age of the machine, of the investor, of improved quantity and quality of goods opened doors to a wide range of underprivileged classes, including the Jews. They streamed into the main currents of whatever nation they called home. Political emancipation followed the economic breakthrough. By 1870 the nations of Western Europe had liberated their Jewish population and given them citizenship. In return, Jewish gratitude was often expressed by ardent patriotism and by their contributions promoting modern progress. Western and Central European Jews were found among factory owners and workers, teachers and shopkeepers, and artists and inventors. Some grew rich and others achieved middle-class status, while many struggled to escape their hand-to-mouth existence. Politically, their affiliations ran the gamut from the radical left to the moderate center to the conservative right. When public schools admitted Jewish children, the youngsters quickly adopted the vernacular, dressed and behaved according to the dominant cultures, and imitated the conduct of their contemporaries. The process of assimilation was underway. Complete acculturation, however, was never achieved. Only if Jews gave up their faith could they hope to "belong," and even then, converts found that many social obstacles were still in place.

TWENTIETH CENTURY

The late nineteenth and early twentieth centuries were years of scientific discoveries that changed man's view of the world. Christians and Jews found their interpretations of the bible questioned. Darwin's theories, the new geology, chemistry, historical research, and psychology stimulated inquiry into every arena of faith and knowledge. Jews asked whether their ancient rites had been set immutably by the patriarchs or was theirs a living, ever-evolving, religion? Would new forms, updated rituals, and modern translations of the holy books destroy Judaism, or would such changes assure its survival? The ferment over reform or tradition was further agitated by the conflict over the degree to which Jews should keep pace with the world around them. Could one be a loyal Frenchman and devout Jew at the same time? The world of business operated on a Christian calendar. Should one work on the Sabbath or not? Can you eat in homes where nonkosher food was served or refuse and give the impression of standing aloof from one's neighbors? Would you place your children in public schools or not? Would intermarriage result from such close contact? The practical and ethical implications were many. By the middle of the nineteenth century, the split between the traditionalists and the liberals had hardened into an open breach. The modernists created their own congregations as Reform Synagogues were established. The founder of this movement, the German Abraham Geiger, was convinced that Judaism must rejuvenate itself in order to better serve man and God. As the second millennium arrived, some of the divisions became permanent features of Jewish life.

It must be noted, however, that the Renaissance and the Reformation, the emergence of the middle class, and the Industrial Age were transformations whose influence stopped along the eastern German boundary. In Poland and Russia, the development of a new economic system was delayed, perhaps by a hundred years. It should be noted that in this region lived the greatest number of Jews, and it was here that their annihilation during the Holocaust was nearly total. In the lands between the Oder and Volga rivers, an entire culture disappeared (to be discussed more fully in the next chapter).

THE NEW ANTI-SEMITISM

The road toward ending anti-Jewish prejudice in Central and Western Europe was neither smooth nor straight, although clearly, industrialism had no religion, and progress required the energies and abilities of all. The medieval preoccupation with the welfare of the soul after death had given way to goals of an earthly heaven of justice and plenty. Increasingly, Jews entered the political and economic fabric of Western society. The granting of civil rights to Jews was viewed by liberals everywhere as symbolic of the enlightened attitude of Western Europe, while the continued anti-Semitism in Russia and Poland was seen as a symptom of their cultural backwardness. Appearances, however, were deceptive. The roots of prejudice were still intact beneath the surface. Different circumstances demanded different modes of venting familiar hatred. The new face of the old aversion was less crude and less obvious, yet was as emotionally charged as the old religious bias. Modern anti-Semitism (the term was introduced in Germany by Wilhelm Marr in 1873) emanated from two related sources: nationalism and racism. The advocates of the former claimed that Jews are forever aliens who cannot share the national ethos; the advocates of the latter asserted that innate racial differences prevented Jews from assimilating with the superior cultures of the host countries.

Nationalism, that deep-rooted sentiment of placing great value on a shared past, language, and culture, emerged in the nineteenth century as a powerful political force. Inspired by Napoleon, it had evolved from rhetoric to political action in the unifications of Germany and Italy and the expulsion of the Turks from nearly all European lands. Pride in one's national heritage swelled everywhere, and in many regions a competitive destructive chauvinism developed. In Germany, sentimentality merged with patriotism to create a mystical concept of Germanness. To be German, truly German, was not a mere matter of citizenship, but was based on an indefinable sense of commonality. Germanic blood and German soil supposedly created an ethos that could not be acquired. Because only an ancient shared heritage could infuse that *Voelkisch* spirit, German romantic writers spoke of a *Volksgeist,* a spirit that is particular to the blood and soil of the German people. The past, particularly the ancient past, was extolled as a time of spiritual perfection. Clearly, Jews could only pretend to be German. Their creativity and contributions in science, philosophy, literature, art, and music notwithstanding, they were forever alien.

Thus, German nationalism was burdened with a romantic, quixotic aspect from the outset. Johann Gottlieb Fichte extolled the notion of the uniqueness and superiority of the German spirit. He argued against Jewish emancipation, which gave ammunition to several generations of anti-Semitic politicians. The composer Richard Wagner wrote with a poisoned pen when he tirelessly and obsessively denounced the Jews. His revulsion seemed to stem from a conviction that German culture was "Judaized," that is, corrupted by Jews. His operas gloried in the Teutonic past, particularly its paganism. The notion that the German essence, its *Voelkisch* nature, went beyond the commonalty of language and heritage was reinforced by other German nationalists. Friedrich Ludwig Jahn (1778–1852) acclaimed the natural, simple German peasant, whereas the city dweller was disconnected from his roots. Georg Wilhelm Friedrich Hegel, founder of the philosophy of dialectics, taught at the University of Berlin during the first quarter of the nineteenth century. He glorified the state and asserted that heroes function outside the norm of history even as they trample on ordinary mortals. A similar note was struck by Heinrich von Treitschke, who persuaded innumerable Germans that unquestioning homage to the state was the ultimate expression of love and duty. Friedrich Nietzsche, whose works were later shamelessly misrepresented by the Nazis, formulated theories concerning heroic individuals who stood high above slavish parliaments and democratic disputations—the original supermen.

ANTI-JEWISH RACISM

German nationalists, whose writings appear rather muddled and self-serving, laid the groundwork for modern anti-Semitism. How deeply did their ideas affect the ordinary German citizen? Tolerance did not vanish; however, it was undermined by the irrationality of the idealized and idolized state, which equated obedience to the state with obedience to a higher spiritual power. From the unification of Germany in 1871 to the rise of the Nazis in 1933, the forces of modernism, that is, progress through material advancement, were challenged time and again by advocates of the idealization of the nation. It is not surprising that the barometer of anti-Semitism rose and fell in tandem with political and economic tensions. Jews, who could never belong to the world of German blood and soil, were held responsible for socialism, capitalism, stock market failures, and labor strikes. Politicians from the ultraconservative right could always count on considerable public approbation when they targeted the Jews for the painful economic dislocations that are part and parcel of industrialization. Anti-Semitism had become a cohesive political issue around which political organizations could be centered.

The division of peoples into races—black, white, and Asian—originated as a system of classification unrelated to any value judgments. Race became racism when innate characteristics were assigned biological attributes by pseudoscientists. The fact that science does not recognize the existence of either a German or a Semitic race was ignored by the supporters of modern racism, and a new, nationally correct biology was created. Eighty years before Hitler became chancellor, the English son-in-law of Richard Wagner, Houston Stewart Chamberlain, influenced millions of readers with his treatise *Foundations of the Nineteenth Century*. He wrote as an oracle, not as an historian or a scientist; his analyses were not the consequence of research, but of insight. He "knew" intuitively that he had discovered nothing less than the mechanism shaping the historical process. According to Chamberlain, the essential traits of a people were determined by the proper or improper racial components of their biological heritage. Creativity, moral fiber, character, and so on were fixed by the interplay of specific racial strains. The Jews, of course, were a fatally bastardized race, while the Germanic people were the inheritors of assured greatness. Chamberlain had no difficulty in corroborating his theory with many hundreds of pages of selected evidence. Considering the fact that the central location of Germany made it a veritable mixing bowl for the genes of tribes crossing her lands and that Jews had been confined to virtual isolation for hundreds of years, Chamberlain's mental acrobatics are astonishing. Nevertheless, Nazi propagandists purported his evidence and repeated Chamberlain's assertion that Jewish blood was hopelessly contaminated.

The racist writers of the nineteenth century did not advocate mass murder, yet their theories played an important role in the coming disaster. Perhaps they hoped to inspire nationalism strong enough to defeat the particularism that delayed German unification until 1871. Whatever the motivation, they fostered the arrogance of racial superiority, which encouraged many Germans to view themselves as different from and better than other nations.

Without Hitler, biological racism may have amounted to nothing more than a footnote in the history of modern Europe, and the theory of an innate, unalterable Jewish malignancy would have remained the purview of quacks. But hatred for the Jews was at the core of Hitler's obsession. The claim that Jews were the bearers of a genetic defect enabled the Nazis to rationalize their nearly successful genocide. If Jews were despicable merely because they did not accept Christ, then conversion and emigration were possible options for them. If Jews could not share the enigmatic ethos of the Teutonic past of the German Volk, they might be excluded from official

Children behind a barbed wire fence at the Nazi concentration camp at Auschwitz. (Hulton Archives/Getty Images Inc.)

positions or be subjected to social discrimination. But if the taint was congenital and if by their presence alone Jews contaminated society, then only their obliteration, including the death of children, even of the unborn, could make Germany safe. And that delusion underlies the tragedy of the Holocaust.

CHAPTER 2

The World that was Annihilated

Although it was strictly forbidden, some members of the *Schutzstaffel* (SS) took pictures of Jews as they reached their concentration camp destinations. The images are heartbreaking, not because the men, women, and children in the pictures look so dreadful but because they look so ordinary, so familiar. They resemble the photographs on grandmother's coffee table of relatives arriving at Ellis Island. These families had been told they would be resettled in the East. They had packed their luggage with items most precious and most needed after the expected resettlement. They look bewildered, confused, and weary rather than frenzied. How could they suspect that they had arrived at a death camp and that in hours, or days, they would die? The officers of the SS Deathhead Squads, who were charged with the execution of Hitler's Final Solution to the Jewish question, were quite successful in their efforts to create a reassuring atmosphere. There might be an orchestra playing on the railroad platform, small patches of grass lined by flower beds, and a clock tower. Orders were shouted to pile the luggage over there, because one would need to find it after the delousing procedure. Arrows painted on the windowless building pointed the way to the disinfecting showers. Ah, these Germans and their fixation on cleanliness. Of course, there were rumors, rumors simply too dreadful to believe, rumors of death camps. Wasn't it terrible, what some people would say? As if the prospect of resettlement was not frightening enough. So, they looked at the flowers and heard the music, and the Nazis were pleased. It would not do at all for hysteria to disrupt the smooth working of the death factory.

Most of the families waiting their turn to enter the infamous showers were Polish, and some were German, with a mixture of Austrians and Czechoslovakians. But as Hitler's armies defeated one nation after another, the victims mirrored their conquests. By 1943, a microcosm of European Jewry was brought to dozens of slave labor and annihilation camps. Some of the victims arrived decently dressed; probably quite recently arrested and held just a few weeks in transfer camps in France, Belgium, or Holland. But those who were shipped east after many months of imprisonment in the ghettos of Polish cities looked gaunt and exhausted and carried their few possessions in cardboard suitcases. Mothers and grandmothers held babies and toddlers in their arms, and fathers grasped the hands of the older boys and girls. The children whimpered, hungry and thirsty, but there is nothing for them, not even a sip of water. And slowly the line moved forward to the deadly showers.

Who were these people? We know that they had no future, their present was compressed into hours or days, but what of their past? Unless we can give them some human dimensions, they remain mere statistics. To understand the meaning of the Holocaust, its victims must be more than entries in German ledgers. The dehumanization of the killing process must be reversed and the faces on the old photographs brought back to life, even if just for a moment.

THE VICTIMS

These men, women, and children were the Jews of Europe. With the exception of Finland, every country allied to or under German control contributed to their numbers. The Germans had cast their net from the outskirts of St. Petersburg to the Ukraine and flung it southward across the Balkan peninsula and, with the exemption of Switzerland (which the Germans preferred to leave neutral), westward over France, the Low Countries, Denmark, and Norway. In 1944 it reached Italy and Hungary, whose governments had been unwilling to surrender their Jews to Himmler's demands but now were occupied by the German army.

Jews had lived in Europe since before the birth of Christ and had adopted, in varying degrees, the customs and mores of their host countries. Surely, there had been intermarriages as well. How else could one explain the great differences in physical appearance among them? There were blue-eyed blondes and dark-eyed brunettes, and freckled redheads. Some men were over six feet tall, others under five. High cheekbones, so prevalent among the Slavic peoples, were well represented, but the round eyes and oval faces of northern lands were also scattered among them.

Not only their appearance varied, but also they came from differing traditions of language and food preferences and dressed according to the country of origin. All were Jewish, but during the Diaspora, the 2,000 years of the dispersion of the Jewish people from their ancient homeland, two major distinctions had evolved. Jews who settled in Central and Eastern Europe are called Ashkinazim, while those who found refuge around the rim of the Mediterranean basin are known as Sephardim. Over the millennia of their separation, they developed variations in ritual and liturgy, although the essence of their faith remained the same. The most notable difference concerned their vernacular language. In Central and Eastern Europe, the spoken and written language was Yiddish, a lingua franca that crossed many borders. Related to medieval German with a generous sprinkling of Hebrew and words adopted from the host nation, Yiddish journalists, poets, and novelists created a literature of great beauty. Isaac Bashevis Singer, a Nobelist in literature, is but one representative among many eminent writers. Sephardic Jews, whose numbers are much fewer, developed Ladino, which was rooted in Latin and Hebrew and was also enriched with the native tongues of their communities, perhaps Turkish, Spanish, or Greek.

Nor were all Ashkinazim alike. Most Western European Jews assimilated to the culture of their environs to a greater degree than Eastern European Jews. This was largely due to the availability of greater opportunities. Although anti-Semitism never disappeared, here the Jews were citizens, they spoke the local language, and, where permitted, they participated in every aspect of national life. It must be remembered that in Germany, France, Holland, and Belgium, as well as in Italy and England, Jews constituted a small minority, 1 percent or less, of the total population. Considering these small numbers, their achievements were impressive. In science, art, and literature their contributions enriched their national life and, in turn, they regarded themselves to be a part of their communities. Social acceptance lagged behind economic and political integration but was also growing as the continuing process of industrialization broke down ancient class barriers. Many Jews became fervently nationalistic and fought in the uniforms of both the Allies and the Central Powers during World War I. At the turn of the twentieth century, they confidently expected that their religious faith would not hinder complete acceptance and that achievement of complete equality was merely a matter of time.

The majority of Jews, however, did not live in Western Europe. Rather they made their homes in Russia, Poland, and the southeastern parts of the Austro-Hungarian Empire. Obviously, European Jewry did not share a single culture. Any attempt here to re-create its diversity, country by country, within the context of a single chapter would serve to confuse rather than clarify. It is more sensible to concentrate on a narrower aspect of the life that vanished, namely Polish Jewry. This choice is justifiable because, first, no other country suffered the magnitude of Holocaust losses as Poland had, which, at three million, constitutes one half of the total. Secondly, their once thriving culture no longer exists. Whereas pockets of Jewish life remain in Western and Southern Europe and a revival of Jewish culture is emerging in Germany, Poland is barren. How strange indeed that Hitler, who despised the Poles, achieved his greatest victory there, for it is Poland, not Germany, that is nearly *Judenrein* ("cleansed of Jews") today.

BRIEF HISTORY OF POLISH JEWRY

The term *Polish Jews* requires definition. The three partitions of Poland in the eighteenth century divided the land and its people among Prussia/Germany, Russia, and Austria. However, even without a political homeland, the Poles continued to foster their native culture and did not blend into the fabric of their conquerors. Poles, and that included Polish Jews, lived for almost 150 years under the flags of Russia, Germany, and Austria. Thus, it is possible to speak of Polish Jewry even when such a designation might refer to Austria's Galicia in the South, to Pinsk in western Russia, or to Posen, which sometimes was part of Germany.

According to German sources, of the approximately six million Jews killed, 4.3 million came from occupied Russia and Poland. In percentages, 85 percent of Polish and 71 percent of western Russian Jews were murdered. Their civilization has vanished. The few thousand Polish Jews who survived the Shoah were met with hostility when they made their way back to their hometowns after the war. The

Polish people who occupied their former homes and places of business often greeted them with hatred, even pogroms. Clearly, the remnant could not reestablish itself on Polish soil. Emigration to Israel, the United States, Canada, or even to Germany was preferable. Cities, towns, and hundreds of villages that once sustained a distinct Jewish life today have little or nothing left to remember the past. Only traces remain: a half-ruined cemetery, a former synagogue now used as a civic center, and perhaps a defunct Talmud–Torah school where now Polish poetry is recited.

Holocaust survivors from western Russia were also unable to revive Jewish cultural life in their former homes. During the more than seven decades of communist control, the government followed a policy of Russification. Similar to czarist aims, the Soviets wanted to homogenize their peoples of diverse backgrounds. Under the guise of equal aversion to all religious worship, Jews were either persecuted or merely discouraged from maintaining their cultural distinctiveness. That policy did not change after the war. In fact, Soviet authorities refused to acknowledge that Jews had specifically been singled out for total destruction by the Nazis. Their commemorative World War II monuments pay homage to all Russian victims without reference to the Jewish catastrophe. Since the disintegration of the Soviet Union into separate nations in 1991, some changes have taken place, and the revival of some Jewish religious institutions is taking place. However, the economic uncertainties which beset the region and occasional outbreaks of anti-Semitism have encouraged emigration, mainly to Israel. Only in the past decade have details of the Holocaust in the German-occupied regions of the Soviet Union become available.

POLISH JEWRY

Jewish history in Poland has deep roots. In the twelfth and thirteenth centuries, the Crusaders attacked Jews in Central Europe with the same zeal they brought to the conquest of the Holy Land. The scream "God wills it" accompanied the burning, looting, rape, and murder that took place. In response, many of the victims fled eastward. They carried with them the medieval German vernacular from which Yiddish developed. The kings of Poland, eager to foster a mercantile middle class, welcomed the refugees. The most enlightened of the Polish medieval kings, Casimir the Great (1333–1370), granted them complete freedom to work, worship, and prosper, despite objections from the church. Even when less enlightened monarchs restricted the economic and social life of the Jews, medieval Poland offered more promise than other European states. Throughout the Middle Ages, when Western European rulers persecuted and expelled their Jewish populations, Polish Jews could work and pray in relative peace. Not restricted to peddling and moneylending, they could live decently in villages and towns. From the thirteenth century to the eve of the Nazi invasion, they provided many of the economic services of a predominantly agricultural society. From blacksmith to goldsmith, tanner to cobbler, miller to baker, weaver to tailor, merchant to banker, and distiller to innkeeper, they made their livelihood. Manufacturing of goods was usually done in homes and small workshops, although some larger factories, particularly in the textile industry, were established. Some Jews plied their goods from village to village; others opened stalls in the town square and sold to the peasants on market days. Because some Jews had financial skills, they found employment as tax collectors for kings and nobles. This was not an unmixed blessing. During periods of want, they were identified with the hated oppressors of the poor and subjected to pogroms.

It is estimated that half a million Jews lived in Polish lands by the middle of the seventeenth century. Depending on the precarious balance of power between king and church and the influence of German merchants who disliked competition, Jewish life fluctuated between prosperity and subsistence. Despite periodic outbursts of anti-Jewish violence, the number of Jews increased. The most devastating attacks occurred in the decade between 1648 and 1658, when the Cossacks revolted against their Polish oppressors and included the Jews in their fury. These massacres in the Ukraine were followed by a Swedish invasion from the north and Russian incursions from the east. In the Polish counterattacks, the Jews were accused of complicity with whatever enemy was at the gates and thousands were killed.

From the seventeenth century on, the promise of coexistence between Poles and Jews was increasingly jeopardized by government decrees. Without the protection of the authorities, prejudice became progressively more overt and extreme, a calamity often instigated by the Catholic Church. Christian hostility was answered in kind by the Jews, but since the latter were virtually defenseless, their insecurity deepened into distrust of the non-Jewish world. Each generation found it more difficult to live decently than the previous one, while the Gentile world responded with indifference or satisfaction to their distress. A widening of the breach between the worlds of Poles and Jews became inevitable.

SHTETL LIFE

The typical shtetl, that is, a town or village with a predominantly Jewish population, was a dreary-looking place. The houses were constructed of unpainted wood, jammed together along unpaved and unlit streets. A well or two provided an often unreliable source of water for the entire community. Family life revolved around the kitchen stove, the only warm spot during the long, cold winter. There were beds or mattresses everywhere, the floors were usually packed earth, and the rooms virtually unventilated. The furnishings were sparse: a table, some chairs, perhaps a hope chest, and a real bed for the parents. Nevertheless, it was a moot question who was better-off, the shtetl dwellers or the nearby peasant, whose animals might share his hut with him and his family.

Jewish life consisted of a rhythm in which the religious and mundane functions were interwoven into a single pattern. The rabbi was generally the most important member of the community because God and his commandments were part and parcel of every activity. Torah and Talmud provided the basis of laws, religious as well as secular. Hundreds of prayers were uttered, not merely during synagogue services but as part of such ordinary activities as washing one's hands or eating the first apple of the season. The search to understand the holy texts was a sacred obligation for those able to cope with the intricacies of commentaries piled upon commentaries. The Almighty of the shtetl was not an unknowable deity who dwelled on high but lived among his people.

Family life was the paramount source of happiness. Children were treasured long before Western civilization discovered the child-centered family. The Sabbath was a joyful celebration, even in the poorest household. Fathers headed the family, but mothers were honored and respected. They made it possible to observe the holy days with special foods, white tablecloths, and Sabbath candles. Grandparents, in-laws, uncles, aunts, and cousins lived sometimes in the same house or down the street, surely not more than a few miles away. Relationships were close, often quarrelsome, but supportive in times of need. When persecution intensified, families and communities sought security from among their own people; it was pointless to hope for help from the world outside.

CULTURAL ACHIEVEMENTS

The fact that during the late Middle Ages many generations of Poles and Jews had lived more or less amicably side by side had become obscured by nineteenth and twentieth century anti-Semitism. In modern Poland, with its institutionalized and grassroots hatred of the Jews, the earlier centuries of coexistence are lost. But it was Polish soil that nourished several vital and enduring elements of Jewish culture. Among these achievements was the study of kabbalah, the preservation of rational orthodoxy, the development of Hasidism, the advocacy of Zionism, and the modernization of many religious practices.

Kabbalah

The quest for God's blessings is as ancient as man himself. Speculation on the mysteries of creation, of man's role in the universe, and on the ways that might lead to an understanding of the creator is a time-honored tradition in Jewish thought. Side by side with the philosophical and devotional search for God, the allure of mysticism also endured. The most abiding form of Jewish mysticism is called kabbalah. Although the invoking of magic symbolism can be traced to the very roots of Judaism, its medieval and modern formulas were largely based on the *Zohar*. This thirteenth-century book has been attributed to Moses de Leon but was based on revelations of a second-century sage named Simeon ben Johai. From the Zohar emanated centuries of occult conjecture and cosmology.

The kabbahlists sought to pierce the mystery of life and death and all the unanswerable questions by discovering God's messages believed to be hidden in the holy texts. Magical powers were assigned to the individual letters of the Scriptures, and it was thought that their specific arrangement concealed some shrouded significance. By manipulating the words and letters, reading them upside down, superimposing one upon another, and even reading them backwards, their secrets might be revealed. Months and years of scrutiny, of poring over every stroke, obscured the simple truths of the holy books. A form of numerology developed, wherein letters were given numerical value and were arranged and rearranged to extract their meaning. The concept that the universe can be made understandable through mathematics strikes a sympathetic chord in the age of space exploration, but Jewish mysticism had no scientific basis. The numbers from one to ten were believed to have radiated directly from God and were assigned supernatural qualities. The longing to penetrate the mystery of God all too often turned into superstition. In times of great suffering, the need to understand God's seeming indifference to human anguish grew especially strong. After the expulsion from Spain, the devotees of kabbalah increased rapidly. Like medieval alchemists, men spent their lives in search of the right formula, and like astrologers, they consulted their books to interpret God's will.

Rational Orthodoxy

Jewish learning of the eighteenth century consisted largely of formalized repetition. The teacher, usually the rebbe (rabbi), accepted boys as young as four or five years of age into his school. They studied Hebrew, the language of prayer, while Yiddish was their mother tongue. Instruction was largely a matter of rote memorization. Although it was permissible to question the meaning of the text, one did not dispute the explanation of the rebbe. Usually, the boys were confined all day in cheerless rooms without an outlet for youthful exuberance. A boy's pale, earnest face was deemed handsome, and the excelling student was the pride of his parents.

Advanced scholarship was equally uninspiring. Endless recitation and argumentation over minutia were the norm, and ritual was exalted over philosophical, even theological, discussions. And yet, the spark for the love of learning remained. Able young men were encouraged to study all their lives. Because Talmud and Torah scholarship was valued above all other attributes, a bright student could hope for a good marriage. It was entirely acceptable that he never earn a living for his family. He was supported either by his proud father-in-law or his approving wife.

Both Jews and Gentiles neglected the education of girls. Their future as wives and mothers was certain. Jewish women accepted their roles as homemakers and obedient wives. The fortunate man was blessed with a wife who filled his home with children, kept a well-ordered house, and was a good cook and caring mother. Sons were valued more highly than daughters because dowries and weddings of daughters were costly, and after marriage, they were expected to become part of their husbands' family. Women could earn respect for kindness and wisdom, but performed only a few of the many religious rites. In the synagogue, the sexes were separated, and Orthodox men avoided touching, even looking at, women who were not close relatives in order to curb any inappropriate desire. Jewish women were probably less subjugated than their Christian contemporaries. Judaism does not acknowledge the doctrine of original sin; Eve is viewed as the mother of mankind rather than as the temptress. The connection between sin and sex, which has rested so heavily on Christian women, does not exist in Judaism. God commanded man to multiply, and sexual urges were the God-given means to that end.

The sterility of the intellectual life of the Polish Jews in the eighteenth century was alleviated by the reforms of Elijah, the Vilna Gaon (wise man). Elijah sparked a revival of Jewish learning by widening its study to include new fields of knowledge. His approach corrected long-existing deficiencies as he urged the cultivation of scholarship rather than memorization. Among his own accomplishments were a translation of Euclid into Hebrew and a treatise on astronomy. His influence left a permanent imprint on the evolution of Eastern Jewry. Fine minds were now able to find within Orthodoxy the challenges of a wider education. Elijah established in Vilna, the capital of Lithuania, a model center of study. His Talmudic academy cracked open a window to the world beyond the confines of shtetl mentality. Under his leadership and that of his followers, philosophy, science, theology, and Hebrew were added to the curriculum. The rabbis who graduated from his school brought a more modern outlook to their congregations.

The breadth of the Gaon's mind was, however, not suitable fare for the masses. The work he required could be mastered by the intellectual elite but was beyond the common man. The laborer, who had to work so that his family could eat, nonetheless sought the divine presence in his life. How could he reach God? Serve God? The question was answered for many Polish Jews by the appearance of the Baal Shem Tov and the development of Hasidism.

The Hasidic Challenge

Hollywood produced several movies that depict Hasidic life in the United States, and residents of large cities have seen the bearded men in black suits and their modestly attired women. Hasidic veneration of their leader, the rebbe, is celebrated and/or decried by Jewish and Christian observers. Sometimes hailed as committed fundamentalists or condemned as religious fanatics, Hasids have carved for themselves a conspicuous and worldwide niche. Their devotion to each other and to their form of Orthodoxy is impressive and so are their almost crime-free, drug-free communities. Although often located in the midst of crowded inner cities, Hasidic enclaves are models of the spirit of neighborliness. In several ways, the intent of the present-day adherents of Hasidism varies from that of the founder of the sect, the Baal Shem Tov ("Master of the Good Name"), but these differences are not part of this discussion. It should be understood, however, that rather than declining in numbers, Hasidism is strong and growing.

The Hasidic movement overcame two insufficiencies within Jewish life in Poland. First, increased persecution caused greater insecurities, which, in turn, intensified the search for spiritual consolation. Second, the unlearned had no access into the tight circle of Talmudic scholarship. Hasidism began as a revolt of the unschooled against the aristocracy of the academics. To serve God was the nearly universal goal, but men who could not spend years in intensive study of the Scriptures felt, and were made to feel, inadequate. The charismatic founder of Hasidism freed the unlettered from that sense of inferiority. Israel of Moldavia, the Baal Shem Tov, believed that devotion to God is rooted in the emotions, not knowledge. Prayer was joy, and joy was prayer. Worship could be expressed through music and dancing. The beauty of nature, seen as a distraction by the Talmudists, was deemed a manifestation of the love bestowed on mankind by the King of the Universe. The Baal Shem Tov elevated faith over ritual, not by discarding the holy books but by interpreting them in an unconventional way. To the Hasids, the presence of God is everywhere in the universe, and one may communicate with God anywhere and at any time. This approach to religion was essentially democratic, since wealth and distinction avail one nothing in the eyes of the Almighty. The emotions of optimism and exultation replenish the whole man, body and soul. Rituals are necessary, but the essence of religion is faith, that is expressed from the depth of feeling. In enthusiasm, ardor, and communal spirit, the religious zeal exhibited by Hasids resembles that of the revivalist churches.

The Baal Shem Tov wrote no instructions for his followers. His personality was the center of the community he created. After his death, the administration of Hasidic life continued to revolve around the figure of a leader. As the movement spread throughout Eastern Europe, it split into several groups. Each chose its own rebbe, from these family dynasties evolved. Such a dynast reigned without a constitution, without an army, and without any but moral force. Nonetheless, he had a great deal of power. His word was law, his decisions final, and the loyalty of his followers absolute. His sphere of jurisdiction was greater than that of any monarch. His disciples awaited his judgment on all questions affecting their lives, be they of an economic or personal nature. The source of this authority was based on the conviction that he stood in a special communion with God and was able to to intercede on behalf of his disciples.

Haskalah

Haskalah, a Hebrew phrase meaning "Let there be light," was a Jewish philosophical movement. Its aim was threefold: to renew Hebrew learning, to bring European culture into Jewish life, and to break down the walls separating Christians and Jews. Its founder was the German philosopher Moses Mendelssohn, a friend of the great dramatist Gotthold Lessing. Both men devoted their considerable talents and fame to teach their contemporaries the meaning of tolerance. Mendelssohn struggled against both Jewish and Gentile bigotry. His devotion to the cause of mutual understanding and his forbearance opened the door through which German and Jewish intellectuals were able to walk together. Jews began to enter the mental world of German thinkers—some of whom acknowledged that Jewishness and Germanness might be compatible. Mendelssohn remained a devout Jew and saw no conflict between Jewish values and Western humanism. With his heart, mind, and powerful pen, he attacked the strictures of empty rituals and rabbinical power. As he sought to open the minds of his people, he also fought for their economic and political emancipation, a goal he did not live to see fulfilled. Predictably, his work earned him the opposition of the Orthodox, who feared that exposure to a Gentile environment would dilute the traditional visions of Judaism. The fact that his children converted to Christianity obviously provided grist for the mill of enemies of Haskalah. Mendelssohn's insistence that his daughters' education equal that of men certainly marked him as a man far ahead of his time.

Mendelssohn's impact was not confined to Central and Western Europe. Gradually, his concepts moved eastward, where a segment of the largely urban strata of Polish Jews fell under the influence of Haskalah. To whatever degree the reluctant Polish authorities permitted, these were the Jews who learned to speak Polish, attended Polish schools, and tried to become part of every aspect of Polish national life. Many entered the middle class, became active in the professions, and owned medium-sized businesses. Others joined the urban proletariat, operated sewing

Jewish boys entering school in Vilna, 1929. (Yivo Institute for Jewish Research.)

machines in small factories, delivered goods by horse and wagon, and finished textiles in their homes. Most were patriotic Poles who chose to live outside the walls of actual or spiritual ghettos, even though they rarely severed all ties with their Jewish past. When they founded hundreds of organizations of mutual assistance, they transplanted some of the closeness of shtetl life to the city. Some went to synagogues, where they prayed from the timeworn books of the Orthodox; others hoped that the Reform movement of Germany would reach Poland. Still others did not pray at all. Nevertheless, they remained Jews.

Roots of Zionism

The two major events in Jewish history in the past century were the Holocaust and the creation of the state of Israel. The 1948 vote by the United Nations that sanctioned the formation of a national homeland for the Jews has been linked by some observers to the Holocaust, but political Zionism had begun much earlier. In the struggle to create a homeland for the Jews, Polish Jewry played a vital role.

The hope of returning to the land of Israel had been kept alive for nearly 2,000 years, ever since the Romans exiled the Judeans. Hundreds of generations had uttered the words "next year in Jerusalem" at the end of the Passover meal. But such hopeful expressions implied an abstract longing, not a blueprint for action. Political Zionism, that is, the organized effort to bring about a national Jewish state, evolved from the confluence of several historic streams. Many Jews recognized that the spirit of Enlightenment had not halted anti-Semitism. Even a secularized Europe had been unable, perhaps unwilling, to stop prejudice. Instead, new forms of the old plague had arisen.

Toward the close of the nineteenth century, pseudoscientific assertions claimed that Jews were racially and ethnically different and that the modern nation-state could not integrate the ever-alien Jew. (A further discussion of the racial aspects of Nazi anti-Semitism follows in the next chapter.) Despite the success of the American experience, the concept that diversity could be a source of strength had not taken hold among many Europeans and was alien to the czars of Russia. The Great Emancipator, Alexander II, had freed the Russian serfs and eased the most repressive measures against the Jews. His tragic assassination in 1881 was blamed on the Jews and was followed by years of officially condoned, perhaps instigated, pogroms. The death toll of those riots in the Pale of Settlement, the southwestern region set aside for Jews, was appalling. Indeed, the physical survival of Russian and Polish Jews was in doubt.

During the final decade of the nineteenth century, the hope to create a Jewish homeland in Palestine had the support of growing numbers of young Eastern European Jews. When the English government expressed interest in such a scheme, the dream began to take shape. But the Holy Land, the focus of the Zionists, was still under Ottoman rule and not yet part of the British Empire; thus the English nod of approval was merely a gesture. Nonetheless, a number of Jewish pioneers settled as farmers on the barren Palestinian land. A nation, however, was not built by the earnest efforts of a vanguard. It required massive support, political negotiation, and excellent leadership. It required, in other words, the ability of Theodor Herzl. Herzl (1860–1904) was a Jewish journalist from Vienna who had been assigned to cover the Dreyfus trial in Paris. Captain Dreyfus' prosecution unleashed an upsurge of anti-Semitism that astounded and dismayed the young journalist, as well as many of the supporters of assimilation. Herzl concluded that only a Jewish state could solve the Jewish problem. He devoted the remainder of his life to effect the reality of nationhood for the Jews. In his book *Der Judenstaat (The Jewish State)*, he outlined the practical steps by which his vision could be realized. The work created a sensation, although much of the response was negative. Many Orthodox Jews protested that the ingathering in the Holy Land could occur only when the promised messiah appeared. Herzl, they argued, was not an observant Jew, how dare he suggest conventional statehood for the chosen people? Other critics contented that Judaism was a religion, not a nationality. Leaders of the assimilated communities held that full integration into the society of the various countries would take place eventually. Patience was called for, not demands for separateness. And then there was the segment of the Jewish population that wanted to remain invisible, who feared any publicity lest it give rise to more persecution. Among many Eastern European Jews, however, particularly the young, the idea of a homeland met enthusiastic support. Here, the ideal of returning to the land of the Scriptures had already taken tentative root. At last, Herzl, a man of action had emerged to provide the essential political leadership.

The First Zionist Congress met in Basel in 1897. For the first time in 1,800 years, Jews from throughout the Diaspora gathered to plan their future. Rich and poor, capitalist and socialist, orthodox and liberal—they had a mission. Though speaking many languages, they were unified in their aim to establish a national home for their people. They marveled at the white flag with the blue star of David, wept upon hearing a Jewish national anthem, and came away believing the impossible dream. They elected Herzl as the first president of their World Zionist Organization. Thus, they laid the foundation for the future state of Israel.

Meanwhile, difficulties mounted. Palestine was Turkish, and land sales for proposed settlements required the sultan's consent. That consent was never given. Herzl believed in diplomatic solutions to the deadlock and tried to enlist the rich and the powerful to promote his plans. He played on the Kaiser's egotism to win his good offices to intercede with the sultan—in vain. He faced the palpable hatred of the Russian foreign minister—in vain. He even applied to the Pope for help—in vain. All his strategies were fruitless. Only Great Britain showed a sympathetic interest by offering Herzl a haven in Uganda, East Africa. Should Uganda be accepted—perhaps as a temporary refuge for the suffering Eastern Jews? Or was Zionism unshakably committed to Zion, that is, Palestine? The organization was split by this controversy when, suddenly, just 44 years old, Herzl died.

Theodor Herzl did not live to establish a Jewish state. In terms of concrete accomplishments, nearly all his diplomatic missions failed. Nevertheless, he is a founder of the state of Israel. His spirit ushered in a dramatic change in the self-perception, and in much of the world's perception, of what it means to be a Jew. The organization he founded spread from village to town and from west to east. The greater the oppression, the greater the impact of the message: We shall live like other peoples, with a national state of our own. Young Jews, mostly Russian and Polish, prepared themselves for a future in Palestine. They studied Hebrew, thus making vital contributions to the transformation of a dead language to one that could serve the modern world. They learned to farm, irrigate, and apply practical knowledge to practical problems. Instead of the Talmud or law or medicine, they read treatises on soil erosion, reforestation, and horticulture. They split rocks, built roads, sang and danced, and rejoiced in the cooperative kibbutz life. The older generation often disapproved, particularly because their children's devotion to religion wore thin; but these young people were done with the meekness of their parents. These new Jews had no faith that assimilation would win them equality within the Gentile world. They would not accept the misery of persecution and poverty with docile hopelessness and look only to God for deliverance.

The religious attitudes of these young men and women ranged from liberal to orthodox, each group creating its own cooperatives. They trained in collective agricultural camps in Poland and Russia and, upon completing their preparatory courses, were expected to live in Palestine, to make *aliyah,* a word that means return to the biblical homeland. Some emigrated legally, others illegally, to become the forerunners of the massive immigration that would follow the First and Second World Wars.

THE REBIRTH OF POLAND

The twentieth century opened with unprecedented optimism. Western Europeans fully expected to expand their domination over the political and economic life of much of the globe. They predicted an end to such anachronisms as war and poverty. Even disease would surely be conquered in the foreseeable future. Science and logic would triumph over all the ills that had escaped from Pandora's box. But then the fantasy was shattered by the catastrophe of World War I. The madness of this devastating war was followed by a hypocritical peace.

After American idealism had raised hopes too high, disillusionment and disappointment at the end of the war were inevitable. Woodrow Wilson was the man of the hour, but many of his expectations were unrealized. The promise of general armament reduction, free trade, and border adjustments based on nationality was broken by the Allies even before they met at Versailles in 1919. But one of the promises that was kept concerned the restoration of Poland.

The new Poland had a bloody beginning. From north to south, its plains had been turned into battlefields during World War I. Already exhausted by the Great War, Poland's newly constituted sovereignty was challenged by its neighbors. Fierce border disputes with the Soviet Union, Lithuania, Estonia, and Czechoslovakia disrupted Poland's attempt to establish an economically viable and politically stable government. The entire interwar period, that is, the 20 years between the rebirth of Poland and its defeat by Nazi Germany in 1939, was an era of tension and limited progress. The anticipation that political liberty would be accompanied by economic well-being was not fulfilled. The euphoria sparked by independence turned to bitter frustration in the face of a difficult reality.

The Polish nation was composed of some 27 million inhabitants, 70 percent of whom were ethnic Poles; the rest of the population consisted of minorities, with Ukrainians and Jews comprising the largest percentages. Most Poles could not understand the complexity of the problems their nation encountered. City workers struggled with unemployment; capitalists lacked money to widen the industrial base; and an unstable parliamentary system composed of too many political parties had too little administrative experience. Patience and endurance were needed, but both were lacking. Millions emigrated, relieving the pressure to some degree. The democratic constitutional government adopted in 1921 was overthrown by a coup in 1926. For the next few years, Poland experienced some economic growth, but just as the recovery gave encouragement to investors, hopes were dashed by the Great Depression of 1929. The origin of the collapse was beyond the comprehension of the masses, and a scapegoat needed to be sacrificed. The Jews were the obvious choice.

Even before the economic disaster, the Polish government between the two world wars had been a moral failure. The treaty that had reestablished Polish sovereignty had specifically stipulated that the rights of ethnic minorities must be protected. But the pledge was not kept. The minorities were oppressed as the government sought to undermine non-Polish culture and force the minorities to abandon their distinctive way of life. For 150 years, the czars had attempted to turn Poles into Russians without success. How quickly that prolonged and painful lesson was forgotten!

THE INTERWAR DECADES

Politicians of the right and left became more radical and, although these extremists agreed on little else, they were as one in their embrace of anti-Semitism. The Jews were held responsible for every calamity that beset the nation. The government sanctioned and encouraged such prejudice and used its legal powers to target the Jews. Laws were enacted that restricted the Jews' economic freedom until fewer and fewer means to earn a livelihood remained. With the exceptions of the textile and some food-refining factories, Jews were denied industrial employment. Jewish workers had usually been the last hired and now were the first fired. Higher educational opportunities were severely limited by a quota system. Jewish students who managed to be accepted into universities were forced to sit on special "ghetto benches," placed in the back of lecture rooms. The social services of the impoverished Jewish communities tried desperately to prevent outright starvation, but only the charity of foreign Jews kept a large percentage of the three million Polish Jews from pauperism.

The impact of this renewed persecution not only resulted in the growth of Zionism, it was also expressed in the organization of the *Bund.* This was a socialist political party founded in 1897 to promote the welfare of the Jewish proletariat. It mirrored other socialist parties in its goals: better wages, improved working conditions, and promoting the election of a socialist government. Jewish workers established their own organization because the conventional socialist parties had no interest in their special needs such as permission to keep Jewish holy days, including the Sabbath, equal educational opportunities for their children, and cessation of the government's official anti-Jewish position. Unlike most of the proletariat, Jewish laborers were well-informed avid readers and involved in a variety of social and cultural activities. In most societies, only the upper and middle classes patronized the arts, but these working people loved literature, art, theater, and music. In western Poland, many Jews spoke, read, and wrote Yiddish, Polish, Hebrew, and German, and in the eastern provinces, Russian.

Despite their oppression, Polish Jewry was remarkably creative during the interval between the two great wars. Odessa and Warsaw became centers of Hebrew literature. Isaac Leib Peretz became the master of poetry, drama, and the short story. Authors such as Sholem Asch, Isaac Bashevis Singer, and his brother Israel Joshua Singer continued the genre. Theater developed from amateur status to professional productions, and popular performers achieved fame as the darlings of their audiences. There were libraries, trade schools, religious education, and magazines and newspapers to satisfy every political leaning. Concerts were performed in simple rooms with wooden benches or in gilded halls with plush seats to give pleasure to both the rich and poor. Jewish composers and musicians were in the forefront of Poland's musical resurgence. Even photography and filmmaking were fostered by Jewish artists. Endless philosophical and political disputations were, of course, accompanied and enhanced by uncounted cups of tea and mountains of cake.

While Polish urban Jewry discovered its great diversity, the shtetl, where God ruled without challenge, still existed in great numbers. Clearly, any attempt to speak of Polish Jewry as homogeneous springs from a flawed premise. The world that vanished had many different faces. A Polish Jew might be Orthodox or atheist, socialist or capitalist, Zionist or patriot. In their dying, however, all differences disappeared. Young or old, healthy or ill, wise or foolish, honest or corrupt, it did not matter. The eyes looking back at us from the photograph of Polish Jews lined up outside the lethal showers of the death camps were the eyes of Everyman.

Business courtyard on Nalewki Street in the Jewish quarter of Warsaw, Poland. (Leopold Page Collection/Library of Congress.)

CHAPTER 3

The Nazis' Rise to Power

The media carry frequent news reports concerning the resurgence of neo-Nazi groups, both in Europe and in America. The sight of swastikas smeared on walls and gravestones sends a shiver of fear and revulsion along the spines of the older generation, the generation that fought or experienced Nazism. Invariably, these hate crimes raise some difficult questions: Can a Holocaust happen again? Can it happen here? Where is the shadowy line that separates overreaction to pranks from disregard of possible danger? At what point does the protection of our civil liberties collide with the constitutional obligation to safeguard the nation?

Some of the answers may be found in the history of the Third Reich. The Nazis were able to reverse the path of Western civilization because three conditions converged that made the Shoah possible. First, the unthinkable had to appear to be not only doable, but also necessary. Persecution, even murder, had to be cloaked as a noble objective for the national welfare—"For the good of the many, a few must suffer." (This topic will be explored in the next chapter.) Second, the government must be a dictatorship and exercise total power over every aspect of the life of the people. When the slogan *Die Juden sind unser Unglueck* ("the Jews are our misfortune") became government policy, the Nazis were able to muster the psychological and the physical power required to remove the said *Unglueck.* Hitler's authority radiated outward from his will—even from his implied wish—to the ranks of his obsequious vassals. No effective resistance remained after the intimidation or physical destruction of all effective opposition.

The third prerequisite is the existence of an overt and/or latent prejudice directed against a targeted minority. This writer does not agree with Daniel Jonah Goldhagen's thesis that the German people were imbued with a special, distinct, murderous form of hatred that made them *Hitler's Willing Executioners.* It is a fact that many Germans viewed Jews with suspicion and antipathy, but it was in Poland and Russia that pogroms erupted. In March 2008, the German magazine *Der Spiegel* published an article entitled "Nazi Atrocities Committed by Ordinary Germans," which estimated that 200,000 Germans and Austrians participated in the perpetration of Nazi atrocities. That (0.25 percent) clearly is not a majority of 80,000,000 population of the two nations. Hitler's control over every means of communication made it possible to create the impression that this minority was representative of a large majority. Had, however, the researchers asked how many Germans knew of the death camps, and had the respondents told the truth, the percentages would have been vastly different.

The implementation of the Shoah required personnel who were asked to perform extraordinary duties. It is simply unbelievable that the men never spoke to their friends and families about their activities. The logistical problems of identifying, arresting, transporting, and killing millions of people while fighting a war were tremendous. It required the work and cooperation of many Germans coming from diverse areas of expertise. Racial "scientists" had to determine who was a full Jew, a half Jew, or a quarter Jew. Economists worked out the dynamics of driving Jews from business, industry, and the professions without interrupting production. The SS (*Schutzstaffel*), Gestapo (secret police), police, and army were needed to hunt down and imprison Jews in ghettos. Transportation experts pored over timetables of trains to ship the victims to the camps. To transform normal men into killers of innocent people who had not been judged guilty by any court, and did not fight back required suppression of all moral principles. As Christopher Browning in *Ordinary Men* analyzed so ably, civil servants who were part of the mobile killing units, the *Einsatzgruppen,* had to be trained to machine-gun naked Jews in open fields. The construction and operation of concentration and death camps demanded many willing hands and minds. The process of dehumanizing the killers, while also attempting to reduce the victims to the level of subhumans, was part of the work of the propaganda ministry. All these operations were possible only in the absence of even the most basic civil liberties and in the presence of a population who, by and large, chose to see nothing, hear nothing, and do nothing. The Jews were disappearing from the community, and the claim that their neighbors had no idea what that really meant has a hollow ring.

THE TOTALITARIAN PREREQUISITE

The German people opted for a dictatorship. They relinquished to their government the right to make all political, economic, and many personal decisions. They handed their individual and public liberties to Hitler like an unwanted gift they wished to return. Many Germans believed that their noninvolvement in the actual process of murder absolved them of all responsibility. Those nebulous "others," who were in charge, who had the power, were the only ones guilty. As long as one did not order or participate in the mass killings, one's hands were clean. The national legislature, the Reichstag, had abdicated its power and became a rubber stamp for Nazi decrees. The principle that resistance to evil was a moral duty did not exist for the vast majority of Germans, while the need to obey one's superiors had been instilled from early childhood. Not until the end of the war did men like Martin Niemoeller and Elie Wiesel arouse the world's conscience to the realization that the bystander cannot escape guilt or shame.

An understanding of the Shoah necessitates a comprehension of the theory and practice of Nazism. However, before discussing what it meant to be a German during the Third Reich, we must clarify the circumstances that allowed Hitler to take control. The Fuehrer (leader) did not forcibly overthrow a legitimate government; he was the officially authorized leader of the Weimar Republic. There was no coup d'état, no revolution. The Nazi Party won a plurality, which resulted in the selection of Hitler as the chancellor by the President of the Republic. Those who voted for the NSDAP, that is, the National Socialist German Workers Party—the Nazis—could not claim ignorance of Hitler's true aims because the press and radio had reported on his agenda for years. His book, *Mein Kampf (My Struggle),* was, in fact, a blueprint for his intentions to create a personal dictatorship. Both his enormously well-received speeches and his writing were punctuated by a loathing for a great many things: democracy, communism, peace, and Jews. Historians still debate just when Hitler's hatred of Jews escalated to annihilation, but it was always clear that their expulsion and persecution were cornerstones of his program.

The question of why a literate, well-informed electorate chose to throw away its freedom puzzles Americans. Why did so many Germans decide to renounce democratic government and vote for a man who had no formal education, never held a responsible job, and was not a German at all, but an Austrian? Were the circumstances that led to the demise of the Weimar Republic so unusual, so singular, that their recurrence is unlikely? Actually, the difficulties experienced by Germans in the early 1930s were not so exceptional that they have no parallel; other nationalities faced comparable distress after the end of the Great War. The victors as well as the losers of World War I experienced economic, social, and political upheavals which paved the road to Fascist and Communist dictatorships in Italy, Spain, and Russia. Nonetheless, it was Germany that plunged the world into World War II and enacted policies that nearly succeeded in destroying Western ideals of human progress toward greater happiness for greater numbers.

THE TREATY OF VERSAILLES

It is not germane to this text to discuss the causes of World War I; however, the results of this devastating conflict have a considerable bearing on Holocaust history. Germany, though allied to Austria–Hungary, Turkey, and Romania, bore the brunt of the bloodletting. Statistics on the number of civilian deaths are difficult to equate because different nations apply different criteria, however, a comparison of military casualties has greater validity. The population of Germany in 1914 was, in round numbers, 65 million. When the armistice was agreed upon in 1918, over 2 million military men had been killed and 4 to 5 million wounded. In percentage, these figures represent casualties of 9.6 percent. Only France, the battleground of most of the fighting, suffered comparatively greater losses, amounting to 14.4 percent of its roughly 40 million French citizens.

After four years of exhausting warfare, Allied armies defeated the Germans in 1918 and the monarchy of Kaiser Wilhelm II ended. The emperor abdicated amid violent political agitation and fled to Holland. The negotiations of the armistice and peace treaty were the unhappy responsibility of the newly established republican government. The exhausted German people wanted an end to hostilities and expected terms to be based on Woodrow Wilson's promise of peace without victory. But the actual treaty the German representatives were forced to sign was punitive, hardly designed to give the fledgling Republic a much-needed vote of confidence. The war guilt clause, placing the blame for the war solely upon Germany, infuriated every level of German society. Many Germans never absolved the signatories for their "betrayal." As a matter of fact, their delegation was not permitted to participate in the negotiations. The first republican government resigned rather than sign the treaty. But the German people were near starvation. Shipments of food and medicines from the United States were withheld until the signatures were affixed. None of these circumstances made any difference; "treason" was the epitaph that followed the men who accepted the Versailles *Diktat.* Field Marshal von Hindenburg, hero of the war, refused to represent the nation at the signing ceremony in the Hall of Mirrors. The civilian head of the Catholic Center Party, Matthias Erzberger, led the hapless delegation. Within three years, that valiant man was assassinated in payment for his courage. The German army was never held accountable by the public for losing the war or for standing aloof at Versailles or for its failure to support the new government.

It must be remembered that no foreign soldiers were on German soil when the armistice was accepted. Even though the human losses and near starvation had caused great suffering, the Germans could not accept that their armies, vaunted as the best in the world, had been beaten. The general reaction to the provisions of the Treaty was outrage. The terms were harsh, that is, unless one considers the severity of the agreement the Germans had forced on the Russians in 1918 at Brest-Litovsk. The Versailles settlement cost Germany one-eighth of her land along the eastern and western borders, her colonies, and her overseas investments. The German army was limited to 100,000 men; her navy was drastically curtailed, and the German people were obligated to pay an enormous, as yet unspecified, reparations bill. In light of today's understanding of international economic linkage among nations, the treaty was bound to obstruct and delay the process of German, or even worldwide, recovery.

THE WEIMAR REPUBLIC

The German government, known as the Weimar Republic (its constitution was drafted in that city), consisted of a legislature, the Reichstag, which was elected by universal suffrage and whose members represented the German people as a whole. A president, also chosen by the voters, served a seven-year term. Unlike his American counterpart, the president was not involved in the day-to-day running of the government but stood above political parties. Following national elections, he usually appointed the leader of the majority party to the office of chancellor to head the executive branch of government. Because it was difficult for any one party to have a clear majority in the Reichstag, all the Weimar governments were coalitions. The constitution also provided for representation from the 18 states to sit as the Reichsrat, but that body played a secondary role in the interwar period. Article 48 of the Constitution permitted the president to suspend many rights granted in the constitution during national emergencies. As will be seen later, this stipulation played a critical part in the final destruction of the Republic.

The political terms of right, left, and center vary over time, and an understanding of their meaning during the first half of the twentieth century is in order. Members of the extreme left were communists or Marxists. They advocated the violent overthrow of the government and redistribution of wealth and abolition of social classes and hoped to create another Moscow in Berlin. They had split from the more moderate and numerous socialist parties of Germany who sought political change through the ballot box. The socialists advocated government control and ownership of major public services, sources of raw materials, and the means of production and distribution. They promoted state direction of the economy and support of the needy from the cradle to the grave. The Catholic Center Party dominated the political middle of the Weimar Republic. It favored gradual changes to improve the lot of its working-class members, improved national stability, and continued religious protection for its minority. The German Democratic Party was never large enough to become a major player in Weimar politics. Its supporters came mainly from the intellectual elite. Among the conservatives were royalists who hoped to restore the Kaiser, militarists, and some members of the nobility. The Nazis, who believed that only a totalitarian dictatorship could save Germany, occupied the extreme right. According to their credo, it was necessary for a single political party to use every means, including terror, to attain conformity and obedience from the citizens. National glory through war and conquest would be achieved under the leadership of a Fuehrer. They judged democracy a hated failure, the consolation of the weak. In addition to these major political divisions, several splinter parties moved in and out of the spectrum, forming and discarding coalitions according to the demands of practical politics.

As a document, the Weimar Constitution was an admirable achievement. It provided for the protection of civil liberties, equality before the law, and free elections of a representative government by universal suffrage. It guaranteed free public education for all and provided safeguards for religious freedom. But this commendable instrument of government was immediately faced with grave problems. With the caveat that an outline of these difficulties may oversimplify some very complicated questions, the following summaries provide an overview.

The communists were disappointed that German socialism was not patterned after the Soviet model. Drawing most of their support from urban workers, they endorsed revolutionary methods to bring down the middle class that dominated the Weimar regime. In order to prevent such a Leninist revolution, the ruling Social Democrats, under President Friedrich Ebert, made a fateful deal with the German army. Generals Wilhelm Groener and Paul von Hindenburg agreed to support the Republic in the event of a communist insurrection. When, in fact, this threat materialized, the army crushed the communists. From this moment on, German democracy was unable to make itself the master of the armed forces. Weimar's civilian government was under constant pressure from its conservative, ever-critical, and still highly esteemed military. Swelling the ranks of the disillusioned were returning veterans. Unable to find work, they joined the *Freikorps*, a disruptive, often vicious, volunteer corps notorious for street fighting for rightist causes. The use of the army by President Ebert had alienated many of the factory workers and radicalized their politics from socialism to communism. The murders of two communist leaders, Karl Liebknecht and Rosa Luxemburg, by former cavalry officers, merely intensified their mistrust. To the upper- and middle-class German, however, communism was the dreaded specter haunting Europe. This resulted in a rather sympathetic, almost forgiving attitude, toward political assassinations, which was reflected by the leniency of the courts toward political assassins.

Members of rightist parties glorified all things German. The misery and shame resulting from the loss of World War I was the dominant source of their resentment. They would not accept the truth that their armies had been defeated. Instead, they covered their humiliation with half-truths and outright lies. The "stab in the back" theory that civilians, mainly Jews, had sold out the army, was particularly popular.

A second attempt to overthrow the Weimar government occurred in 1920. This venture was organized by the political right. Members of the old military–aristocratic alliance, secretly joined by a number of industrialists, marched to Berlin to topple the government. Known as the Kapp Putsch, it was a total failure. The ill-conceived plan misfired because the workers in Berlin staged a general strike. This time the military did not respond to the call to defend the Republic, but remarkably the labor unions united to crush the rebellion. The workers refused to provide the city with basic services: no power, no mail, and no transportation. Within five days, Wolfgang Kapp found that he could not establish a government in a paralyzed city. This fiasco, however, did not spell an end to rightist politics. Other, ever more extreme parties emerged. Among these was the Nazi party, whose actual name was *NAtionalsoZIalistische Deutsche Arbeiterpartei* (National-Socialist German Workers' Party).

The center's major objective was the protection of religious and civil rights of Catholics in a nation dominated by Protestants. In national elections, the number of centrists was usually second only to the number of socialists. Seen as moderate, centrists actually furnished more chancellors than any other party during the Weimar years. Without their cooperation and/or leadership, no government could effectively function. Trying to meet the needs of all Catholics meant that the Party tried to serve widely opposing interests beneath a single umbrella. Workers were courted to join Catholic trade unions, at the same time that many Catholic employers and aristocrats opposed major labor reforms. Agricultural, military, and commercial concerns also were frequently at odds. Only on the issue of communism was there unanimity; here, the Center Party stood in absolute opposition. Obviously, it was difficult to find a choirmaster to harmonize so many diverse voices. The brilliant Mattias Erzberger was an outstanding leader of the Center. He had seen it as his duty to sign the Treaty of Versailles, thus sparing the army and Marshal von Hindenburg the disgrace of doing so. In the eyes of violent nationalists that act was unforgivable. He was murdered by young rightists in 1921.

The Democrats suffered from the brutal politics of the 1920s as well. One of their most gifted statesmen, Walter Rathenau, head of the Foreign Office, was assassinated in 1922. The fact that Rathenau was a Jew and that his religion became a point of anti-Semitic inflammatory rhetoric was a bad omen. He incurred the hatred of the extreme right because he believed that the signature of German delegates on the Treaty of Versailles obligated the nation to honor its provisions. The nationalists hailed his murder as a victory despite the fact that Rathenau had earned international renown when he concluded the Treaty of Rapollo with the Soviet Union. This 1922 rapprochement of two pariahs in the family of nations benefited both participants; it ended their isolation. Germany gained an outlet for her industrial output, which was needed by the Soviet states that were aiming for greater economic self-sufficiency.

The death of the first president of the Republic, Friedrich Ebert, might be called murder by defamation. This man, who so richly deserved the gratitude of the German people, was hounded to death in the poisoned atmosphere of the era. He was vilified by the right and the left for doing his duty, namely, trying to make German democracy function. While working people accused him of catering to the middle class, conservatives despised him for his humble beginnings as a saddler. He was publicly denounced as a traitor and went to court to defend his name. Ebert sued the libeler and won the verdict. But the court also found that because Ebert had taken part in an illegal strike in 1918, he was technically guilty. The action and counteraction cost Ebert his life; he delayed a necessary appendectomy for too long and died in 1925 at the age of 54. His successor was the elderly Marshal von Hindenburg, the man fated to reluctantly hand the chancellor's office to Adolf Hitler.

Economic Problems

While the questions concerning payment or nonpayment of the huge reparations bill caused intense debate in the Reichstag, the French declared Germany in default over a rather minor delivery deficit. No doubt, the lasting bitterness over their defeat during the Franco-Prussian war and the German attack in World War I still festered in France. Supposedly to assure future payments, the French sent troops to occupy the industrial German Ruhr region. This escalated the long-standing enmity between Germany and France. The German public was incensed at this insult to German sovereignty. The former Allies opposed the French move, yet they did nothing. The inability of the Weimar administration to exercise full control within its own borders emphasized its weakness. But more serious still was the terrible inflation largely triggered by the occupation of the Ruhr.

The German government urged the workers of the occupied Ruhr region to strike rather than work for the French. The men complied but needed financial support from the government. Thousands of miners and industrial workers were supported by payments from the national treasury. This new burden was a further drain on Germany's fiscal health, already in difficulty due to the debts incurred during the war, the cost of demobilization, and the huge penalties demanded by the Treaty of Versailles. The government responded by printing more and more paper money, not backed by gold. The consequence was predictable: inflation. The continued effects of a lost war, the economic dislocation, the losses of territories, and finally the deluge of cheap money to buy scarce goods—all contributed to the problem. Debtors obviously like to get rid of their obligations with inflated currency, but as the problem intensified, the whole monetary system was undermined. Each rise in prices activated higher wages, and the resulting spiral drove the economy to ridiculous extremes. People rushed with their earnings to stores lest prices double within the next hour. In 1918, at the end of the war, the mark had been valued at 8.4 to the dollar; in 1922, the ratio was 70,000 marks to the dollar; by December 1923, the rate of exchange was astronomical, trillions of worthless marks for a single dollar.

This wild inflation ruined the German economy. Savings intended to provide for the needs of old age suddenly bought only a single loaf of bread. Investments quite literally were not worth the paper on which the certificates were printed. Labor unions were nearly destroyed because they were unable to provide their members with job security or a living wage. Large segments of the middle class were ruined financially. Some of the industrial giants, on the other hand, profited mightily. Their debts melted away, paid off with cheap money. Real estate speculators increased their holdings. The political reverberation of the economic chaos resulted in the further polarization of the right and the left. As will be noted in the following chapter, the newly organized Nazi party attempted and failed in its premature Putsch to use this crisis to commandeer the Bavarian government.

Finally, beginning in 1923, the administration was able to control the runaway inflation by placing the mark on par with its prewar value. This was strong medicine, and many of the already weakened businesses collapsed; the standard of living declined further as unemployment and low wages demoralized the breadwinners. But the bitter pill was swallowed and digested and resulted in a partial economic recovery.

Brief Recovery

The international community, somewhat belatedly, made an effort to support Germany's struggle to recover. The Dawes Plan and later the Young Plan, both formulated by Americans, provided for an orderly reparations schedule. Payments were adjusted, gradually reduced, or altogether forgiven. The French troops withdrew from the Ruhr and a major international crisis was averted. The ensuing recovery expanded as foreign investors acknowledged the fine performance of German industry and labor. German companies extended their organizations into giant vertical trusts. These were conglomerates that brought under a single management every process of manufacturing, from extracting raw materials to the distribution of finished goods. Among such successful, monopolistic international combinations, IG Farben Industrie was probably the best known. By concentrating vast business and technical power in the hands of only one group of managing directors, it was possible to compete successfully in domestic and foreign markets. Prices and profits were controlled, competition was bought out or eliminated, yet the quality of the output was high. The Weimar constitution provided greater freedom for organized labor and protected the right of collective bargaining, resulting in higher wages and improved working conditions. As unemployment fell, optimism rose. It is fair to say that in the mid-1920s, despite political uncertainties, the German people were rebuilding their economic life.

In the realm of world politics too, the horizon brightened. In 1926, Germany was admitted into the League of Nations, a step that encouraged greater national and international support for the Republic. If this trend had continued, political stability might well have followed. But, disastrously, this period of revival was short-lived.

Conditions outside the control of the German people plunged the nation into new danger. This time there would be no last-minute reprieve.

The Great Depression

The shaky foundations of the German Republic were subjected to an unexpected shock by the worldwide depression. The Wall Street crash of 1929 destabilized the American economy, and driven by a domino effect, the European economies were pulled down one after another. The Great Depression slashed production, employment, and the purchasing power of individuals as well as corporations. Many banks struggled in vain to remain viable, but when debtors were unable to meet their obligations, the number of foreclosures and bankruptcies multiplied. Farmers were the first to suffer economic decline and the dreaded forced sales deprived many thousands of their homesteads. Hunger once more undermined the physical and mental health of many Germans. Despair and rage competed within the hearts and minds of men and women who had worked hard all their lives and now faced a daily struggle for mere survival. The abiding and energizing hope of parents that their children might have a better future faded away.

German recovery had relied heavily on foreign loans and exports. Financial institutions from the United States had been the most generous creditors but now they were forced to call in their outstanding loans. American importers who had bought German products curtailed or completely withdrew from these markets, ever deepening the downturn of the economic cycle. No wonder doubts were voiced concerning the ability of a capitalistic free-market system to provide industrial societies with economic security. Centrally planned economies, supposedly free of foreign interference or dependence, found new supporters. The tycoons, of course, wanted no part of communist or socialist state planning. The mere suggestion of a possible nationalization of their companies pushed the conservative barons of industry to search for alternative remedies. Even the rhetoric of the Nazis won supporters because the Nazis promised to place no restrictions on private property and vowed that they would manage the nation's business life without depending on foreign support.

The Weimar Republic could not cope with the destitution of millions of its people. The unemployed who were affiliated with labor unions received small social security stipends, but many of the self-employed and unorganized workers were reduced to pauperism. Once again, the middle class, barely emerging from the chaos of inflation, was victimized by economic disaster. No wonder the quick-fix solutions offered by the Nazis appealed to these groups. The Social Democrats, in power since 1928, were unable to alleviate these mounting problems. The voters replaced them with the Center Party under the leadership of Chancellor Heinrich Bruening. The new chancellor, nicknamed *der Hunger Kanzler,* failed to get several of his projects through the Reichstag. With no other solution at hand, he persuaded President Hindenburg, then 82 years old, to invoke Article 48 of the Constitution. According to that provision, the nation was declared to be in a state of emergency and the parliamentary system was suspended. The measure was to be temporary, but in effect, marked the beginning of the end of the Republic. Officially, the takeover by the Nazi party did not occur until 1933, three years later, but the democratic process ground to a standstill as the nation tottered from crisis to crisis. The conviction grew that democracy could not work in Germany and that supposition attracted many voters to the parties of the extreme right and left.

THE NAZIS ENTER HISTORY

The soil in which the Nazi party took root and grew powerful had been well tilled. Since their defeat at the end of World War I, the German people had experienced international humiliation, political convulsions, economic disasters, and cultural escapism. Every calamity left a trail of discontent which fueled the hope that something new, something extreme, would come along and set the world right. Conservatives remembered the past in ever more glowing terms, extremists on the left looked with yearning and rose-colored glasses toward the Soviet Union, and rightists lent their ears, their conscience, and their money to the several ultranationalist parties. The success achieved by Hitler and the Nazi party was the result of a historic intersection of a man and his time.

By any measurement, Adolf Hitler's career was phenomenal. Technically, as an Austrian citizen, he was a foreigner in Germany. His education was incomplete, he had not graduated from high school, and he had never held a paying job; his appearance, except for the power of his eyes, was ordinary at best. In a nation where the right family background was highly valued, his *Kinderstube* was surely unimpressive. Yet this man held sway over a culturally mature nation and was idolized by millions of followers.

Adolf Hitler was born in 1889 in Lower Austria, the son of a minor customs official and his third wife. The boy showed no special promise, and he failed the entrance examination to attend the Vienna Academy of Fine Arts. It appears that this rejection turned the young Hitler into a homeless vagabond. For four years he tried to earn pennies peddling the picture postcards he painted. The Vienna interval was also associated with the development of his violent anti-Semitism. Vienna, the capital of the Austro-Hungarian Empire, had been a magnet for many poor Jews from the eastern provinces and from Poland. As is usually the case, the newcomers, often with odd customs, unfamiliar religious practices, and a strange mode of dress, were resented. Between 1895 and 1910, the political life of the city was dominated by its Christian Socialist mayor, Karl Lueger. To stay afloat in the cauldron of Austrian politics, Lueger tied himself to the hopes and frustrations of the lower classes. Among his formulae for retaining the support of the masses was anti-Semitism. The young destitute Hitler was deeply impressed by Lueger's simplistic solution of ascribing all calamities to the evil influence of the Jews. Lueger was popular and powerful. He was also an eloquent speaker—all in all a striking model for the future dictator.

World War I gave Hitler's life the direction it had lacked. He moved to Munich in 1913 and volunteered for the German army when the war broke out. From all accounts, he was a good soldier. The fact that he only achieved the rank of corporal would indicate that although he was awarded an Iron Cross First Class for bravery, he did not impress his superiors as officer material. When the armistice was reached, Hitler, by his own admission, was devastated. He went to Munich, where, in 1919, he joined a small political party, the German Workers' Party. Its founder was a railroad worker named Anton Drexler. Hitler's membership card read 555, but to inflate the roster, the numbering started at 500! Almost immediately he was elected to the executive committee of the *Deutsche Arbeiter Partei.* Most of the group were nearly penniless veterans, whose extreme nationalism included purging Jews and foreigners from German soil. Hitler very quickly reshaped this handful of malcontents into an effective organization. Here he discovered his exceptional powers as an orator. His words, his gestures, and his blazing eyes had an almost hypnotic effect on his listeners as his own inner conviction transfixed his audience. He spoke with certainty when others equivocated; he offered simple, bold solutions with an air of absolute assurance. His world was black and white; he wooed the crowd with his love for Germany and indulged their self-deceptions by assuring them that they represented the best among the races of the world. During this process he probably became certain that indeed he was destined to rescue the Fatherland from the clutches of communist and Jewish depravity. This mere splinter of an organization, one among hundreds, was lifted from obscurity to prominence by this fervor and his persuasive rhetoric.

THE PARTY PLATFORM

In 1920, the Party, soon to be renamed the National Socialist German Workers' Party, or Nazi Party, drafted the program designed to attract money and members. There was something in this agenda to appeal to nearly every discontented or frightened German. Among the 25 enumerated principles, the following are of particular interest in light of future events:

1. We demand on the basis of the right of national self-determination, the union of all Germans into a Greater Germany.
2. We demand equality for the German nation among other nations and the revocation of the peace treaties of Versailles and Saint Germain. [The latter had been concluded between the Allies and Austria.]
4. Only a racial comrade can be a citizen. Only a person of German blood, regardless of religious denomination, can be a racial comrade. No Jew, therefore, can be a racial comrade.
5. Noncitizens shall be able to live in Germany as guests only and must be placed under alien legislation.
6. Only citizens may hold public office, no matter what kind, and no matter whether it is national, state, or local.
8. Any further immigration of non-Germans must be prevented. All non-Germans who entered Germany after August 2, 1914, will be forced to leave the Reich without delay.

10. It must be the first duty of every citizen to perform mental or physical work. Individual activity must not violate the general interest, but must be exercised within the framework of the community and must be for the general good.

25. The creation of a strong central government is a requisite to the implementation of the above listed reforms. [Among these were included the confiscation of war profits, mandatory profit sharing of large business enterprises, old age insurance, land reform, the death penalty for many criminals, government-sponsored educational and health service, newspaper censorship, and the curtailment of religious freedom.]

Considering the fact that most party platforms contain empty verbiage rather than a plan for governing, this document came close to being a blueprint for the conduct of the Nazis in office. The union with Austria, the scrapping of the treaties ending World War I, discrimination against the Jews—all were outlined and centralization of political power was also forecast. Hitler's preoccupation with so-called German blood, so vital in his Aryan superiority ideology, was given several references. Article 10 asserted that citizens exist for the nation, not vice versa, a concept of central importance in the Third Reich.

THE SA

In 1921, Hitler created the SA (*Sturmabteilung,* best translated as storm division) to function as a semi-military organization for the protection of Nazi Party meetings and to harass rival organizations. The troopers wore brown shirts, pants, and boots and were often referred to as the Brownshirts. Most were unemployed toughs; some had seen military service. Their antisocial behavior was glamorized as heroism in defense of the Fatherland. They brawled in the streets with the militant members of opposition parties, threatened voters near the balloting places, and beat up Jews and other targeted civilians. Under the leadership of Hitler's friend Ernst Roehm, their numbers swelled to reach 400,000 in 1932. When Hitler became chancellor, he enhanced the SA's powers by converting it to a national political police force. While ordinary policemen were expected to enforce the law, the SA was accountable only to its own commanders. But Roehm's ambitions for the SA were even greater. Roehm aspired to create a truly military force, one to rival and equal the regular army. As will be noted later, the feud between the *Wehrmacht* (regular German army) and the SA was decided in 1934 during the Night of the Long Knives in favor of the traditional army. After the eclipse of SA power, the function of terrorizing the public was taken over by the SS (*Schutzstaffel,* storm troopers, also known as the Blackshirts), the better-trained, better-schooled elite of Hitler's political army.

THE FAILED BEER HALL PUTSCH

Hitler's first attempt to attain political power was a local affair. He planned to unseat the Bavarian state administration with a coup d'état in 1923 in Munich. Named after the beer hall where the attempt began, its scenario resembled a comic opera performance rather than a serious political strategy. Act I opened in the cellar where some 3,000 Bavarians, including political, military, and social leaders, had gathered to hear a speech by Gustav von Kahr, the state commissioner. Outside, 600 SA men surrounded the building. They set up a machine gun with its muzzle pointed toward the main entrance of the building. In the beer hall, meanwhile, there was shock and high drama. Von Kahr was droning on when suddenly an excited man with a mustache jumped on a chair, fired a shot toward the ceiling, and shouted that the national revolution had begun. Hitler, in the company of a few followers, then exclaimed that the SA had already taken over the police and army barracks and that soldiers and police had joined the revolution. (They were all lies.) Several of the dignitaries hustled the shooter into a back room. There a very tense Hitler informed them that the new head of the German nation was the renowned General von Ludendorff. The stunned circle of officials recovered enough to tell Hitler to stop his nonsense. The enraged Hitler screamed that tomorrow would find Germany either with a new government or he and his comrades would be dead. (Neither prediction was accurate.) One by one the officials of the Bavarian government managed to escape from the beer hall and prepare for the coming showdown with these would-be revolutionaries.

Ludendorff, the war hero turned right-wing eccentric, arrived in time to lend his considerable prestige to the coup. Meanwhile, news of the Bavarian uprising had reached the head of the national army. Its leadership promised to stand by the Republic and declared its willingness to commit troops to quell the insurrection in the event that Bavarian authorities needed help. As it turned out, such assistance was not required.

The next scene was enacted on the streets of Munich. The SA, led by Ludendorff and Hitler, marched toward a confrontation with Bavarian police. Three thousand Nazis were stopped by a barricade of 100 policemen. Hitler's demand that they surrender was answered with bullets. The line of Brownshirts melted away. Neither Hitler nor Ludendorff was injured, but the Putsch was over. The 16 Nazis who were killed that November morning became the glorified martyrs of the movement; their praises were sung many thousands of times in the "Horst Wessel Song," the Nazi anthem.

The last act of the attempted insurrection was played out at Hitler's trial. Indicted for treason, he did not stand as a penitent at the bar of justice. Quite the opposite, he used the public prosecution as a propaganda platform and turned failure into a publicity success. The whole nation suddenly knew who he was. He was found guilty and sentenced to five years' imprisonment. Actually, he served less than two years and used that interval to further advance his cause. While rather comfortably confined, he dictated the holy writ of Nazism, *Mein Kampf (My Struggle),* to his friend and secretary Rudolf Hess. The lesson of the failed takeover was not lost on Hitler; he was now certain that although he was fated to resurrect Germany, it must be done through legitimate means. In other words, the way to victory was ballots rather than bullets. The acquittal of Ludendorff, so obviously a conspirator against the Republic, was a clear indication that the judicial system remained unduly awed by the military. Hitler's brief sentence and comfortable incarceration were examples of the indulgence of the judicial system toward the extreme right.

It is difficult to judge the actual impact of Hitler's book. During the Nazi era it was found in most German households; it replaced the Bible as an almost mandatory wedding present. Every student could quote passages from its pages. Hitler became a millionaire from the ten million copies sold by 1945. (He placed the profits in Swiss banks.) How much of the volume was actually read and understood by the general public one cannot guess. The first edition was almost unreadable. It was a jumble of Hitler's racial and political invective against the evils of the contemporary political and economic systems. He admonished Germans to value their *Volksgemeinschaft*, their special relationship to German blood and soil. He insisted that Aryans are the crowning glory of creation, and Jews the eternal parasitic enemy. The book was so poorly organized and contained so many grammatical errors that subsequent editions had to be cleaned up by the editors. In retrospect, the German people, in fact, the entire world, would have done well to pay greater attention to Hitler's stated objectives. Those who actually bothered to plow through the volume had few surprises when Hitler ultimately achieved power.

Among the major propositions postulated in *Mein Kampf* are the following:

1. Unconditional authority belongs to the leader. This concept, often called the *Fuehrer Prinzip,* regards democracy as a despicable form of government and the Weimar Republic as one of its most depraved examples.
2. The Germans are a superior race. As Aryans, they are the bearers of the highest expression of racial fulfillment. Aryan racial purity must be maintained at all cost. No diseased or weak people must be allowed to have children.
3. The Jews are the essential enemy in Hitler's pseudo-Darwinistic concept of survival of the fittest. Jews seek to ruin Germany and all civilization; they have no culture, and Jewish men desperately want to seduce Aryan women.
4. All life is a struggle for survival; war is the natural and honorable expression of that struggle.
5. Marxism is the other great enemy of Germany. Often the Marxist and Jewish menace are depicted as one and the same.
6. Germany's economy must become self-sufficient. Dependence on foreign loans and trade was designed to keep the nation enslaved to interest payments.
7. Nationality and race are innate, and only birth and heritage can bestow the German birthright, not language or religion or cultural imitation.
8. Large economic complexes must be broken up, and all businesses must share profits with their workers.

With the exception of the last item, most of the ideas expressed in the book became Nazi policy after 1933.

THE ARYAN SUPERIORITY MYTH

At the center of Hitler's beliefs was the racial doctrine. Since it was the theoretical basis and the rationale for the destruction of so many millions deemed unfit to live in the Nazi universe, it requires further elaboration.

Who was the Jew according to Nazi doctrine? No logical answer emerges from the thousands of pages dedicated to the topic. The Goebbels' propaganda machine and the pages of Julius Streicher's *Stuermer,* a weekly newspaper dedicated to Jew baiting, reveal the Jew to be an enigma: powerful enough to threaten every civilization but also cowardly and servile and racially pure (although totally evil), yet lusting after Nordic women. He was the capitalist with an insatiable appetite for money but also responsible for organizing labor into hated unions; he was responsible for that turn-the-other-cheek religion of meekness, Christianity, yet Christ was depicted as an Aryan chieftain. In other words, the Jew was whatever the Nazis needed him to be at any given moment.

How did the German people manage such confusion? It seems that they divided their judgment into two categories. First, there were their Jewish neighbors, the ones they knew in flesh and blood, folks no better or worse than most Germans. But then there were the other ones, the despicable ones. They lived somewhere else, in some vague sphere beyond their horizon. They must exist because it was unthinkable that the authorities would lie.

Herbert Spencer had theorized that Charles Darwin's survival of the fittest was a concept that could be applied to human societies. Might makes right; that is nature's way. Nazi "racial philosophers" adopted the theme. It dovetailed with their doctrine of the warrior as the highest expression of mankind. From this assumption and the pseudoscientific pretensions of other exponents, the theory of Aryan superiority was advanced. The fact that there is no Aryan race was no deterrent. The term "Aryan" is actually the designation of an Indo-European language group. By virtue of skillful manipulation, a lie was elevated into a so-called science. From kindergartens to universities, racial studies were presented to students as objective truth. Aryan superiority was "proven" with concocted data of biological measurements and historical "evidence" of past greatness. The ideal men and women were blond, blue-eyed, tall, straight-backed, and had high foreheads and straight noses. Side by side with the physical attributes of the Aryans were their spiritual qualities: courage, honesty, intellect, inventiveness, and artistic excellence. These traits were genetically embedded in the bloodline. The superiority of the Nordic race permitted, no, demanded, the right to subjugate less advantaged people, such as the Eastern European Slavs. Thus, counterfeit biological factors were given momentous significance in this perverted form of Darwinism. The race most fit to dominate had the natural right to mastery over lesser races; the nation able to subdue the weak is endowed by nature with the right to conquest.

The spurious scientists of the Third Reich elevated the theories of the fertile minds of Houston Stewart Chamberlain and Alfred Rosenberg to the level of dogma. Chamberlain (1855–1927) was born an Englishman who turned his back on his native country. He married the daughter of composer Richard Wagner and became fanatical in his admiration of all things German. His mental acrobatics were astounding. He admired Galileo, Dante, Michelangelo, and Leonardo da Vinci and insisted that these historic figures were racial Teutons. In fact, all benefactors of mankind, all gifts enjoyed by humanity, stemmed from the Nordic race. Even Jesus was given an Aryan heritage. The Teutonic/Germanic people stood in direct opposition to the destructive power of the only other pure race, the Jews. In his lofty, metaphysical style, Chamberlain rewrote history. Racial impurity was blamed for the fall of ancient Rome, and the Jews were the bearers of the ethnic disorder that felled mighty Rome. It is difficult to believe that such nonsense found so many advocates; nevertheless, his books were best sellers and won critical praise in Germany.

Alfred Rosenberg (1893–1946), a Lithuanian by birth, was the chief ideologist of the Nazi party. After a stint as editor of the Nazi newspaper *Voelkische Beobachter*, Rosenberg was offered several political positions by Hitler. His final post was as Reichsminister for the Eastern Occupied Territories, where he promoted the brutal Germanization of conquered Poland, supervised slave laborers, and aided in the mass murder of Jews. His dreadful career ended on the gallows upon his conviction by the International Military Tribunal at Nuremberg in 1945.

Influenced by Chamberlain, Rosenberg's best seller, *The Myth of the Twentieth Century,* reiterated the claim of Nordic racial superiority but added a new concept—namely, a virulent anti-Christian element. The Catholic Church was held responsible for accepting and spreading the destructive spirit of a Semitic/Latin faith. In pseudoscientific terms, Rosenberg reshaped the loving Christ into an Aryan warrior who fought with sword in hand. From this spurious reasoning, Rosenberg leaped to the conclusion that the Jews were answerable not only for their own crimes but also for all evil, past and present, committed by the Christian world. His attempts to return to the ancient pagan faith, called rather paradoxically, Positive Christianity, was cut short by the war. The pagan god Wotan of Norse legend could not replace Jesus even among ardent Nazis, and Rosenberg's theories never seriously damaged Christian doctrines.

LEGITIMIZING HITLER

As noted earlier, the Depression had given the Nazi movement the opportunity to increase its membership dramatically as the disillusioned electorate turned to radical parties in growing numbers. City workers found their way into both the Nazi and the communist movements. The radical left and its *Rotfrontkaempferbund* (Red Front Fighter Group) and the SA of the Nazis fought pitched battles on city streets. Speakers representing every political point of view harangued the public with their rhetoric. Every sort of uniform was resurrected from attics and cellars. Prominent among these was the gray worn by the *Stahlhelmers* (the Steel Helmets), a paramilitary umbrella organization of nationalistic ex-servicemen. Their smart marching ranks welcomed most monarchists as well as other assorted enemies of the Weimar Republic. However, the Steel Helmets only rarely clashed with the Nazi militia. Hitler had forbidden such conflicts. The connection between the *Stahlhelm* and the regular military forces was too close for comfort, and Hitler had no wish to alienate the army.

Political warfare was expensive, even in the 1930s. The Nazis campaigned hard in every local and national election. The SA, the propaganda campaigns, the sea of swastikas, the ancient symbol the Nazis had adopted as their insignia, the uniforms, and marching bands—all these trappings necessitated fundraising. Hitler needed money, or preferably, he needed support from people with money. But would members of the financial and industrial establishment take him seriously? Could their snobbish attitude toward an Austrian upstart be overcome?

Fear of communism gave Hitler a passport into the world of power and money. He was seen as a possible champion, a counterweight against the dreaded Red Menace. When the number of Nazi Reichstag representatives rose from 12 to 107 in the 1930 election, it became the second largest party in the parliament. The communists, too, had made dangerous gains, from 54 to 77 seats. In the absence of a better candidate, Herr Hitler, so the magnates believed, would do. Indeed, he was a little uncouth, not from the background they preferred, but he would be useful as their tool, their means to fight communism. No doubt, this Austrian corporal would be malleable in their experienced hands, a man to be molded to their will.

Two events contributed to the improved standing of the Nazis among the upper classes. The first occurred in 1931 when a conclave of political rightist party leaders allowed Hitler into their vaunted company of important, well-established nationalists. In attendance were the *Stahlhelm*'s chief, Franz Seldte; the director of the United Steelworks, Fritz Thyssen; the renowned banker and economic wizard Hjalmar Schacht; and the head of the Nationalist Party, Alfred Hugenberg. The meeting took place in the small town of Harzburg and was thus dubbed the Harzburg Front. Hitler, always an impressive speaker, made a good impression on the assemblage. Acceptance, endorsement, and financial support by the mainstream of rightist organizations allowed the Nazis to take a giant step up the ladder to power.

During the following year, Hitler was invited to address the members of the elite Industry Club. Here, in Duesseldorf, at the center of German manufacturing, Hitler again worked his oratorical charm. He spoke for two and a half hours, shouting much of the time. He persuaded his audience that his party would safeguard capitalism, protect private property, end the communist danger, and keep the trade unions in check. This was music to the ears of the coal and steel barons of the Ruhr. Hitler was given a standing ovation, and more importantly, his future political campaigns were well financed.

THE END OF THE REPUBLIC

The moderate parties of the Weimar Republic had been unable to solve Germany's economic distress nor could they remedy the political morass. At this juncture, in 1932, Hindenburg's first presidential term ended. Hitler decided his time had come and ran against him. It was an election campaign characterized by frequent violence, particularly between communists and Nazis. The voters at the polls were threatened by the Brownshirts who swarmed around the polling places. Hitler won 30 percent of the vote; this necessitated a run-off election with Hindenburg. The aging war hero was returned to office, but his was a hollow victory. Later that year, in the Reichstag elections, the Nazis won 230 seats. Although they did not have a majority, they had become the largest single party in the legislature.

By precedent, Hitler should now have been appointed chancellor, but the venerable president of the Republic could not bring himself to hand the government to this ex-corporal from Austria. Hindenburg was 84 years, and his mind and body had lost much strength, yet he had an almost instinctive mistrust of this gesticulating man with the black mustache. So, he tried to give Germany a government without Hitler.

Chancellor Bruening had been dismissed. Who could fill the post? The Machiavellian role played by General Kurt von Schleicher underlined the continuing deterioration of German politics. Schleicher had been at the periphery of power for years. He now suggested that Hindenburg proffer the chancellorship to a mediocre member of the aristocracy, Franz von Papen. The debonair von Papen sought to curb the power of the Nazis by bringing Hitler into his fold. The maneuver failed; Hitler did not want to become vice-chancellor. He was certain his time to realize complete power was near at hand. Von Papen decided that a new election would reduce the Nazi vote. He was only partially correct. The number of NSDAP members in the Reichstag was cut by 34 seats. A small victory, but it changed nothing. Von Papen resigned, and Schleicher moved up into the chancellor's office. His was the last administration of the Weimar Republic.

Schleicher tried to check the Nazi menace by creating an anti-Nazi coalition of the army and the trade unions, but even fear of Hitler could not hold together such an unnatural pairing. With no other option in sight, the chancellor tried to convince Hindenburg that only a military dictatorship could save the Fatherland, but the old field marshal had sworn to uphold the constitution and would not sign such an order. Schleicher had no choice but to offer his resignation. Hitler never forgot nor forgave Schleicher's attempt to block his road to power. In 1934, during the Night of the Long Knives, also known as the Blood Purge, six Nazi murderers entered Schleicher's home and killed him and his wife in the presence of his family.

The curtain fell on the Republic when Hindenburg, under pressure from his son Oskar, was finally persuaded to ask Hitler to form a government. Von Papen, still under the illusion that his titles, his background, and his diplomatic experience would impress the son of a minor customs official, accepted the vice-chancellor's office. He, like so many others, underestimated Hitler. For the field marshal, it was a painful duty to appoint the Austrian ex-corporal; he had vowed that never would he hand the government to Hitler. Upon hearing this, Hitler said, "Hindenburg is 85 years old, I am 45. I can wait." He did not wait very long. Within a year he occupied the president's office as well.

CHAPTER 4

Masters of the Third Reich

The Holocaust was implemented by men, not mechanical robots or spineless puppets. Men planned, executed, and exulted in the commission of modern history's most despicable crime. The more we learn about the methods used to realize Hitler's vision of a world without Jews, the more insistently the question recurs: What kind of people could have committed such unspeakable acts?

Hatred of the Jews was Hitler's central passion. The man and the Shoah cannot be separated. The suggestion that the Fuehrer did not order, in fact did not know of the mass killings, flies in the face of all we know about the administrative apparatus of the regime. No one would have dared to execute such a momentous scheme without Hitler's actual or implied order. Even though a written directive for the Holocaust has not, as of this writing, been uncovered, veritable mountains of research indicate that Hitler's elite vied with one another to do their master's will. Often, the heads of agencies dealing with Jewish issues anticipated Hitler's wishes and converted assumptions to orders. It would have been suicidal for any subordinate to act in opposition to the Fuehrer's instruction or his implied intentions because others within Hitler's inner circle would have denounced any rival in order to further their own careers.

HITLER'S IDEOLOGICAL ANTECEDENTS

In *Mein Kampf* Hitler gave little indication of how his early personality was shaped. He stated that upon passing a group of religious Jews on the street during his stay in Vienna, he experienced a mystical insight that these bearded, black-garbed men represented a deadly cancer upon the Germanic spirit. Actually, during the period of 1907–1913, the young Hitler had adopted his racial and political concepts from ideas promulgated by others. For example, an ex-monk who called himself Lanz von Liebenfels wrote extensively on Aryan superiority and flew a flag with a swastika over his castle. Liebenfels insisted that Jews headed the list of inferior races and must make way for the superior Aryans. His notion of "making way" included deportations, slave labor, sterilization, and killing—all methods later used in the Third Reich. Another precursor of Nazi theory was Georg Ritter von Schoenerer. He was the leader of the Austrian pan-German movement, which urged the union of all Germans into a single nation. He, too, exhorted his followers to recognize Jews as a national menace. The previously mentioned mayor of Vienna, Karl Lueger of the Austrian Christian Social Party, became Hitler's mentor in two areas: First, he accused the Jews of shameless financial exploitation and held them responsible for whatever ills beset society. Second, Lueger manipulated the masses, creating a prototype for the masterful use of dramatic and emotional propaganda techniques.

Few of the methods Hitler employed during his war against the Jews were new. Anti-Jewish malevolence was practiced in the ancient, medieval, and modern world. These antecedents foreshadowed the Nazis' program rather explicitly; only the use of death camps was an innovation. Clearly, Jews have a long history of persecution and served as scapegoats for floods, droughts, plagues, missing children, cattle decease, and whatever harm befell Europe. The Christian Church had institutionalized this hatred. It gave its blessing to kings, who made Jews their personal chattel and repeatedly expelled and readmitted them, barred them from most occupations for hundreds of years, and shut them into ghettos. Yet, none of these precedents explain the Holocaust. The persecutions of the past were based on objectives or motivations that made sense to the persecutors; something advantageous was expected to result from the mistreatment of the Jewish minority. But how did the Holocaust benefit Germany?

THE IRRATIONALITY OF THE HOLOCAUST

Before we attempt to understand Hitler's *Weltanschauung,* his worldview, some misconceptions need to be dispelled. Governments, we know, have killed segments of their own people since the dawn of history. But such atrocities were committed with the expectation that the carnage would advance some groups and solve some problems. It would be reasonable to expect this concept to hold true for the Nazi era as well. But that supposition is not born out. As will be explained below, killing six million Jews did not benefit Germany. The Holocaust rendered no political, social, economic, or military advantage to the Nazis. In fact, killing the Jews was detrimental to Hitler's domestic and foreign policy goals. Then why was it done? To examine that question, it is necessary to dispel some of the erroneous notions still given credence.

Hitler's determination to make Europe *Judenrein* was not based on economic motivation. Yes, in the first years of his dictatorship there was high unemployment, and depriving the Jews of their jobs and businesses allowed some Gentile Germans to find work. However, when the killing process was initiated, increased production had already provided full employment. Keeping the Jews alive as unpaid slaves would have made economic sense. Instead, their annihilation cost the Germans many millions of working hours. The argument that Hitler needed the wealth of the Jews to fuel his military plans is equally wrong. Jewish assets were never large enough to fund his wars. At any rate, he ordered the seizure of the Jews' properties and bank accounts and all their valuables, from jewelry to wool coats, pauperized them, and still shipped them into death camps. In places like Auschwitz the considerable skills of Jewish prisoners were wasted.

Is it possible that the Jews were killed for political reasons? Hitler once stated that if there were no Jews he would have needed to invent them. In other words, they were useful scapegoats. But does that view correspond with their destruction? It does not. Dead scapegoats have no value. Once gone, they can no longer absolve the living of their failures. A new scapegoat would then be required, but the Jews would be difficult to replace—historically they were unsurpassed as objects of blame.

Did the Jews at any time pose an actual political danger to the Third Reich? Again, the answer is no. Joseph Goebbels, minister of Propaganda and Public Enlightenment, denounced them as Marxists, communists, saboteurs, greedy capitalists, union organizers, and traitors in league with the enemy, but he furnished no evidence to substantiate his words. The Jews of Germany, at most 1 percent of the population, never constituted a political bloc. They did not support any single political ideology or candidate. A diverse group, they included urban workers, lower and upper middle-class artisans, businessmen, and a wide range of professionals. Not even the minister of Public Enlightenment thought it expedient to accuse them of conspiracy to usurp the political order. His assertion that the Jews were both greedy capitalists as well as leaders of subversive labor unions undermined both allegations. His revival of the rather well-worn accusation that Jews planned to overthrow all Christian civilizations, a claim made in that old czarist forgery known as *The Protocols of the Elders of Zion,* was pure fiction. The *Protocols,* published in 1903, had been written at the behest of the Russian secret police and purported to be the minutes of a secret meeting of the leaders of international Jewry. The alleged aim of the cabal was nothing less than the domination of the Christian world. Here the pathetic Jew of the Middle Ages was replaced by a new version, the sly, powerful, brilliant, and very dangerous modern Jew. The old scapegoat was dressed in new clothes befitting for the twentieth century industrial era.

Hitler often coupled Jew and communist to form a single word, a device that played on the fears of the German middle and upper classes. Actually, Jews were no threat to the government because they had no political power. The very success of the Holocaust demonstrates their weakness and their inability to exert any influence in Germany or internationally.

PSEUDO INTELLECTUAL ROOTS

Some scholars assert that German philosophers during the past two centuries prepared a unique Teutonic predisposition for the Holocaust. Their arguments are not convincing. It is questionable how much influence was exerted on ordinary Germans by such learned professors as Imanuel Kant, Johann Gottlieb Fichte, Georg Hegel, and Heinrich von Treitschke. Until the rise of Hitler, the ebb and flow of anti-Semitism had washed the shores of Spain, France, Germany, Poland, and Russia without partiality. One could make an equally dubious case for the opposite *Weltanschauung* by quoting from the works of Germans who urged tolerance and acceptance of differences among people. Finally, we must not assume that Hitler's racial ideology was derived from reading the works of philosophers whose theories were often unintelligible even to the educated elite. Neither Hitler nor the men who sat at his feet were philosophical thinkers. They took pride in action, not debating, and often sneered at the intellectuals whom they considered useless baggage.

It is very difficult for rational human beings to acknowledge that the causes of the Shoah are not rational at all. Neither economic, political, religious nor social motivations can account for the gas chambers. How then can we explain this reversal of Western values that idealized progress for improving the lives of the greatest number of people? One is persuaded to believe that the death of the Jews gratified some destructive imperative within Hitler's mind.

PSYCHOLOGICAL HYPOTHESES

Why did Hitler hate the Jews? We will ignore the aberrant theory that Hitler's brain was damaged by syphilis or the equally insupportable opinion that Hitler became deranged because he had only a single testicle. Can psychiatry provide some

Hitler, the orator. (AP Wide World Photos.)

answers? Perhaps, but it must be remembered that at best, psychological analyses of Hitler result in theories, in probabilities, and in presumptions. As social scientists, historians prefer to place emphasis on the term *scientist* and seek hard evidence rather than rely on conjecture. Any attempt to discover a dead man's motivation cannot yield measurable, conclusive data. Nonetheless, as students of the Holocaust we cannot evade the central question concerning the state of Hitler's mind and thus we are compelled to step into these uncertain waters. Always, however, we must remember that theories are open to interpretation.

Was Hitler insane? The search for an answer begins with Adolf the child. There is no doubt that the boy lived in an unhealthy family environment. The father seems to have been a nasty brute and the mother pious in the extreme. But a miserable childhood is an all too common problem and need not lead to a warped adult. No doubt, early childhood traumas play a role in the development of personality, but that is not analogous to producing a Hitler. Surely, the world would be a place of unremitting savagery if painful childhood experiences produced destructive, depraved adults.

Among the several psychological analyses offered, the most compelling account, in this writer's view, was elaborated by Robert G. L. Waite in his book *The Psychopathic God: Adolf Hitler.* Waite and others maintained that the paradoxical, irrational, and sexually aberrant Hitler was reared in circumstances that were destructive to proper maturation. Waite's Hitler combined a number of abnormalities to form a neurotic individual, who, toward the end of his life, became psychotic.

HITLER: A MAN OF PARADOXES

Biographies of Hitler delineate his personality as paradoxical. He was brutal, but also capable of kindness, particularly to children and animals. Sometimes his honesty could be disarming, but lies served him with equal ease. His grasp of reality was a matter of timing; sometimes it seemed firmly based, at other times his fantasies seemed to overpower his mind. His life was marked by acts of courage as well as of cowardice. In public, he exhibited superb self-assurance; in private, he worried about the impression he made. He saw others only in two diametrically opposing shades, black or white, blind supporter or dangerous enemy. His moods could swing from rage to gentleness in a moment. His capacity for hatred, coupled with his conviction that destiny had singled him out for a messianic role, made him the most dangerous man in a perilous century.

Hitler glorified the concept of the perfect Aryan specimen, but his appearance hardly met his own criteria. Furthermore, his inner circle included a number of misfits. When facts contradicted a concept in his mental world, Hitler did not change his mind, he altered the facts. Thus, for example, it became Nazi lore that Jesus was not a Jew, that Jews were infectious vermin, that Franklin D. Roosevelt and most of the English nobility were Jewish, that Judaism was a race not a religion, that only Aryan blood was creative, and non-Aryans were merely fit for enslavement. The determining factor of good and evil, right and wrong, was blood and blood alone. His preoccupation with blood, and Jewish blood in particular, ran like a refrain through his mind. One cannot but wonder why.

The Parents

Hitler's father, Alois, was the illegitimate child of Anna Marie Schickelgruber and Georg Hiedler. The father's brother Johann adopted and reared the boy in his home. Later, Alois changed the spelling of his name to Hitler. The uncertainty of his ancestry may have contributed to his son's fixation on genetics and raised questions concerning his own bloodline. Many Austrians were anti-Semitic, and it is not unreasonable to presume that young Adolf heard anti-Jewish comments during his childhood. Such early indoctrination, when coupled with insecurity concerning his parentage, may have caused Hitler's fascination with blood. If he feared that his own heritage could be tainted with Jewish genes, then his many references to poisoned blood, his refusal to father any children, and his strange eagerness to endure leeches as part of medical treatments become comprehensible. Consciously or not, doubts regarding his Aryan purity may have resulted in some strange personal habits. For example, he was obsessively clean (Jews are dirty); he drew attention away from his nose with a mustache (Jews have large noses); in 1935, just two years after he became chancellor, he banned Gentile females under the age of 45 from working in Jewish households (his grandmother had been a maid, although not in a Jewish household); and sexual intercourse between Jews and Gentiles was declared a capital crime. The razing of the entire village where his father was born was certainly bizarre. Surely, there were other sites where an artillery testing ground could have been installed without moving the residents to new homes. Did Hitler hope that the disappearance of the village would cause his father's memory to go up in smoke as well?

Robert Waite is not alone in his allegation that Alois Hitler was a mean and cruel man. He had risen from peasant stock to become a minor customs official on the Austro-German border. Clara, Adolf's mother, was his third wife. She was 23 years younger than her husband. It would not be unusual if Alois expected, and was given, total and silent obedience from his family. Nor would it have created any stir if he beat his wife and children, either drunk or sober. The adult Hitler rarely mentioned his father. As a matter of fact, he did not commonly refer to Germany as the Fatherland. It is the Motherland he promised to save, the Motherland he extolled endlessly.

Alois seemed to interpret the duties of fatherhood to consist of either ignoring or browbeating his son. Erik Erikson, the renowned psychologist, used the term "negation" in just such a context and stated that a child who is negated develops the desire to destroy.

Hitler's mother was pictured as a deeply troubled, pious Catholic. She had lived with Alois before they were married, and that sin seemed to consume her conscience. She probably interpreted the early death of two of her children as God's punishment for her weakness. If Waite is correct, then Adolf was not only the object of her maternal love, he also represented the possibility of God's forgiveness. So she clung to him, doted on him, and adored and spoiled him. She hoped the boy would enter the priesthood, but Adolf was expelled from the religious school he briefly attended when he was caught smoking. While there is no doubt that the boy loved his mother, he surely must have hated her as well. Why did she allow herself to be beaten? Why was she so powerless? And even more tormenting was her inability to protect her children. How could she love them and do nothing when the father abused them? Why did this wide-eyed, pale woman work so hard to please her despicable husband? What secrets did the mother and the father share when they closed their bedroom door?

Growing up with a brutal, all-powerful father and a loving, indulgently permissive but weak mother does not bode well for the future of any child. The resulting confusion is commonly identified by family counselors as receiving "double messages." Hitler's mother died when he was 19. By then the ingredients for future neurosis may already have been in place.

A Psychosexual View

According to Freudian analysts, the personality of the adult Hitler points to unresolved problems in his psychosexual development. As is typical of incomplete oral sexual maturation, the Fuehrer was a compulsive talker; he was given to uncontrolled tantrums (German anti-Nazis called him *Teppichfresser,* one who chews on carpets). Nor did he seem to resolve his Oedipal conflict; his relationships with women were never normal. There is general agreement that the most important woman in his life was a young niece, Angela Raubal. Hitler kept her a virtual prisoner until she succeeded in her efforts to kill herself. His most lasting attachment was to Eva Braun. She was by his side for 12 years; during this time she too attempted to end her life. Eva was Hitler's wife for one day, April 30, 1945. She was Hitler's partner in death when together they committed suicide in their Berlin bunker. Eva matched Hitler's concept of the ideal woman: quiet, loyal, disinterested in politics, undemanding, and shallow. Hitler once commented to Albert Speer, his personal architect and wartime production chief, that a highly intelligent man should *take* a primitive and stupid woman. The wording is revealing not only in connection with Eva, but that a man should *take* a woman. This contemptuous statement was made in Eva's presence.

An Uncertain Conclusion

Was Hitler mentally ill? Unfortunately, a simple yes or no is not possible. Within the legal context, he would have been pronounced sane. He knew right from wrong and chose wrong. It seems clear that his personality was deviant. He was unable to change his mind. Errors of judgment were never his, others had to bear the blame. Unable to be a friend, he had no friends. The line between imagination and reality was often blurred—his sniffing of his own body and repeated washing were neurotic. His disposition was rigid, indeed; he was proud of the "granite foundation" of his philosophy and confused inflexibility with strength of character.

Could the psychiatric community have argued that he was not responsible for his actions? Not in a court of law, but perhaps as a medical analysis. Hitler was neurotic but not consistently psychotic. In other words, as Robert Waite construed, he was able to function effectively despite certain obsessive and sadomasochistic traits. In the early years of his regime, his very pathology, his certainty that heaven itself had mandated his mission to save Germany, gave him the appearance of commanding authority. As Fuehrer, he brushed aside all opposing opinions in favor of the dictates of an inner voice that only he could hear. After the German armies had failed at Stalingrad, his behavior was described as abnormal. Like a demented man, he ordered armies about that no longer existed, had uncontrollable fits of rage, and saw treachery everywhere. Defeat may have pushed him from the realm of neurosis into madness.

While German soldiers were freezing to death from the rigors of a terrible Russian winter and supplies were urgently needed at the front, the German railroad system delivered trainloads of Jewish victims to German death camps in Poland. On April 29, 1945, one day before Hitler's death, while Berlin turned into blazing rubble, he wrote his so-called political testament. The final sentence reads as follows:

> Above all I charge the leaders of the nation and those under them to the scrupulous observance of the laws of race and to the merciless opposition to the universal poisoner of all peoples, International Jewry.

We return now to the original question. Why did Hitler hate the Jews? Our response, largely based on Waite's analysis, is a theory, well reasoned, but nonetheless a theory. To this observer, it seems the most acceptable of the various attempts to explain Hitler. Certainly he was subject to mental and emotional problems. Because he did not fit in, he felt isolated, inadequate, and, at the same time, vastly superior to others. It is possible that the ferocity of Hitler's hatred of the Jews may have stemmed from a latent sense of self-hatred. No one can map the unconscious mind, but the damage done by his parents, his early anti-Jewish environment, his failure as an artist, and his happiness to serve in the army followed by desolation when the war was lost are parts of the puzzle. What emerges is a hypothesis that the troubled child and unhappy teenager grew into a sexually deviant man *who despised himself.* But because the human ego is very fragile, it protects itself from unpleasant truths and builds elaborate defenses. Among such defensive mechanisms is scapegoating, the transfer of guilt and shame to the shoulders of others. Hitler's self-hatred, constantly fed by his dreadful crimes, may well have turned outward. Since the dawn of history, scapegoats have been used actually and symbolically to rid sinners of guilt. The greater the offenses, the greater must be the suffering of the sin-offering. If we accept that premise, then the Jews were well-suited to play that role. The sacrificial offering must be docile, without powerful friends or allies, and have a past that marks them with a long-established burden of culpability. This description fit the majority of European Jewry between 1935 and 1945.

The theory that Hitler's self-hatred externalized into anti-Jewish hatred offers a glimpse to account for the irrationality of the Holocaust. In Hitler's mind, the death of every single Jew may have destroyed some atomic particle of the self he wished to obliterate. Thus it may be possible to understand why a million victims could never be enough, nor 10 million. All Jews everywhere had to die, but even that would not be enough. Other scapegoats would have to be driven to their death. A terrible image strikes the inner eye: a picture of Europe if Hitler had won the war.

THREE EXECUTIONERS OF THE FUEHRER'S WILL

If we accept the explanation that Hitler tried to extinguish the fire of his self-hatred with the burnt offerings of European Jewry, the insatiability of his destructive impulses becomes comprehensible. This, however, leaves the historian with the still unanswered questions concerning the motivations of the men who so willingly carried out the genocide. Excluding the officials who "merely" expedited the paper trails that ended in mounds of human ashes, thousands of Schutzstaffel (SS) troopers were organized into special killing squads, the infamous *Einsatzgruppen.* These were the men who carried out the physical execution of men, women, and children, who were guilty of nothing at all. What do we know about members of these special task forces? Their work was not abstract, their own eyes met those of their victims, their hands held the guns that killed an estimated 1.5 million Jews— one, by one, by one. What did such men say to their wives, their children, or their parents at the end of a day's work? It would be convenient but wrong to dismiss them as brutes or savage animals outside the perimeter of civilized society. The commanders of the four individual detachments of mobile killing units, the *Einsatzkommandos,* were professional men with many academic degrees who were quite at home among Germany's cultural elite. Some members of the *Einsatzgruppen* were volunteers; others had been conscripted into this ghastly duty. A few objected to the assignment of supervising and participating in mass killings and were given other duties, as far as we can determine, without penalty. Once again, students of the Holocaust must face the fact that morality and education can march to different drummers.

We cannot comfort ourselves with the belief that the torturers and killers were of a different species. Christopher Browning's *Ordinary Men* is recommended to the student interested in further exploration of this topic. Here we cannot explore this enigma further and must be content to discuss, albeit briefly, three criminals at the top of the Nazi hierarchy. The choices of Hermann Goering, Joseph Goebbels, and Heinrich Himmler are based on their importance in carrying out the Final Solution, the Nazi's euphemism for the annihilation of the Jews.

HERMANN GOERING

Life is a struggle. Hitler, in the very title of his book, proclaimed this to be his mantra. The leaders who operated in the upper realms of the Nazi hierarchy shared that *Weltanschauung.* Goering's appearance, overweight, with a charming smile, and his fondness for flamboyant uniforms, could easily lead the observer to think he was a pleasure-loving dandy. That would be a mistake. Although he liked to call himself a Renaissance man, he began his rise within the Nazi government as a soldier. He craved power and the adulation of the masses who saw only a whitewashed version of his character—the avuncular officer who combined the attributes of a hail-fellow-well-met with that of a war hero. His ridiculous vanity, appetite for luxury, and megalomaniacal cruelty were largely unknown to the public. In the end, Hitler called him his greatest disappointment and deprived him of all honors and authority.

Hermann Goering (1883–1946) was born into a "good" Bavarian family. Among the political and social nonentities leading the Third Reich, he stood out as a welcome exception to the rule. His father, a distinguished colonial official, had been the first governor of the German protectorate of West Africa. Hermann's first wife, Karin von Katzow, came from a well-connected aristocratic background. Young Goering's career before he discovered the Nazi Party had been in the military. He was a much-decorated fighter pilot in the infant *Luftwaffe,* the tiny air force of World War I. After the death of its famed ace, Baron von Richthofen, Goering took over his command and served with distinction. At the end of the war, Goering, like so many of his contemporaries, found it difficult to adjust to civilian life. He joined the fledgling Nazi party in 1922, and thus qualified as an "early fighter." Hitler was delighted with this supposedly wealthy, famous new recruit and made him commander of the Brownshirts, the *Sturmabteilung* (SA). Goering was by his Fuehrer's side during the Beer Hall Putsch, the failed Nazi attempt to overthrow the Bavarian government. In the melee, Goering was severely wounded but managed to escape before he could be arrested. Apparently, these injuries launched his addiction to morphine. When a declaration of political amnesty cleared the way for his return, he was assured of high rank in the Nazi Party.

Ascent and Descent

Goering's rise was rapid indeed. Among the positions he held were President of the Reichstag, Reich's Minister Without Portfolio, Commander in Chief of the *Luftwaffe,* Minister President of Prussia, and Prussian Minister of the Interior. He created the Prussian Political Police, which was soon (1934) incorporated into the Gestapo, Hitler's Secret Police. These were not empty titles. Goering enjoyed the exercise of personal power. If ever he had scruples, they did not prevent him from directing the execution of old comrades. During the assassinations of the SA leaders on the Night of the Long Knives (see Chapter 5), he was in charge of the Berlin region. It was Goering who established the first concentration camp at Oranienburg. To the delight of many Germans, "our Hermann" was made a full general in 1936 and shortly thereafter he became the czar of the Four Year Plan for economic development. In that capacity he directed German industry and its effort to achieve self-sufficiency and military preparedness. As chief executive of the state-owned *Reichswerke Hermann Goering,* a huge mining and industrial complex, he amassed enormous personal wealth. He became an avid collector of great works of art, acquired sometimes by purchase, sometimes by forced gifts, and finally by theft from the great collections of defeated nations. He built a small palace, Karinhall, named after his deceased first wife but presided over by Emmy, his second wife. Emmy had been an actress who continued to perform in style as Hitler's official hostess during state functions. The Goerings became notorious for the exorbitance of their parties—so lavish were they, and so outrageous, that they rivaled the circuses of the emperors of ancient Rome.

Goering did not advocate Hitler's policy of expansion through war, although he played a central role in the annexation of Austria and Czechoslovakia. The day before the attack on Poland, Hitler, never at a loss to take advantage of a dramatic

Hermann Goering. (Corbis/Bettmann.)

moment, declared that in case he, the Fuehrer, died in battle, Goering was his designated successor. A new title, Chairman for the Reich Council of National Defense, was added to the many he already held. Within the year he was named *Reichsmarschall,* a high military rank.

The mantle of success did not fit Goering very well. His love for the decorative aspects of power was not in tandem with his growing disinclination to work. Although he relished his titles, he did not enjoy the performance of the many accompanying duties. The search for wealth in order to enhance his personal pleasures occupied much of his time and energies. His rivals for Hitler's favors, such as Goebbels and Himmler, used every opportunity to whittle away at his authority. Although the *Reichsmarschall's* tailors created fantastic costumes and uniforms in every color, it was impossible to hide his ever-increasing girth. Not only did he change his wardrobe many times a day, but with each new outfit, a different set of jewels adorned his fingers and glittering waistband. By the 1940s, the ace of World War I looked gross and grotesque.

Some early doubts notwithstanding, once Germany was committed to war, Goering gave it his full public support. In fact, the *Reichsmarschall's* power and popularity reached their greatest heights during the Polish and French campaigns. The blitzkrieg, or lightning war (adopted from the theory of mobile warfare suggested by a French officer named Charles de Gaulle and rejected by the French General Staff!), depended largely on the air force. After the fall of France and Poland, the German media used every word of praise in its vocabulary to laud the *Luftwaffe* and its chief. But unexpectedly, the promised quick defeat of England did not happen, and despite air force bombardments, Goering's pilots could not prevent the escape of British and French troops from Dunkirk. To the embarrassment of the *Luftwaffe* and sorrow of the civilian population, the English Royal Air Force would not yield its domination of the skies over the English Channel. As a result, the invasion of the British Isles had to be delayed again and again, and finally it had to be abandoned. Goering's inability to protect the Fatherland from Allied bombing raids greatly diminished his popularity. Hitler turned cool toward his erstwhile comrade. Perhaps, if the *Reichsmarschall* had boasted less and paid more attention to his duties, his star might not have descended so rapidly. He even neglected to keep his darling *Luftwaffe* abreast of new developments in the field of aviation. By 1943, it was clear that Goering was a shell, left standing with empty titles and a chest full of medals but no authority.

Despite the fact that Goering was not a fanatical anti-Semite, he played an important role in the persecution of the Jews. His participation in almost every aspect of the destruction of European Jewry was not borne from conviction but from subservience to the stronger will of the Fuehrer although seizure of Jewish property dovetailed with his insatiable greed.

In 1938, he played the major role in international negotiations between the German government and an intergovernmental committee proposing to speed up the emigration of German Jews to foreign countries. Nothing came of the negotiations, but his participation refuted his claim that he had always been certain that the annihilation of Jews was necessary to secure Germany's future.

Whenever, wherever Nazi policy presented possibilities of increasing his personal wealth, Goering was sure to be in the picture. As head of the economic Four Year Plan, he controlled the profitable Aryanization campaign. Aryanization was the euphemism for the legalized theft of Jewish assets by permitting Germans, usually members of the Nazi Party, to purchase such properties for a fraction of their actual value. Even these greatly reduced payments did not go to the seller, instead were deposited in specified banks. The former owners were permitted to make small monthly withdrawals, but if they emigrated, that bank account was confiscated by the state. Obviously, Aryanization was replete with opportunities for private bargain hunting by Germans with the right connections.

In 1938, Goering commented that it might be necessary to place Jews into ghettos at some future time. Within two years he called for the physical separation of the Jews from the Aryan Germans. The idea of using Jewish work brigades also germinated in his mind, a concept that was issued as an order in 1938. After the destruction of Jewish property during the *Kristallnacht* pogrom (see Chapter 6), it was Goering who proclaimed that the insurance companies must pay compensation, however, not to the insured but to the state, while the owners of the ruined stores were ordered to pay for their repair. Always eager to cloak theft with legal justification, the Nazis proclaimed that this action was proper because the Jews were responsible for causing the pogrom in the first place.

Goering hoped to maintain permanent control over the Jews, but he was outmaneuvered by Himmler. It is doubtful, however, whether the Jews would have fared any better if Goering had retained command. In 1939, he appointed Reinhard Heydrich, one of the Jews' most deadly enemies, to head the Reich Central Office for Jewish Emigration. The selection of this man to positions of ever-expanding power was in itself a crushing blow to Jewish survival. Before Himmler and his SS usurped mastery over all the Jews within the Nazi grasp, Goering had nominally been Himmler's chief. Thus it was the *Reichsmarschall* who decreed the emptying of the ghettos and the deportations of its inhabitants to concentration camps in Poland.

Despite these blows against the Jews, Goering did not share Hitler's fanatical views on the super race theory. He never accepted the Fuehrer's assessment that the Jews, by their very existence, threatened Germany. Jews had usefulness, first, by virtue of their possessions and second, as slave laborers. But whatever their value, their destruction was vital to Hitler, and one did not argue with the Fuehrer. In July 1941, Goering asked Heydrich to prepare a final solution to the Jewish question. Although he did not attend the fateful Wannsee Conference of January 20, 1942 (see Chapter 9), he absolutely shared responsibility for the death of six million Jews.

Goering brought on his own collapse. The war was going badly for the Germans, yet he paid less attention to his work than to his tailor. His behavior grew increasingly bizarre; even Hitler lost patience with him. At first, the Nazi leadership merely bypassed him in their decision-making processes, but that made no impact on Goering's lethargy. His drug addiction and regression into infantile theatrics intensified. Shortly before the end of the war, he was dismissed from all his posts. Hitler believed that his old comrade had conspired to replace him and ordered him to be shot. In the chaos of the final days of the Reich, however, there was no opportunity to carry out that order.

For a few belated moments, at the moment of the German collapse, some of the old vitality seemed to surge again in that bloated body. He claimed, upon hearing of Hitler's suicide, that now he was the new Fuehrer, the one and only man to represent the German government in dealing with the Allies. He actually demanded a meeting with General Eisenhower. Instead, he was captured by American troops and placed before the International Military Tribunal at Nuremberg. During his incarceration, while awaiting judgment, he was cured of his addiction. His body regained some shape, and he defended himself with considerable vigor. Nevertheless, he was found guilty of crimes against humanity. In the end, his flair for theatrics outmaneuvered the waiting hangman. He swallowed a vial of poison two hours before his scheduled execution. The mystery of how he obtained the poison and the drama of his final exit gave him the attention he had craved all his life.

JOSEPH GOEBBELS

Among the intellectual lightweights at the top of the Nazi elite, Goebbels was an oddity. He had attended several renowned German universities and earned a doctorate in literature. He was often called brilliant, even by people who despised him. Under his stewardship, propaganda, once merely the art of persuasion, became the medium for mass manipulation. He combined applied science and technology with total ruthlessness to create a hypnotic vacuum for his audience, which, at a precisely timed moment, he filled with an emotional frenzy of either Fuehrer worship and/or rage against the supposed enemies of the Fatherland. Among all of Hitler's henchmen, Goebbels was the best educated and the most cunning. He was the physical and intellectual misfit among the dullards who surrounded the Fuehrer.

Goebbels could not live up to the image of the Aryan he so relentlessly acclaimed as perfect. He had neither the long, sturdy legs, the slim waist, and wide chest nor the fair skin, blue eyes, and blond hair of the idealized German. His importance to Hitler had to be great indeed to forgive his puny frame, the large head sitting atop a spindly body, the brown hair and eyes, and swarthy complexion. Worst of all, he walked with a distinct limp and had to wear a special shoe and brace. His left leg was several inches shorter than his right. This was the result of an operation he underwent as a boy when he was ill with osteomyelitis, an inflammation of the bone marrow. Even the most touched-up photos could not erase his physical shortcomings. Many Germans believed he was born with a clubfoot. Among his enemies, gossip was spread that he was partly Jewish. Obviously, Goebbels' body and mind were at odds with Aryan doctrine; the fact that he rose to great power nonetheless demonstrated the strength of his will. Ashamed of his physique and reluctant to display his intellect, he forced himself to live a cynical life. He often pretended that his lameness was due to a war wound; he appeared at public meetings in SA uniform at the head of a contingent of SA troopers. In order to appear as "one of the boys," he expressed distaste for intellectuals and erudition. His diaries were filled with adulation for Hitler, whose private conversations were notoriously long-winded and boring. Whether these entries revealed his true feelings remains questionable; after all, he was a professional liar.

Goebbels was born in 1897 into a devoutly Catholic Rhineland family. His father had been a manual laborer who rose to a lower middle-class position. The young man, already painfully aware of his handicap, was desolate when other youths went to war in 1914 and he was rejected. He never came to terms with his inability to serve as a soldier. Success at university life gave him status, but it could not mend the anguish over his deformed leg. He was awarded a doctorate at Heidelberg and from then on insisted upon being addressed as "Herr Doktor." The attempt to win fame and fortune as a writer floundered when his book *Michael* and two plays were received with critical scorn. His career as a journalist was short-lived. His keen and restless mind was searching for a calling when in 1922, quite accidentally, Goebbels heard Hitler speak in Munich. The die was cast; the Austrian with the black mustache and the spellbinding voice was the means by which his own star would rise.

Goebbels' first propaganda campaign was designed to ingratiate himself with Hitler's inner circle. The Fuehrer responded to his flattery despite the nasty comments whispered about the "little mouse-doctor." The Nazi Party needed him, a man who was not only an impassioned speaker, almost as intoxicating as Hitler himself, but also a master of the written word. The fact that this new recruit combined a cunning mind with a complete absence of integrity increased his value. From 1927 to 1935 Goebbels edited a newspaper, *Der Angriff (Attack),* to promote national socialism without even minimal regard for the truth. Even his detractors were awed at his exploitation of the concept of "the big lie," that is, a lie so blatant, so outrageous, and repeated so often that the public accepted it as truth.

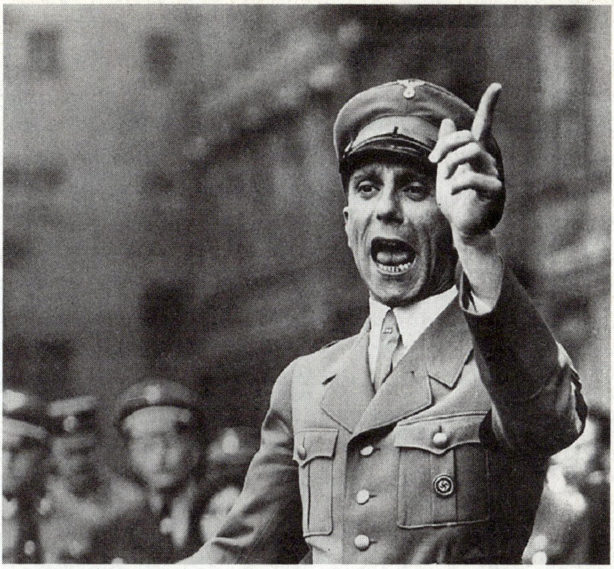

Joseph Goebbels. (Corbis/Bettmann.)

When Hitler appointed him Gauleiter (district Party leader) of Berlin, Goebbels created the highly effective political theater that would soon dazzle all of Germany. He was credited with playing a vital part in the great gains made by the Nazis in the Reichstag elections of 1932. Herr Doktor, the PhD from Heidelberg, cheered at the Berlin book burning when across the nation some 20,000 books were thrown into bonfires. Among the volumes fed to the flames by university students and some of their professors were the works of Jewish, communist, and pacifist authors, among them Thomas Mann, Sigmund Freud, and Maxim Gorki.

Goebbels had an instinct for judging the mood of the masses and catered to their appetite for sensationalism with slander, rumors, and personal attacks. Some of his SA Brownshirts walked the streets with red bandages to feign injuries suffered during street fights in defense of the fatherland. He wrote articles under an assumed name in which he lauded Dr. Goebbels as a man of extraordinary valor. After the death of a contemptible SA rioter named Horst Wessel, Goebbels fabricated martyrdom for the street brawler, and for a dozen years, Germans sang the Horst Wessel Song as their second national anthem. The refrain of this Nazi hymn ran, "Yes, when the blood of Jews spurts from our knives, then things go twice as well."

In 1928, five years before Hitler became chancellor, Goebbels became propaganda chief for the Party. This assured his appointment as National Minister of Public Enlightenment and Propaganda in 1933. The title did not indicate the dimensions of power that he wrung from his position. He built an empire that encompassed jurisdiction over the cultural life of the nation in which propaganda was but one of many facets. His commitment to Hitler was total. He never abandoned the core of his mission: to glorify the Fuehrer and his vision of the new Germany.

King of Propaganda and Culture

As cultural czar, Goebbels had the authority to dictate the literary, artistic, journalistic, and musical tastes of a nation. His power included jurisdiction over sports events, films, plays, even operas. He masterminded and managed the spectacular rallies that imitated the pomp and solemnity of religious ceremonies. He was the arbiter of painting and sculpture and decided what was acceptable Aryan artistic expression. Propaganda, he stated, had no relationship to truth, only to effectiveness.

The outbreak of World War II caused Goebbels' fortune to lapse for several years. He was jubilant over the early victories, but his public assurances of a quick end to the struggle were proven wrong, and the public felt deceived. He further blundered when he treated the Allied forces with contempt rather than with the respect due a worthy adversary, unmindful that victories over an ignoble foe earn no glory. His pledge that German civilians would be safe in the virtual fortress the Fuehrer had built around them flew in the face of reality, as night after night, Allied bombers delivered a message that belied his words. At this point Goebbels' enemies within the Party believed the little man was finished.

However, when the possibility of defeat, though unspoken, was no longer unthinkable, Goebbels' services were again in great demand. The nation must be readied to fight to its last breath. Now his approach was to instill fear and hatred for the enemies of the Reich: for the Jews, of course, but also for England, the Soviet Union, and the United States. If defeated, he warned, the German people could expect no mercy. Rape and pillage, particularly at the hands of the "Asiatic hordes," would be their fate. In an effort to reverse the spirit of weariness and hopelessness, and prevent panic, he promised them a marvelous secret weapon that would turn the tide of the war. His glee at the death of Franklin D. Roosevelt was obscene. Hitler was still the child of destiny, so Goebbels assured the public, with the cursed "Rosenfeld" gone, the American war effort would wither away. But German defeat was inevitable. Goebbels' appointment in 1944 as general plenipotentiary for the war effort was, in effect, a gesture. Germany had no reserves left to prevent the invasions from either direction, the east or the west.

Is it possible to reconstruct Goebbels' actual views on the fate of the Jews? On the Holocaust? Not with precision because his ambition erased any vestige of concern over the fate of others. Nothing in his early life points to youthful hatred of the Jews, but when he realized that an attitude of indifference toward the Jews would prevent his rise in the ranks of the Party, he conformed to the required, politically correct anti-Semitism. Whether or not he believed what he said and wrote is debatable, but it hardly matters. His portrayal of the Jew as a dehumanized caricature was effective in persuading millions of Germans that there "must be something to it." The assassination of a German official in Paris by a Jew (see Chapter 6) gave Goebbels the opportunity to demonstrate the sincerity of his anti-Semitism. He turned the shooting into a nationwide pogrom from which German Jewry never recovered. Known as *Kristallnacht,* the organized rampage was largely of his making—this was his answer to rivals who thought him soft on the "Jewish Question."

Murder and Suicide

Certain aspects of Goebbels' life and death bore resemblance to those of Hitler's. Both men appear to have been driven by self-hatred. In Hitler's case, Jews became his personal sacrificial scapegoats; for Goebbels, all of humanity was the enemy; he spared none but Hitler from his scathing pen. He was a homely man, small and lame—the antithesis of the Aryan superman he so masterfully glorified and so consummately envied. Although the details differ, both men had difficulty in their relationships with women. Goebbels had many affairs, before and after he was married. As a politically powerful man, he had no difficulty in proving his virility with ambitious starlets, eager to further their careers. His wife, Magda, was ready to ask for a divorce when his philandering became a public scandal. Only Hitler's personal intervention prevented the breakup of the marriage.

In their suicides, the similarities between Goebbels' and Hitler's personalities were striking. Goebbels actually orchestrated Hitler's death. He urged his Fuehrer to die like a hero portrayed in German mythology, a godlike superman who leaves this world in a blaze of destruction. Only suicide and flames could feed the future legend of his greatness. The drama must end like a climactic scene from Wagner's *Götterdämmerung.* Afraid of capture by the Russians, Hitler agreed. He paid the faithful Goebbels a final tribute. In his last testament, Hitler appointed him to a leading role in a future German government, a nomination that can only be characterized as bizarre.

But Goebbels had decided to play out his own drama. In his last words, he apologized to Hitler for disobeying his order to leave the bunker as the Russian army approached. Goebbels had decided to die because life without the Fuehrer had no value. His wife, he wrote, had chosen to die with him. But Joseph and Magda had brought their six children to Hitler's underground bunker. They refused the offer to have them flown out to safety. Goebbels' final crime violated the most basic norms of humanity. He claimed that if his children had been old enough to speak for themselves, they too would rather die than live in a world without Hitler. The picture of the father (it is unclear whether the mother participated in the actual commission of this crime) going from bed to bed handing his children a lethal drink was the penultimate scene of Goebbels' life. The curtain came down on May 1, 1945. With Russian tanks entering the chancellery garden, his wife took poison and Goebbels shot himself.

HEINRICH HIMMLER

Himmler is often called the architect of the Holocaust. The epithet denotes more than theoretical planning: Himmler supervised the day-to-day reality of the killing process. He did not conceive of the Shoah, Hitler did, but the efficiency required to murder such great numbers in less than five years was largely Himmler's work. Some writers have called him the perfect bureaucrat, the man who carried out orders with the mechanical efficiency of a robot. But that characterization does not take into account the man's fanaticism nor his political acumen. The smooth implementation of the Holocaust required the resources of a master of deceit. Everything about Himmler, including his appearance, was deceptive. It must also be remembered that the threshold leading to Hitler's office was always crowded with ambitious men jostling to get nearer to the seat of power. Himmler's success in that perilous arena indicates that the man cannot be reduced to a single, simple caption.

Himmler was the most feared and hated man of the Third Reich because he deliberately inspired terror not only among Jews, but also in the general population. The arm of his Gestapo (Secret Police), his SS (Storm Troopers/Blackshirts), and finally his authority over the nation's entire police force seemed able to reach into every home and workplace. Himmler silenced opposition to the Nazi state by fostering the perception that his agents were everywhere, saw everything, and even listened to private telephone conversations. There were whispers of terrible tortures inflicted during Gestapo interrogations and of unspeakable conditions in concentration camps. Himmler did not have the manpower to actually regiment the entire German population, but his reputation was enough to silence political criticism. It was best to say nothing, to trust no one.

Hannah Arendt, the author of *The Origins of Totalitarianism* and *Eichmann in Jerusalem,* might have named Himmler along with Eichmann as confirmation of her theory of the banality of evil. The man was so ordinary, so conventional, that it is very difficult to see him as a fanatical mass murderer. His upbringing was comfortably middle class—a devout Catholic home, the father an educator with connections to Bavarian nobility, and the mother attentive to her home and her three sons. Psychiatrists cannot point to cruelty or abnormality in the visible workings of this family. Heinrich was the middle child, born in 1900. The young boy was already unattractive, though not repulsively so; his small eyes, thin lips, and weak chin gave him a ratlike expression. He attended a technical college and was awarded a diploma in agricultural studies. He married a nurse who shared his interest in such para-scientific subjects as herbalism, mesmerism, and homeopathy. We know little of the marriage. Heinrich was not a faithful husband and fathered several children out of wedlock while neglecting his own family. After he achieved great power, he became interested in mysticism, and his superstitions often bordered on the absurd. During his boyhood his schoolmates noticed none of these oddities. They described him as methodical, hard working, attentive to detail, but utterly without charisma. He was a plodder, adequate but not outstanding.

When World War I erupted, Heinrich was in school. At age 17, he served for a year in a Bavarian infantry regiment without duties at the front. The end of the war and the politics of the Weimar Republic disappointed young Heinrich, and he joined a rightist paramilitary organization. He met Hitler and joined the National Socialist Party. At the Beer Hall Putsch of 1923, Himmler stood next to SA Commander Ernst Roehm and therefore could claim the vaunted "early fighter" honorific. During the six years following the failed Putsch in Munich, Himmler functioned in various capacities in the Nazi Party while earning a living as a chicken farmer and fertilizer salesman. Up to this point, his career was in no way distinguished. But his subservience and slavish loyalty had made an impression on Hitler, and the "faithful Heinrich" was assigned to head the SS, or *Schutzstaffel* (Defense Echelon, better known as Storm Troops), in 1929. With this appointment, a new chapter opened for Himmler, for Germany, and tragically, for the Jews.

Heinrich Himmler. (AP Wide World Photos.)

Himmler's advancement cannot be separated from the evolution of the SS. Its membership consisted of a mere 300 men when Himmler became their chief. The troop's original duty was to protect Hitler during public appearances. Taking a page from the praetorian guards of ancient Rome, virile, handsome men were selected to enhance the Fuehrer's presence. Their emblems were symbols rather than decorations, the double lightning, a stylized form of the letters SS, the skull or death head on neckband and ring, the dagger in the belt, the black tunic, trousers, and boots—all were calculated to instill awe among civilians. Their appearance was no mere facade. It represented careful training, a strict code of conduct, total dedication to Hitler personally—as opposed to service to the nation—and readiness to perform any assignment, no matter how repulsive. Since the SS became the instrument of the Holocaust, its development will be detailed in Chapter 9. Here it suffices to say that the SS as a cult and as the implement of terror was Himmler's work. He created a state within the state where ordinary rules of morality and law did not apply. He brought a businesslike approach to fanaticism that made mass murder a product to be manufactured with all the efficiency of modern technology.

Himmler was given the opportunity to show Hitler his loyalty during the massacre of the SA leadership during the Night of the Long Knives. After the SS murdered a number of veteran leaders of the Nazi movement, the reliability of the

Blackshirts to the Fuehrer could never be questioned again. From their original duties as bodyguards, their job description expanded to include identification and elimination of all alleged internal enemies of the regime. The organization operated without oversight or interference from the customary courts of justice, its authority was legitimized by the following phrase: "In the name of the Fuehrer I order you."

Master Race Mania

Himmler was obsessed with the scheme of using his SS to advance Aryan racial purity for Germany. He concocted a blueprint to turn this fixation into his own version of a brave new world. A student of agriculture, he was familiar with methods of improving cattle through selective insemination, and now the *Reichsfuehrer* (National Leader) envisioned the use of breeding techniques to produce the master race. He was convinced that genetics, or blood as the Nazis often called it, determined all the characteristics of a people. Valuable Aryan blood must be nurtured; inferior blood, such as Jewish, Gypsy, or Slavic blood, must be prevented from further polluting the Nordic race. Himmler not only believed this but devised plans to implement this fantasy.

The SS was at the center of his plan; these were the men and their carefully selected wives who would validate his theory. Candidates for membership in the SS were required to trace their racial purity for three generations; they took an oath to marry only "qualified" and approved Aryan women and promised to father many children. Racially acceptable out-of-wedlock offspring were welcomed and were financially supported by the SS organization. The first home for unmarried expectant mothers opened its doors in Munich in 1936 and at the height of the Nazi regime the number had grown to 13.

Himmler's scheme to produce this race of masters entailed the settlement of SS families on land appropriated from Polish and West Russian owners. Like feudal lords, the Blackshirts were projected to hold sway over their farm workers in a revisit of feudal lord and serf relationships. "Surplus" Poles would be eliminated, moved eastward, or killed; it was immaterial which method was employed. These SS-owned estates were expected to Germanize in perpetuity the *Lebensraum* conquered in the East. In order to prevent the native peoples from rebelling against this new order, potential leaders among the Poles, such as the university-educated scholars, army officers, priests, and communists and, of course, Jews, would have to be eliminated.

Himmler also planned to save, in his words, to "harvest," the genetically superior material carried in the genes of Aryans who lived in the eastern lands. A monumental process involving the forced transfer of hundreds of thousands of so-called ethnic Germans, the *Volksdeutschen*, was well on the way between 1940 and 1944. Their resettlement was halted only when the German army suffered reverses.

Himmler exhibited similar obsession when he directed the murder of Germans whose physical and/or mental imperfections made them "unworthy" of life. His so-called euthanasia program sanctioned the killing of children and adults whose progeny could pollute the racial integrity of the nation. Only the fit were allowed to survive, and only he could determine who was or was not fit to live in his German world (See Chapter 5). Yet another aspect of his racial purity mania was called *Lebensborn* (fountain of life). It involved the kidnapping of racially acceptable young children from their families in the conquered countries and offering them for adoption by German Aryans. Blonde, blue-eyed Polish children were particularly vulnerable to be snatched from their parents. It is estimated that several hundred thousand children disappeared in these secret raids, never again to be seen by their biological mothers and fathers. The code name for these crimes was "Haymaking."

At the height of his power, Himmler commanded a virtual empire. In 1939, he became the Reich's Commissar for the Consolidation of the German Nation. The title was grandiose but so was the power it yielded: He was commander of an enormously expanded SS, which included control over the "racial degenerates," concentration and death camps, and the *Einsatzgruppen* (see Chapter 9). He headed the political administration of the Eastern Occupied Territories, the Gestapo, and all police organizations; was Minister of the Interior; and was supreme commander of the People's Army, the *Volksturm,* or Home Guard. Even the teenagers of the Werewolf troops, boys who had sworn to defend the Fatherland when all else was lost, were part of his realm.

The personal files of the *Reichsfuehrer* were destroyed at his orders. Nevertheless, enough evidence remains from other sources to give succeeding generations a portrait of a man who was slavishly devoted to Hitler, who was totally indifferent to the fate of millions, and whose unrealistic racial theories bordered on the demented. His rise to power from obscurity confirmed his stamina as an infighter and his skill as an administrator. His character was devoid of any ethical code save that of loyalty to his Fuehrer.

Himmler's power emanated from the single source of Hitler's will. But everything depended on winning the war, and even the Fuehrer could not order that miracle. Finally, when even the faithful Heinrich realized that all was lost, he tried to approach the Allies with peace feelers. Apparently, he had no idea that he was the very last man with whom the victorious commanders would deal. Hitler was furious with the last-minute desertion of his paladin and ordered his arrest—a futile gesture reminiscent of Goering's fate.

Himmler tried to escape in disguise after the German surrender. He was captured by the British, and while undergoing a physical examination, he bit down on a vial of cyanide hidden in his mouth. He had made the mistake of masquerading as a low-ranking Gestapo agent, unaware that that entire organization had been declared criminal. He died almost instantly; thus he, like Hitler, Goering, and Goebbels, slipped out of the hangman's noose. Unloved in life, he was unlamented in death.

CHAPTER 5

Germany Under the Nazis

The once popular assessment that the Nazis ran Germany with clockwork precision has been rejected by historians. The uniformity of marching feet, of arms outstretched at a precise angle for the Hitler salute, the vaunted punctuality of the trains, and the conformity of the faces of Hitler Youth beneath the swastika banners—all created the myth that these appearances mirrored German political life. The facts, however, paint a different picture. Conflicts, uncertainties, and unclear lines of authority muddied the Nazi administration. Hitler worked sporadically, preferably late at night; often his orders were vague hints rather than commands; and he encouraged interservice rivalries among his deputies. As long as the men around him vied with each other for a scrap of his power, his own position was secure. The fact that no serious contender ever challenged Hitler's authority indicated that this approach produced the desired results.

DESTRUCTION OF THE REPUBLIC

On January 30, 1933, Field Marshal von Hindenburg, the President of the Weimar Republic, reluctantly agreed to the appointment of Adolf Hitler as chancellor of Germany. Thus, the government was now headed by the former corporal who achieved power in accordance with the Weimar Constitution. The choice of Franz von Papen as vice-chancellor had finally convinced the old President that Hitler could be reined in if necessary. The elegant Franz was a man from the old school of diplomats who assured Hindenburg that Hitler could be managed. After all, the Nazis held only three other cabinet posts out of eleven, and the important ministries were in the hands of conservatives. The fact that the Nazis had attained their greatest popularity in 1932 and still only received 37 percent of the votes gave this reasoning the appearance of logic. Nazi election rhetoric had emphasized nationalism, a rather nebulous form of socialism, vicious anti-communism, denunciation of the Treaty of

Versailles, and the promise of relief from economic woes. The old guard opposed only the socialist allusions. It should be noted that anti-Semitic tirades had been muted because they proved to be an ineffective election tactic, a point lost on historians who claim hatred of Jews was endemic in Germany.

Although Hitler began his political career within the laws of the Weimar Constitution, in only two years he transformed the government into his personal dictatorship. Civil rights disappeared, long-established institutions became unrecognizable, and conventional social and cultural mores were challenged. The myth of Jewish debasement and its obverse, Aryan supremacy, came to play central roles. One of the most totalitarian governments in history was installed, and only defeat on the battlefield would dislodge it. This was Hitler's work. No matter how abhorrent the man and his crimes, such extraordinary ability must be acknowledged. The caricature of the mustached buffoon distorts the truth as much as the heroic image created by Goebbels.

The Nazification of the nation was a process, not an event. As processes go, the transformation was implemented at breakneck speed. It is not possible to assess exactly who bears the greatest blame for ending the German Republic—there is plenty of guilt to go around. Three factors played major roles in the fiasco. First, the opposition parties in the legislature, the Reichstag, were unwilling or unable to put aside their differences and present a united opposition to the Nazis; second, the leaders of the Weimar Republic had been unable to convince the German public to cherish their democratic freedoms; and third, in their narcissism, the conservative upper classes overestimated their own power and underestimated Hitler.

THE LAST ELECTION

So was he given power before the vote

? Even before he took office, Hitler asked for and was granted new Reichstag elections. He hoped to win a clear majority so that he could reshape the government with the endorsement of a supportive legislature. This desire to disguise every procedure with the veneer of legality was apparent throughout his political life, perhaps as a result of the failed and unlawful *Bierhall Putsch* in Munich. The new election was scheduled for March 1933. With the resources of the government behind him, the new chancellor ran an effective, often coercive, campaign. But electioneering cost money, lots of money. Hitler addressed a conclave of Germany's industrial magnates and pledged to the heads of such giants as the Krupp Works, IG Farben, and the German United Steel Works that the coming election would be the last one. He vowed to preserve private property and hinted broadly that regardless of the wishes of the voters, he would stay in power, he would find a way. It seems inconceivable that such a speech was actually applauded. When Goering passed the hat, he collected three million marks. One may wonder if Hitler intentionally played upon the vanity of these men, by creating the impression that he would be useful to them as their front man, a puppet whose strings they held.

Hitler kept his word; this would be the last German election until 1949. The Communist and Socialist Parties were unable to present their candidates to the public effectively. The *Sturmabteilung* (SA) disrupted their meetings, arrested their leaders, and smashed their printing presses. In Prussia, Hermann Goering, now Minister of the Interior, urged his police to shoot anti-Nazi suspects. Although the words "Socialist Workers" were part of the proper name of Hitler's Nationalist Socialist German Workers' Party (NSDAP), trade unionists were beaten regardless of their political affiliation. Street fights escalated into killings, and still neither the German people nor any of their institutions rose in protest. The churches, professional and labor organizations, university faculty and students, civil servants, and most importantly, the armed forces remained passive. By their moderation (or was it cowardice?), they further encouraged the street gang methods of the brown-shirted battalions.

Hitler had hoped to provoke the communists into acts of violence that would provide him with an excuse to destroy their organization once and for all. In the Reichstag, the Communist Party held 100 seats of a total of 600, and if these delegates could be dislodged, Hitler would have a clear majority. How this problem was solved reads like the plot from a B movie.

THE REICHSTAG FIRE

The word *Reichstag*, similar to the U.S. House of Representatives, denotes both the legislative body and the building. On February 27, 1933, just a week before the elections, the Berlin Reichstag building was torched. Without question, the blaze was the result of arson; the large amount of incendiary material found on the premises left no doubt on that issue. But who set the fire? The Berlin police arrested a young Dutch communist Marinus van der Lubbe, hysterical and half-naked, at the scene. Hitler and his team seized the moment and accused the communists of instigating the crime. Most historians, Hans Mommsen among them, agree that van der Lubbe was probably guilty, although a suspicion that the Nazis set the fire lingers on. At any rate, the arson was a gift for Hitler. The communist deputies of the Reichstag were arrested; the remainder of their party's leadership went into hiding. The Nazi press shouted Red conspiracy and hailed the illegal seizure of the duly elected communist legislators as a triumph of law and order.

There was a trial. Five men—the incoherent Dutchman, a former Reichstag deputy, and three Bulgarian communists residing in the Reich—were charged with arson and intent to instigate a rebellion. The world was watching; possibly this saved all but the pathetic van der Lubbe. No one who knew this confused and obviously disturbed young man believed him capable of high treason. Nevertheless, a guilty verdict cut short his life several days before his twenty-fifth birthday. The other defendants were acquitted.

The day after the fire, Hitler succeeded in persuading von Hindenburg to sign a decree "for the protection of the people and the state." The otherwise liberal and progressive Weimar Constitution contained a clause, Article 48, whereby in times of crisis, the President, with consent of the Reichstag, may temporarily suspend the fundamental rights of German citizens. By invoking this article, supposedly to prevent a communist coup d'état, Hitler was given temporary dictatorial powers. Thus, on February 28, 1933, the freedom to speak, to write, to assemble, to have privacy in one's home, and to elect representatives and the guarantee of due process of the law—all were swept away. Also known as the Enabling Act, it was passed by the Reichstag on March 24th, by a vote of 441 to 94, well within the required two-third majority. Most Germans cried no tears over the disappearance of the communist leadership; many believed that even an abuse of power was laudable if it rid Germany of the Red menance. Of course, once Hitler had the right to rule without the restraints of constitutional government, the road to totalitarianism was open before him.

The election that followed the Reichstag fire was tainted by many abuses. Uniformed SA men confronted voters at the ballot boxes and "persuaded" many to vote the Nazi ticket. Despite these tactics, however, Hitler did not gain the victory he had expected. When the ballots were counted, the Center Party and the socialists held their own; even the leaderless communists lost fewer votes than anticipated. Instead of a landslide, just 44 percent of the votes went to the Nazis. Only in conjunction with another ultrarightist party, the Nationalists, did the Nazis achieve a simple majority.

The end of the Weimar Republic was predictable when Hindenburg signed the order to invoke Article 48 and the influential Center Party acquiesced with its vote. The Catholic delegates justified their support of the bill with the claim that their endorsement would grant them some influence over the Nazis—a familiar refrain. Only the Social Democrats opposed, but their dissent could not prevent the Reichstag from signing its own suicide note.

POLITICAL CENTRALIZATION

The consolidation of political power, the *Gleichschaltung* (coordination), took place during the next several months. One by one the separate strands of authority were pulled together into Hitler's chancellery. All political parties except the NSDAP were outlawed, labor unions disbanded, and freedom of speech, press, and assembly abrogated. The federal system of government was reorganized into a unified, highly centralized administration; state and local legislatures were deprived of any meaningful autonomy. A single appointed individual, the political *Gauleiter,* usually a reliable Nazi who took his orders from Berlin, headed each of the new political units, the *Gaue.* The various departments of the national administration were Nazified by means of a purge, which was camouflaged as The Law for the Restoration of the Professional Civil Service. All Jews and many anti-Nazi bureaucrats were ousted from their positions. It was not possible to remove all "unreliable" officials and keep the government functioning, but whenever and wherever possible, they were supplanted by Party members. It must be remembered that teachers, including university professors, were also civil service appointees; thus, the impact on education was nothing less than revolutionary.

How could this revocation of civil rights be effected without serious opposition? Why were there no strikes, riots, marches, or protests? Although no definitive answer can be offered, surely, fear of retribution silenced the voices of protest. Also many Germans had been bitterly disappointed by the failures of the Weimar Republic and wondered if Germany was suited for democracy. The national mood can be summed up in the phrase: "Let's give Hitler a chance."

THE PARTY AND THE GOVERNMENT

Hitler had inherited the oldest civil service bureaucracy in the Western world. By his order, these established administrative departments were largely, although never entirely, dismantled and absorbed by appointed Nazi functionaries. Ever concerned to give some legal camouflage to his actions, Nazi theorists stated that Hitler's unlimited power was rightfully vested in the Fuehrer as the sole representative of the will of the German people.

The *Fuehrerprinzip,* a theory that total power must be confined to a single leader, had already been delineated in *Mein Kampf.* Hitler believed that parliamentary governments were cumbersome, unreliable, unmanageable, and symbolic of weakness. Every aspect of his dictatorship was organized so that departmental executives derived their authority from him alone. For example, the head of the *Frauenschaften* (women's organizations), Gertrud Scholtz-Klink, was entitled to call herself the *Fuehrerin,* the female Fuehrer.

To ensure his totalitarianism, the loyalty of the military was essential. Members of the armed forces were required to swear a new oath of obedience, not to

Hitler addressing a giant Nazi demonstration, 1933. (AP Wide World Photos.)

the Fatherland but to Hitler personally. Thus the generals lost the independence they claimed to hold so dear. When the voters were asked to legalize the dictatorship by means of a plebiscite, 90 percent gave their approval. No doubt, many votes cast for Hitler were expressions of fear rather than political conviction. Nevertheless, Goebbels could proclaim that the nation had approved to end the Weimar Republic and the personal rule of the Fuehrer.

Implementation of totalitarianism was well underway within a year of Hitler's appointment as chancellor. During the next decade, the grip of the Nazi Party grew stronger until its activities dominated or duplicated the work of the regular bureaucracy. Inevitably, Hitler's deputies created a maze of overlapping competitions and rivalries. In some cases, remnants of the old civil service continued to exist, often in apposition to Nazi officials with similar job descriptions. Thus, some agencies had parallel organizations, while others were wholly swallowed by Party officials. For example, Germany's police departments had been under the jurisdiction of the Ministry of the Interior until Henrich Himmler incorporated them wholesale onto his own organization; the old agency for economic affairs was simply sidestepped when Hitler appointed Hermann Goering to head the Four Year Plan; and two legal and court systems operated at the same time, one for Party members and one for the rest of the population. Loyalty to the Fuehrer and rank in the hierarchy of the Party were crucial in obtaining positions in the government. In other words, political perceptions were the most important criteria for bureaucratic appointments. This was true for the file clerk in a village town hall as well as the foreign minister in Berlin. Obviously, many good workers who did not have the right connections or had not joined the Nazi Party, lost their positions. Men and a few women who had displayed their swastika armband early on were given preference as a matter of course, with little concern regarding their qualifications. Such blatant patronage raises the question: "How could, how did, the Nazi government function?" Those who lived during these years in Germany were apt to reply: "Not very well."

GOVERNING THE REICH

Hitler's personal power was the overriding force in the administration. No institution, and certainly no individual, not the churches, not the aristocrats, not tradition, not the working classes nor the industrialists curbed his authority. His pronouncements became the law of the land in all political, economic, and even cultural affairs. Several rather ineffectual challenges to his personal rule were overcome quickly, and he was obeyed even when the nation lay in rubble.

Hitler's style of governance was rather haphazard. It suited him to encourage rivalry among his administrators. Often his vague pronouncements required interpretation by his subordinates, who used this lack of preciseness and clarity to construe the Fuehrer's casual comments as orders. Like the emperors of ancient Rome, Hitler retained a facade of the old political institutions. Ministries continued to exist, even the Reichstag met to rubber-stamp his decrees. Cabinet members continued to meet, but Hitler was not interested in supervising their affairs and did not participate in their sessions. A State Secretary of the Chancellery ferried papers between the ministers and the Fuehrer. The difficulty in carrying on the business of state was further complicated by Hitler's nepotism. He appointed certain favorites to powerful posts and granted them the privilege of riding roughshod over other bureaucrats. For example, Fritz Todt, who built the *Autobahn,* the famous German road system, was responsible to no one but Hitler and received his funds directly from the chancellery.

The Nazis could not fill all administrative jobs with their own people; thus, some positions remained in the hands of experts. To prevent a collapse of governmental services, some non-Party members remained at their civil service posts. This was principally true during the first several years of the regime. Many of the old employees of such departments as the foreign ministry, the national banking system, the economics ministry, post office, railroads, police, education, courts, and public health were needed to conduct the nation's business. But their future was uncertain. The more responsible the position, the more eager were the *Gauleiters,* the highest-ranking regional Nazi Party officials, to install their comrades. Many of the older bureaucrats found that their duties were hampered by the constant interference from Party officials, but fear of losing status and pensions kept them at their desks.

Adolf Hitler and Paul von Hindenburg, Potsdam, 1933. (Brown Brothers.)

PARTY ORGANIZATION

The framework of the Nazi Party resembled a pyramid; Hitler stood at the apex, and below him were the *Gauleiters,* the functionaries whose territories roughly matched the old German states. Further divisions, from provinces to counties to villages, were headed by Party men. As noted earlier, lines of authority were often confused, and the judge, the school principal, the museum director, the postmaster, and so on worked in a morass of conflicting directives. Many civil servants solved their dilemmas by becoming active members of the Nazi Party. Then they needed only to follow orders issued by the Party and could ignore the directives coming from other authorities.

The reorganization of the government into a dictatorship pointed to a significant shift from the originally proclaimed goals of the Nazi Party. As Hitler's aims to expand the German borders became central, his earlier interest in the welfare of the working poor was dropped. He needed the magnates of capital and industry to secure the nation's rearmament program. But not all Nazis approved of Hitler's ultrarightist shift and his abandonment of "national socialism." The primary protest came not from the workers whose leaders had disappeared, but from within the Party itself. The ensuing internal crisis was settled during a bloody showdown known as the Night of the Long Knives and/or the Blood Purge.

THE BLOOD PURGE

Hitler's flirtation with the conservative, even reactionary elite—the generals and the barons of industry—created problems. In the center of discontent was the SA and its chief, Ernst Roehm. No doubt, this swashbuckling adventurer and his Brownshirts had contributed greatly to his friend Adolf's victory. Roehm had been remarkably successful in attracting young men to his ranks. In 1933, they numbered two million strong. Despite his past contributions, Roehm was becoming a liability. He had taken seriously the socialist pronouncements of the Fuehrer and urged a second revolution to bring about the promised shift of the nation to the political left. Obviously, the regime had no intention of curbing the profits of the powerful few in order to promote the interests of the workers. In addition, Hitler and Roehm differed in their view of the role of the SA. Hitler wanted the corps to function as the paramilitary strong arm of the Party. Roehm was ambitious and demanded a greater arena for himself and his men. He wanted his units incorporated into the regular army, a suggestion the generals found totally unacceptable. The officers of the high command were appalled at the notion of a "people's army" under the personal command of Roehm, whose homosexual lifestyle raised eyebrows. It was no secret that he and other leaders of the SA engaged in all sorts of debauchery. This alone made the SA leadership unacceptable to the great majority of Germans.

Faced with the choice of appeasing either the regular army, which had the power to topple Hitler if it had the will, or Ernst Roehm, his longtime friend, Hitler made his decision. Goering and Goebbels agreed that the old comrade and his cronies had to be sacrificed. The fact that Heinrich Himmler's Schutzstaffel (SS) was willing, perhaps even eager, to carry out the assassinations removed any practical difficulties. With one blow the power of the SA would be broken, and, no doubt, the generals would be grateful.

The arrests and most of the executions took place on June 30, 1934—the Night of the Long Knives or Blood Purge. Hitler himself participated in the arrest of Ernst Roehm. Some SA leaders were murdered immediately, others, like Roehm, within a few days. The liquidation of the chiefs of the SA also served as an excuse to settle some old scores between rivals. The exact number of victims has never been firmly established, perhaps as few as 100 or as many as 1,000 were killed. No indictments were filed; no due process of the law granted. After the assassinations were carried out, the public was told that Roehm and the SA had planned to usurp the government in a counterrevolution, and for the sake of public peace and order, the authorities had been obliged to strike quickly. Actually, nearly all of the alleged plotters were surprised in their beds; thus, no credence can be given to the official justification. The SS, of course, earned the Fuehrer's gratitude, and its growing importance can be traced to this moment marked by the murder of old comrades.

As usual, the Nazis attempted to mask their crimes as legally sanctioned acts. An obedient Reichstag passed a law that retroactively legitimized the assassinations. There would be no other challenges to Hitler's power from within the Nazi Party during the Third Reich.

WORKERS

On May 1, 1933, Hitler celebrated the labor's contribution to the past and future greatness of the Reich. With laudatory speeches and parades, workers were lulled into wishful thinking about their role in the new regime. That was the calm before the storm. On the following day, all trade union headquarters were raided, their assets confiscated, and their leaders sent to concentration camps. Within the week, labor unions were dissolved, and strikes were declared illegal.

Clearly, the National Socialist German Workers' Party (Nazi or NSDAP) had expunged the socialist component of its name. There was no resistance to these draconic measures; in part due to the growing fear of arrest, in part due to the disappearance of communist and union leaders, and certainly, as the unemployment rate was falling, the expectation to find a job.

Hitler had no patience with and no understanding of the intricacies of economics. He simply wanted to realize certain highly visible objectives, regardless of any long-range implications. Foremost was his goal to reduce the unemployment rate. When he came to power, some six million Germans were out of work. Within the next four years that number was reduced to one million. Production rose more than 100 percent in this period, and hope for the future kept the rather poorly paid workers acquiescent. Public works, from grandiose construction schemes to the innovative *Autobahn* road system, and the revival of the arms industry alleviated the worst economic suffering.

In place of independent unions, the Nazis organized the German Labor Front. Hitler appointed Robert Ley to head the Workmen's League, designed to assure the submission of labor to the nationalistic goals of the Reich. Germany's more than 20 million workers were given glowing assurances of better pay, an end to industrial strife, emergency financial assistance, greater educational opportunities, and stable wages. These pledges were repeated over and over but never fulfilled. Some cosmetic changes were made. For example, factory managers were urged to make working conditions more pleasant; Ley instituted "Strength through Joy," a program of complimentary vacations for the most productive workers, gifts of tickets to attend theaters and sports events. The Volkswagen project was a unique scheme. Workers by the hundreds of thousands permitted the government to make deductions from their wages toward ownership of a Volkswagen. It must be remembered that very few German factory workers boasted possession of a car, an important status symbol for the middle class. Goebbels' propaganda press waxed ecstatic about the respected status of workingmen and issued posters depicting the well-muscled laborer as the indispensable counterpart of the soldier.

But Germany was not the new Eden for the working class. No Volkswagens rolled off the assembly lines for the men; the money withheld went into the production of tanks instead. Wages remained low as civilian production was subordinated to the rearmament demands of Hitler's quest for *Lebensraum* (space to live). After 1939, the status of labor, in the view of some historians, its enserfment, deteriorated further. The requirements of war production pushed the men to the limit of their endurance. There were no pay raises, only declarations of gratitude from the government. No longer could a worker choose his occupation freely; a state agency had the right to approve or disapprove changes of employment and residence. Goebbels' office reiterated endlessly that as a good soldier must do his duty without complaint, so must the German laborer. The effectiveness of that appeal may be judged by the fact that workers remained at their tasks until the Allies destroyed their factories. It is noteworthy that relatively few German women were hired even during wartime shortages, but the slave labor of foreign and Jewish females was used in fields and factories.

ECONOMIC POLICY

Hitler's ambitions were in the arena of foreign affairs. The expansion of the Reich and German hegemony over Europe were always a vital part of his grand design. Because he saw war as a part of the natural battleground between the fit and the unfit, preparations began as soon as possible. Rearmament required money, but the details of financing his aims were other people's concerns. He was fortunate to have the wizardry of Hjalmar Schacht at his disposal. Schacht was brilliant and opportunistic; he claimed to be a monarchist, but was a founder of the German Democratic Party. In 1931, he declared that he was not a Nazi, but he enabled Hitler to achieve important economic gains. During the Weimar Republic, he had earned fame for his genius in finance and had been largely responsible for curbing the runaway inflation of 1923. Within a year of Hitler's appointment as chancellor, he accepted the post of *Reichsminister* of Economics. He masterminded the early economic successes of the Reich despite his objections to some Nazi policies, including the violent anti-Semitism. Claiming opposition to Hitler's military aggression, he nonetheless readied the German economy to prepare for war. He printed money and manipulated currencies. When foreign creditors feared that they might lose their German investments, Schacht convinced them to invest more money in order to recoup a shaky debt. Hitler, of course, was delighted to have such a renowned banker in his service who allowed him to transfer vast sums to the military and finance projects that reduced unemployment.

Schacht became disillusioned with Nazism and secretly flirted with opponents of the regime. At this point he was no longer the economic czar; much of his authority had been usurped by Goering, who was in control of the Four Year Plan. This plan, devised in 1936, attempted to make Germany self-sufficient and independent of foreign imports. Despite the creation of various synthetics and ersatz fabrications, Germany was never able to free itself of the need for certain imports, gasoline and fats in particular.

After the attempt on Hitler's life in July 1944, Schacht was arrested, and he spent the following year in several concentration camps. He was one of the defendants during the postwar Nuremberg Trials and was acquitted by the international tribunal.

FARMERS

When Hitler assumed power, German agriculture had been in crisis for five years. The peasantry, 29 percent of the population, had provided important support for the NSDAP, and Hitler promised to alleviate their distress. Specifically, farmers sought to curtail agricultural imports to prop up prices for their products and get relief from debts. Farm foreclosures were threatening small and medium landowners in ever-growing numbers. For a landholder to lose his property was more than a financial disaster, to descend from the position of an owner to that of a laborer was a serious loss of social status as well.

Richard Darré, the man appointed to lead the reform, added another facet when he declared the peasantry to be the stronghold of racial health. Darré, a general in the SS and devotee of the Nazi racial ideology, believed that German soil together with German blood were the mainsprings of a uniquely German Volk ethos. Peasants, with their large family, were extolled as representative of Aryan excellence. How many farmers were persuaded by that propaganda is impossible to estimate, but it is doubtful that many were impressed by Darré's flattering words.

Darré hoped to make German farmers independent of the fluctuations of world market conditions. Although the government raised duties on imports, it was not possible for German agriculture to provide for all the needs of the nation. Even when the ministry instituted price controls and production quotas, farmers' plight persisted. While improved prices raised farmers' incomes, the required quotas deprived them of their freedom to grow the crops of their choice. The enactment of the Reich's Hereditary Farm Law was also a mixed blessing. To ensure that farms of less than 308 acres remained intact, the owner could not sell his property or divide it among his children. He was forced to pass it on to a single heir, the oldest or youngest son according to local custom. The heir was then obligated to provide for the basic needs of his siblings. Such inherited and entailed farms could not be divided, mortgaged, or foreclosed. While this legislation provided security, it also tied farmers to the soil. As the military drained young men from the fields into the army and the industrial requirements of rearmament called them into factories, the agricultural labor shortage became acute. The government decreed that all young men and women between the ages of 18 and 25 spend a year working on farms or as domestic workers (the *Landjahr*), but inexperienced youngsters from the cities could not replace seasoned farm hands. During the war years, hundred of thousands of men from conquered countries were forced to work on German farms. Depending on good or ill luck, these foreign laborers received varying treatment from their masters, but they were generally better off than the starved men and women impressed into factory work.

The German government also requisitioned shipments of food from the countries they occupied in order to feed German civilians and the army. Despite all these efforts, the goal of an agriculturally self-sufficient Germany could not be met. When Goering offered the people "guns, not butter," he encapsulated the priorities of the government perfectly, though his growing girth indicated no shortage of butter in his diet.

BUSINESS

The gulf between election rhetoric and the actuality of governing was also exemplified by the Nazi attitude toward small businesses. The craftsmen and small shop owners had been promised the breakup of their giant competitors, such as chain and department stores. Large numbers from the lower middle class had voted for the NSDAP, expecting protection for their vulnerable enterprises. Such help was never given. The associations created to protect small businesses were quickly dominated by the Nazis, who discouraged political action among their membership. Even when the Jews had been driven from the economy, the plight of small shops did not improve. The welfare of individuals was never a concern of the Nazi hierarchy; the emphasis was always on doing what must be done to assure Germany's victory in the coming war.

The subordination of domestic needs to foreign policy goals enabled the great manufacturers and industrialists to thrive. During the first six years of the Third Reich, they increased their profits from 1.75 million marks to 5 billion marks. Although the government issued innumerable rules and regulations dealing with production, import and export, prices and wages, allotments of raw materials, and the size of the work force, the great corporations flourished. No attempt was made to break them up or curb their profits. Hitler knew that their productivity was a vital component of his plans of conquest. If, in the pursuit of his larger goals, the hopes of others for a better life were sacrificed, so be it.

The rearming of Germany was to be carried out with a maximum of self-sufficiency and a minimum of imports. The manufacture of substitute products, the ersatz materials, resulted in various synthetics, but such replacements could not meet the nation's fuel, rubber, and food requirements. Germans might reluctantly drink coffee made from grain, but tanks and planes could not operate without gasoline. Hitler admitted that even his best scientists could not reproduce in laboratories certain needed raw materials, and only conquest of Balkan and Eastern Europe could fill that need. Until the nation was ready to go to war, workers and farmers and tradesmen must accept their hardships.

PUBLIC EDUCATION

"How could the Holocaust have happened in the land of Goethe and Beethoven?"—This often-asked question implies a connection between culture and ethics. In this context, the term *culture* refers to a people's art, music, literature, institutions, and prevailing attitudes. These values are passed from one generation to the next and may be accepted, questioned, or altered. Ethics, on the other hand, denotes principles of morality and behavior. The long-held assumption that educated people have higher ethical standards than uneducated people was refuted by Nazi Germany. University degrees and an appreciation for the classics did not influence the well-educated commanders of the *Einsatzgruppen,* the mobile killing units, as they carried out their bloody business.

The Nazis viewed education of the young as the most important vehicle for the perpetuation of the Nazi doctrine. To insure their hope for a Thousand Year Reich, the role of education was paramount, and education became indoctrination. Before 1933 German children were taught that intelligence was an asset, and that degrees from universities opened the way to successful careers. Good students justified their parents' pride and hope. The Nazi ethos, however, adopted an anti-intellectual posture that flew in the face of tradition. The strong body was valued above the brilliant mind, obedience above critical thinking, patriotism above family loyalty, and conformity above individualism. German youth was to be recast in a new image.

The man appointed to Nazify the educational system was an old friend and supporter of Hitler, Bernhard Rust. He had not been a successful pedagogue; his teaching career had ended when he was fired for molesting a schoolgirl. Nonetheless, Rust supervised the centralization of the educational system and the dissolution of local school boards. All professional decisions, including teaching appointments, were under his jurisdiction. He promised to do no less than transform the German system. To a rather frightening degree, he succeeded.

Rust was able to rely on the enthusiastic support of those faculty members who were already committed Nazis. Many were veterans of the Great War, nationalistic to the point of chauvinism, and conservative to right wing in their politics. Even before membership was mandatory, the percentage of educators in the Party was considerably larger than the 20 percent of the general population. Remarkably, the proportion of university professors was highest of all. It should be noted that the partnership between school and parents, so familiar to Americans, hardly existed in Germany. The teacher was in charge, period. Most educators fell in line with Rust's new directives; some conformed merely to keep their jobs, others left the profession. Parents did what they had always done: told their children to mind the teacher.

The needs of the state, not the welfare of the child, was the basis of Nazi pedagogy. To guarantee classroom application of this philosophy, only the politically reliable were permitted to teach. Jews were excluded immediately. Teachers with records of democratic or socialist sympathies were dismissed as soon as replacements became available. At the universities of Berlin and Frankfurt, 32 percent of the staff was purged. Over a quarter of physics professors were fired, among them were 20 past and future Nobelists, including Albert Einstein. All academic associations were automatically incorporated into the National Socialist Teachers Organization, which, in effect, became an extension of Goebbels' propaganda network. Eventually, all teaching staff were required to enroll in the Party and swear an oath of obedience to the Fuehrer. Faculty, from kindergarten to graduate school, was obliged to attend intensive training courses on the new education goals. Even the innocuous prayer of the children that traditionally opened the school day was replaced with the Heil Hitler salute and an expression of gratitude to the Fuehrer for saving Germany.

Rust initiated fundamental changes in order to transform German youth into zealous, anti-Semitic, obedient Nazis. Physical education (PE) was given top priority, usually scheduled for five hours per week. Students who did not complete their PE requirements, regardless of any physical handicaps, could not receive their graduation diplomas. Girls were also compelled to participate in rigorous bodybuilding programs. As the fatherland needed healthy soldiers, so it needed strong, fertile mothers. The revised program emphasized changes in history, biology, and German literature. Aryan racial theories were accorded the pretensions of scientific study, and students were required to trace their personal racial inheritance as far back as possible. Readings were purged of the works of Jewish and liberal authors. Every field of instruction was twisted to follow Nazi ideology. For example, a geography lesson emphasized Germany's need for *Lebensraum;* an ancient history class instructed students that the culture of the Germanic tribes was superior to that of the Romans; physiology became a vehicle to demonstrate the biological inferiority of the Jews; and mathematical problems related to the number of bullets needed to kill Germany's enemies. Before Jewish children were excluded from school, they often were directed to stand in front of their classmates, while their features were analyzed as examples of their subhuman heritage. The racial superiority of Germans found expression in almost every topic, and a pupil could not spend a single day without learning something about the perfidy of all Jews. Questioning the material was discouraged. Students who came to class wearing the uniform of the *Hitler Jugend,* the Nazi youth organization for boys, or that of the *Bund Deutscher Maedel* (BDM), for girls, were especially welcome. Physical punishment, usually caning, was not discouraged. Boys and girls who wore glasses, were physically weak, whose parents were not members of the Nazi Party, or were serious about scholarship found the atmosphere hostile.

TRAINING THE NAZI OF THE FUTURE

The most intense ideological indoctrination of German youth took place within the Nazi Youth movement. The young Baldur von Schirach, a poet by avocation and professional Nazi by vocation, was Hitler's choice to head the Hitler Youth organization. In 1936, all other youth organizations, including church groups and the

Boys and Girls Scouts, were outlawed. Membership in the Hitler Youth movement was made compulsory, and the state, rather than the Party, became its sponsor and financed its budget. Most of the youngsters enjoyed the activities and the bonds of comradeship these groups fostered. The programs included camping, hiking, day and night marches, and many sport competitions. Some groups offered instructions in flying model planes, participation in marching bands, and singing contests. Indoctrination into Nazi concepts of race and reverence for the Fuehrer were included at every opportunity. Parental complaints that their children had so little time at home merely assured the troop leaders that they were doing a good job.

Large amounts of money were expended to mold the next generation in the Nazi image. From the ages of 6 to 19 and often beyond, the greatest influence on the development of German youngsters was not the parents, not the schools, but the *Hitler Jugend.* Six-year old boys were inducted and called *Pimpfe.* Usually around 10 years of age, they advanced to the status of *Jungfolk,* having demonstrated their physical fitness and shouting Nazi slogans. Within three years, they were eligible to be installed in the *Jugend.* Acceptance was not automatic; it depended on passing some highly competitive examinations that tested strength, courage, and the ability to follow orders without question. Some youngsters demonstrated their competence by completing such tasks as laying telephone wire and reading semaphore. Graduation at 18 promoted the young man into the NSDAP and/or the SA.

Girls were subject to similar regimentation. According to Nazi ideology, the natural sphere for women was the nursery and the kitchen. Members of the *Bund Deutscher Maedel* (BDM, Union of German Girls) were ordered to braid their hair into two pigtails and wear blue skirts and white blouses. When they marched in parades, they usually created a stir of admiration. They too underwent rigorous physical training in order to become healthy mothers of healthy children. Advancement up the organizational ladder depended on enthusiasm and mastery of the tasks tested. There were, however, only three schools to train leaders in the Nazi women's movement. Older girls received instruction in cooking, childcare, and homemaking. The desire of girls to enter the workplace was denigrated; the ideal woman was a mother and an adjunct to her man. Any ambition for independence and equality was characterized as a Jewish–Bolshevik plot.

Even at the age of 19, young Germans' commitment to the state was not completed. Both men and women were required to give six months, later extended to a year, of labor service to the nation. Called the *Landjahre,* this innovation was to promote solidarity between rural and urban citizens by sending city youths to work on farms and country youths to factories. After completing this obligation, men entered the military for their compulsory service. Women were not accepted into the military; they were expected to marry. However, out-of-wedlock children were fully accepted by the Party. Pregnant girls were offered the opportunity to deliver their babies in cost-free maternity homes. If they wished, they could rear their children and receive help from the government, or could offer them for adoption. As one would expect, all university enrollment declined during the Nazi era, but that of women dropped most sharply.

The Nazis established three types of schools to train future leaders of the movement—the *Adolf Hitler Schulen* (Adolf Hitler Schools), the *NAPOIAS*

(National-Political Training Institutes), and the *Ordensburgen* (Order Castles). The *Hitler Schulen* selected students of promise from among the *Jungvolk.* Racial background, particularly blond hair and blue eyes, was of the greatest importance. Their training emphasized military ideals with five periods of physical training and one-and-a-half periods of academic study per week. Nonetheless, after completing the course, the young men were considered ready to enter universities.

The second of the training institutions, the *NAPOIAS,* aimed to educate officials for important posts in the Third Reich. Although under the direction of the Nazi Party, the old Prussian academies that had offered academic and military instruction served as models. Of course, the sons of loyal Nazis were given preference in the enrollment. By 1938, there were 23 such schools, but few cadets were able to fulfill their ambitions; the war pulled the graduates into the army.

Candidates who had been judged fit for future roles in the highest echelon of the Party might be placed into one of the four *Ordensburge.* These students were older alumni of the Adolf Hitler schools, usually in their mid-twenties when they were offered the chance to be among the Nazi elite. They lived in castles amid medieval settings and ceremonies designed to create a mystique of brotherhood and service. The philosophy underlying their training is best summed up by their motto: "Believe, Obey, Fight." The SS ran these institutions and expected its graduates to join its officer corps. Again, the war absorbed most of them before they could reach their intended goal.

Visitors to Germany in the prewar Nazi years were often charmed by its polite, good-looking youth. Healthy, respectful, and active, they compared favorably with children of other nations. That was one side of the coin. The other side involved the rapid decline of the intellectual standards in German schools and universities. Everyone was overtaxed with rounds of endless activities that had no connection to studies. One might assume that juvenile delinquency disappeared inasmuch as young people seemed to live in a perpetual, albeit highly regulated, summer camp. The facts refute such assumptions. Gangs were still active, and juvenile lawlessness continued to exist.

THE CATHOLIC CHURCH

Hitler did not destroy the external structure of the major Christian institutions. While no church was burned down or turned into a museum, the spirit of Christianity was placed under siege. Even though the official philosopher of the NSDAP, Alfred Rosenberg, denounced Christianity and tried to promote a cult of pagan worship, the German masses rejected his *Mythus.* Rosenberg's claim that Jesus was an aggressive, revolutionary Nordic, whose essence was perverted into a faith of Christian meekness, fell on deaf ears, as few Germans accepted his gospel of racial purity. Not even the Protestants sanctioned his denigration of popes as mere merchants of snake oil.

Hitler wanted no confrontation with the churches—it was enough to bring them into line by restricting many of their functions. Most religious schools were closed, religious fraternal organizations were outlawed, and the freedom to teach the tenets of the faith was severely curtailed. But persecution is a relative concept. The doors of the churches remained open; services were held. Some individual members of the clergy, both Catholic and Protestant, were arrested and imprisoned for preaching anti-Nazi sermons. The vast majority of priests and ministers, however, went about their business as best they could and kept clear of dangerous topics. That list included such essential ideals as love thy neighbor, turn the other cheek, and the concept that obedience to God takes precedence over obedience to man. The churches continued to provide ritual observances, while the spirit of Christianity was diluted. German religious institutions did not battle the Nazi anti-Christ; instead, by their silence they permitted the perpetration of terrible wrongs. Hymns were sung, masses said, and baptisms celebrated, but the doctrines of mercy, love, peace, and equality before God were suspended.

Hitler and The Papacy

The Catholic Center Party had opposed the Nazis even after the *Gleichschaltung* of all political parties. Hitler, a nonpracticing Catholic, feared the potential opposition of the centrists and the power of religious faith. He hoped to avoid an all-out conflict with German Catholics and tried to win their support. Shortly after coming to power in 1933, he concluded a concordat with Pope Pius XI. This agreement guaranteed, to quote the document, "freedom of the profession and the public exercise of the Catholic religion." Other clauses guaranteed the continuation of Catholic religious instruction in public schools, the protection of church institutions, and the appointment of a bishop to serve the armed forces. The Vatican, in return, gave official recognition to the regime and consented to the dissolution of its church-sponsored social and political organizations including labor unions.

Hitler derived immediate benefits from the treaty; it enhanced his image and raised hope among German Catholics that the Nazis would not interfere with their practices and educational institutions. It was a vain hope, because the concordat was quickly violated until, step by step, all the promises made by Hitler were breached. The Catholic Youth League was dissolved, religious instruction in public schools banned, Catholic publications prohibited, members of Catholic clergy, including nuns, arrested, and convents and monasteries closed. In 1937, the Pope issued an encyclical known as *With Burning Concern*, which accused the Nazi government of deifying race, nation, and the state. The message was smuggled out of Italy and secretly distributed among the Catholic clergy, who read it to their congregations on Palm Sunday. If the Pope had hoped to influence Hitler's position, he was disillusioned. The government harassment of observant Catholics continued. Another more forceful anti-Nazi document had been written and was on the Pope's desk when he died in February 1939.

The Nazi design to create a perfect race ran counter to the Christian obligation to love all creations of the Lord, no matter how impaired. When the Nazis enforced their plan to sterilize those Germans judged too "defective" to have children, the churches objected strongly. Nevertheless, the medical procedures continued. By 1937, some 200,000 people had been sterilized for reasons such as schizophrenia, alcoholism, and a range of physical problems. The objective of creating the master race took an even more heartbreaking turn when it was decided to stop feeding "useless eaters." These so-called misfits were quietly, secretly murdered. When Cardinal/Archbishop Clemens von Galen of Muenster became aware of these "euthanasia" killings, he declared from the pulpit that this practice was a grievous sin. Fear of public reaction officially ended the use of lethal injections and gassings of children and adults though it continued in greater secrecy. The number of victims is estimated at 275,000.

HITLER AND THE PROTESTANT CHURCHES

The relationship between the Nazi state and the Protestant communities failed to develop into a consistent policy. Neither the government nor the religious groups found a satisfactory method of dealing with the other. The official stance was to reduce the influence of traditional religion without causing serious opposition. Several different approaches were tried, sometimes simultaneously. The attempt to crush the independence of the churches by placing them under the control of a synod of pro-Nazi ministers was not successful. The Nazis were unable to unify or completely control the church federation they had established under the Evangelical theologian Ludwig Mueller. Mueller was given the title of Reich Bishop, but the so-called German Faith Movement failed to attract mass support. The notion of combining Christianity with Nordic paganism merely revealed the muddled thinking of Alfred Rosenberg. The great majority of Protestants did not abandon their faith, Hitler himself remained aloof. Finally, the Nazis had to settle for weakening the churches by the tactics they had found most successful: intimidation, harassment, and even terror. Protestant ministers, like priests, were arrested during services in front of worshipers. Both the fear and the reality of imprisonment in concentration camps stilled all but a few voices of protest among the clergy.

German Protestants, numbering about 45 million of a total population of some 60 million, were not a homogeneous group. The majority were Lutherans, followed by Calvinists, with smaller representations of Methodists and Baptists. The several thousand Jehovah's Witnesses deserve mention because the Nazis persecuted them relentlessly for their steadfast adherence to the doctrine of the superiority of God to an and for their dedication to peace. Further divisions occurred within the denominations over the issue of cooperation with the Nazis. It is important to remember that Martin Luther, the towering figure of the Reformation, was fiercely anti-Semitic. His unrestrained verbal attacks on the Jews were not equaled until Goebbels' rhetoric. The Nazis, of course, invoked these denunciations to fortify the concept that it was possible to remain a good Protestant while becoming an equally good Nazi. The great reformer had exhorted his followers to give unquestioning and complete obedience to civil authority. Thus, Nazi aims dovetailed with Lutheran doctrine.

Most of the reformed churches tried to avoid running afoul of the authorities by preaching "safe" sermons. In the process, essential Christian doctrine was watered down to mere observance of rites and rituals in an atmosphere of disquiet. Some Christians, however, raised their voices in opposition. The best known among these was the Reverend Martin Niemoeller. A highly decorated U-boat captain of

World War I, he had described his wartime experiences in a best seller; thus, his name was familiar to most Germans. A fervent nationalist, he had supported the rising Hitler. But the actuality of Nazis in power and their racial and anti-Christian policies offended and disillusioned him. An activist by nature, he became the leader of a religious resistance movement. His Confessional Church and the Pastors Emergency League were a counterweight, albeit an ineffectual one, to Hitler's German Faith Organization. In 1934 these ministers drafted a statement declaring their opposition to Nazi interference in church affairs and to the doctrine that might makes right. They also declared that Christianity was irreconcilable with the Nazis' German Faith Movement. At its height, Niemoeller's organization included some 7,000 of approximately 17,000 Lutheran ministers.

The Gestapo responded swiftly. More than 700 ministers were arrested and usually sent home after a brief but highly "educational" imprisonment. Pastors who were deemed unlikely to fall into line, numbering about 50, were sent to concentration camps. Hitler preferred a gradual rather than an abrupt weakening of the power of the church and direct pressure eased. Niemoeller, however, was seen as the spark of the movement. In 1937, after preaching a sermon on obedience to God, not man, he was arrested. He was tried in a special court on charges of "abuse of the pulpit." Since his sentence was shorter than the time already served while awaiting trial, the court ordered his release. As he left the courtroom, however, he was arrested by the Gestapo and placed under "protective custody." He survived seven years in various concentration camps until, in 1945, he was finally liberated by the Allies.

It would be misleading to see Pastor Niemoeller as spearheading an army of righteous Christians. During the seven years he endured hardships in the Sachsenhausen and Dachau camps, he was almost forgotten by the German people. The brief candle of protest, the Confessional Church, was snuffed out by the Gestapo. Only after the German defeat did Pastor Niemoeller become a hero once again. He had been a "good German," a symbol of German decency and courage in the face of the general submission of the Protestants to the repression of religious freedom. It also needs to be said that he had no interest in the fate of the Jews.

NAZI JUSTICE

In his official stance, Hitler was an advocate of law and order; privately he declared that the human conscience was a Jewish invention designed to enslave other races. It was no surprise that justice was one more sphere to be subordinated to the ideal of the *Volksgemeinschaft,* that is, the racial, ideological, and organizational unity of the German people. Individual rights had to give way to communal rights; persons and institutions were valued in direct proportion to their ability to promote Nazi goals. Those who failed to advance the Nazi *Weltanschauung* were pronounced useless; those who stood in the way, decreed to be enemies to be rooted out. Ruthlessness, even cruelty, became a virtue in the battle to destroy the real and imagined enemies of the new order. Concepts of justice were based on the decisions of men, not on the rule of immutable laws designed to secure lives and property in a civilized society.

The Third Reich did not issue a new legal code. The existing system was reinterpreted to suit the contemporary realities. All judges were appointed; most of the sitting judges were already nationalistic and conservative, and some were committed Nazis. With the exception of Jewish jurists, there was no wholesale dismissal of judges, and courts continued to function. New harsh laws poured forth from Berlin in a constant stream, mainly related to safeguarding racial purity and protecting the regime from opposition. By 1945, there were 43 crimes punishable by execution, including *Rassenschande*—defilement of race by sexual intercourse between Aryan and non-Aryan. Crimes committed by juveniles were tried in adult courts. The criminal justice code sanctioned beating of prisoners during questioning—but not more than 25 blows delivered to the buttocks. Also, officially approved was the use of torture by the Gestapo and SS when questioning accused prisoners.

For some Germans it was still possible to get justice in a German court, most often in civil matters dealing with contracts, wills, and other such issues. But in cases that pitted a member of the Nazi Party against a nonmember, a verdict in favor of the Party member was practically assured. An individual suing a community wasted his time and money; his effort was doomed from the start. While prosecutors were given greater powers, those of defense counsels' were reduced. Gauleiters routinely interfered in court proceedings.

The Nazis were unceasingly preoccupied with the possibility of political counteraction. The Gestapo alone employed thousands of informers, *Spitzels,* whose identity was unknown to the public. Remarks implying criticism, even a political joke, could be interpreted as a crime under the Law Against Malicious Attacks on State and Party. But the most distorted aberration of justice was the *Volksgericht,* the People Court.

To deal with the spate of accusations following the attempted assassination of Hitler on July 20, 1944, a special court was established whose judges were fiercely loyal to the regime. Cases involving treason were heard by the People's Court, which consisted of a combination of Party jurists and high-ranking Nazi officials. The proceedings had little resemblance to our understanding of justice. Defendants were threatened, denounced, and shouted down by the judges. There was no appeal of the verdicts. The attempt on Hitler's life resulted in the execution of between 180 and 200 accused conspirators. Cases involving Party members were tried by yet another innovation, *Parteigerichte* (the Party Courts). These tribunals were generally used to discipline members of the NSDAP and punish administrative irregularities.

The most tragic perversion of justice was, of course, the Holocaust. In its sphere, the criminals, that is, the SS, were empowered to act as judges, juries, and executioners. The question of wrongdoing was irrelevant; simply to be a Jew was a capital crime. Himmler had become their master, and the SS had the right to take their possessions and their liberty and passed the death penalty upon them six million times in four years.

CHAPTER 6

History of German Jews to 1939

The term "anti-Semitism" originated in Germany. It was first introduced into the vocabulary in the 1870s by Wilhelm Marr in his book *The Victory of Judaism over Germanism* and popularized by the diverse factions that opposed the integration of Jews into the life of the German Empire. The fact that hatred of Jews was given a new designation in the recently unified nation confirmed that a new dimension had been added to an ancient prejudice. No longer was the age-old aversion based solely on its Christian antecedents, rather the taint of racial inferiority was now superimposed on the long-accepted religious bias. Anti-Semitism became the catchword that sanctioned the notion that an inherent incompatibility existed between Jews and Gentiles. Thus, the theory evolved that a number of supposed negative "Jewish characteristics" existed, which ranged from avarice to zealousness. As a result, Jews could never be part of the Germanic people, even if they converted to Christianity. Nor would their residency on German soil, be it of hundreds of years in duration, alter their inability to be part of the *Volk.* The acceptance by some Germans of such sophistry in the nineteenth century marked a reversal, perhaps a conservative reaction, of the generally more liberal attitude of the era.

EMANCIPATION

The medieval persecution of the Jewish people in Europe had been deeply rooted in the deicide, the Christ-killing myth. Thus, the miserable state of Jewish life, though caused by severe economic restrictions, was explained in religious terms: This was God's punishment for the rejection of the Savior. All past sins, however, could be absolved through conversion. Beginning with the Age of Reason (also called the Age of Enlightenment), during the eighteenth century, some of the old assumptions concerning the Jews were challenged. The great writers of the era, the *philosophes,* such as Jean Jaques Rousseau, Voltaire, and Montesquieu, who agitated for fundamental political and social changes, paved the way for the coming French Revolution. They insisted that human institution must be based on logic, not tradition or religious doctrine. They attacked the political absolutism of the French government and its compliant sister, the church. In the process, the prevailing anti-Jewish prejudices were questioned. When Napoleon made himself the ruler of France and beyond, his soldiers carried the revolutionary ideals of liberty, equality, and fraternity into central Europe. Political liberty was slow in coming, fraternity was still a dream, but the concept of equal treatment before the law had significant effectiveness and influenced the treatment of the Jews. By the end of the eighteenth century, Jews in central Europe, France, and England had been granted most civil rights. As the ghetto walls fell, its former occupants were grateful and hopeful that the forces of rationalism would allow them to live peacefully as citizens in the Gentile world.

CAN JEWS BE GERMANS?

In Germany, the Jews lived on a roller coaster of hope and despair for more than a century. The pull of the old conservatives and push of the Enlightenment contracted and advanced their hopes of acceptance. The achievements of Moses Mendelssohn (1729–1786) had raised their expectations of entering into the full rhythm of German life. Mendelssohn, the "German Plato," exhorted the Jews to emulate educated Germans, speak their language, read their literature, and study the natural sciences, history, and philosophy. In the intellectual salons, where men and women of learning came together, Jews and Gentiles met as equals. The eagerness of German Jewry to be accepted inspired them to embrace German culture enthusiastically. The voices of admonition raised by the Orthodox rabbinate could not hold back the desire of most German Jews to join the mainstream of national life. They hoped that cultural conversion could accomplish what religious conversion had done in the past, but without the loss of their Jewish faith.

Germany was not unified into a single nation until 1871. Otto von Bismarck's political achievements were followed by rapid economic growth, as German industry competed to manufacture goods for international markets. German Jews eagerly participated in these expanding economic opportunities. As they entered and succeeded in various business and professional pursuits, voices of opposition grew stronger. Even though this renewed anti-Jewish agitation rested upon the old overt and covert religious antipathies, now the claim of ethnic incompatibility opened a new anti-Jewish front. The indictment alleged that Jews were ethnically and culturally different, "aliens in our midst," who could never be true Germans. Modern German anti-Semitism had found a new theory to support an old resentment.

ECONOMIC ANTI-SEMITISM

Throughout the Middle Ages and beyond, Jews had been subjected to severe economic restrictions, but in the first half of the nineteenth century, the door to economic opportunity opened a crack. The Napoleonic wars (ended in 1815) were followed by the gradual emancipation of western and central European Jews. Most German states (their number had been reduced from over 300 to 30 by Napoleon) permitted Jews to do business with the Gentile world on a more equitable footing. The unification of Germany and the ensuing industrial expansion had given larger numbers of Jews entry into growing trade and manufacturing activities. Mechanization and mass production required modernization of business methods, particularly in finance and banking. Now the middlemen, the traders, the storekeepers, the men who understood investments and the raising of capital, were in demand. Workers were needed to man the machines, and factory owners were not interested in the religious affiliation of their labor force.

For the German Jews, such economic changes were not obstacles; rather, they offered opportunities. Many took full advantage of these new possibilities, and often they succeeded. Within a generation or two, many poor Jews had entered the middle class, and a few became rich and powerful. As they embraced bourgeois economic values, they usually adopted the prevailing German moral and cultural standards as well. With an enthusiasm often typical of newcomers seeking acceptance, they plunged into German art and literature as well as science and education as admirers and contributors. The German language replaced Yiddish in their homes; modern dress replaced the somber traditional garb; and many women stopped the customary covering of their hair. These changes permitted Jews to enjoy less isolated and less restrictive lives. For Jewish intellectuals, the bounty of European culture, its literature, and scientific and artistic accomplishments were a feast for the senses.

German Jews, by and large, espoused emancipation and acculturation. Their successes, however, reawakened a barely dormant anti-Semitism. The economic upheaval that accompanied the development of German industry frustrated those who did not or could not benefit from it. Social and political power was no longer limited to the landholding nobility as the power of money contested old and respected family position. The cycles of boom and bust, the hardships caused by recurring periods of unemployment, and the emergence of new wealth and new poverty—all were factors in creating insecurity and anxiety. Who could be blamed for ushering in this new and, for some, frightening state of affairs?

Because there is no connection between prejudice and reality, it was not difficult to target the Jews. Capitalists, unhappy with the growing socialist movement among their workers, noted that some of the labor leaders were Jews. Factory workers, protesting the avarice of the owners, pointed to Jewish manufacturers. When wild speculation resulted in the crash of 1873, articles in the press singled out Jews for condemnation. Although the name of Rothschild was held in high esteem in financial circles, it was the opinion of the anti-Jewish establishment that the banking house had become entirely too rich and powerful.

POLITICAL ANTI-SEMITISM

Expansion of suffrage in national and state elections in the German Empire stimulated the development of political parties, ranging from the reactionary to the radical. The majority of German Jews supported liberal politicians, which aroused the antagonism of some factions within conservative and reactionary circles. German conservatives discovered that anti-Semitic propaganda had vote-getting power. In courting the blue-collar middle class, shopkeepers, craftsmen, and petty officials, the promise to restrict Jewish competition was effective ammunition.

The Christian Social Workingmen's Party had been founded in 1878 by Adolf Stoecker, the official court chaplain of Emperor William I. Its centerpiece was vilification of Jews and the demand that they convert to Christianity. Stoecker, like Hitler, was an eloquent speaker, a rabid anti-Semite, and a good organizer. With his endorsement, several international anti-Jewish congresses were convened in Germany, and for the first time, but certainly not the last, a delegate from an overtly anti-Jewish party took his seat in the Reichstag. Stoecker called for the revocation of citizenship for Jews and their removal from certain professions. But his diatribes were too regressive, even for the revered Chancellor Otto von Bismarck, who declared that the nation would not permit religious affiliation to intrude on the rights of citizenship.

The Christian Social Workingmen's Party was the most blatant but not the only political organization to advocate limitations of the rights of Jews. In 1880, some 250,000 Germans signed petitions to ban Jews from attending German schools and universities. The Catholic Center Party and conservatives included a promise to combat the "oppressive and disintegrating Jewish influence on our national life" in their political platforms. Ambitious politicians gave assurances that Jews would be "kept in their place" and promised to enact laws banning non-Christians from teaching their children or serving as magistrates.

The phrase, so often repeated by the Nazis, "the Jews are our misfortune" was given legitimacy, even respectability, when used by the renowned historian Heinrich von Treitschke. So effective were the accusations coming from the extreme nationalists, some of the clergymen and the ever-present clique of opportunists that anti-Semitic violence broke out during the last quarter of the nineteenth century, which resulted in destruction of property and beatings. Only the socialists expressed concern over this lawlessness. Many German Jews, however, recognized that they needed to exert themselves on their own behalf. What forms their self-defense should take remained a divisive question until Hitler supplied the answer.

JEWISH REACTION: THE REFORM MOVEMENT

The Jews of Imperial Germany, citizens under the law but attacked by significant forces, were facing a dilemma. The great majority continued to await complete acceptance by their Christian fellow nationals. They believed that it was possible to serve two masters, to be patriotic Germans and retain their religious attachment to the ancient faith. There were Catholic Germans and Lutheran Germans, then why not Jewish Germans? *Deutschtum* was not incompatible with *Judentum.* For theological and philosophical reasons as well as the desire to facilitate the process of acculturation, German Jews initiated the modernization of religious practices. Rites and beliefs that were obsolete or considered contrary to the judgments of science were discarded or changed. Dietary prohibitions, the use of phylacteries in prayer, and the separation of men and women in synagogues were held to be outdated. Choirs and organ music were introduced to enhance the religious service; sermons were preached in German; prayer books were revised; and German translations of Hebrew texts were provided. Orthodox Jews, who remained the most numerous, were appalled and accused the reformers of abandoning Judaism for Germanism. The fact that members of Reform congregations were more likely to marry outside their faith and were often lost to the Jewish people gave substance to their fears.

But there was more to the Reform movement than the search for public acceptance. It was a revitalization of the faith. The need to bring harmony to Jewish civil and spiritual life was real. The foremost advocate of reform was Abraham Geiger, a noted scholar and critic who became chief rabbi of the synagogue of Breslau. He believed that the outward forms of Judaism must not be dictated from antiquity, but must reflect a vital living faith. In his view the ethical essence of the religion was not altered by the elimination of archaic ritual. To the distress of the Orthodox rabbinate, prayers for the coming of the messiah and the Jews' return to Zion were eliminated because German Jews must look upon Germany as their one and only homeland. It should be stressed that Reform Judaism removed none of the moral requisites from the Judaic faith. The command to act with righteousness and the struggle for social justice, two concepts rooted in the Torah, remained central in the Reform movement. Predictably, the very success of the reformers widened the gap between the traditionalists and the modernists, and theological debates sometimes disintegrated into factious quarrels.

IS ZIONISM THE ANSWER?

The desire of the German Jews to be treated as equals with their Christian neighbors was not commonly shared by the Gentile world. No matter how sincerely the Jews proclaimed their patriotism, how eagerly they embraced the German culture, how successfully they advanced German economic progress, anti-Semitism did not disappear. Most German Jews continued to hope that time and education would work on their behalf, but increasing numbers of individuals, especially among the young, faced the reality of their insecurity and wondered: What should we do? One answer, indeed an ancient one, was to flee. The modern equivalent of flight, that is, emigration, caused many to seek asylum beneath the outstretched arm of the Statue of Liberty. By 1880, the United States had opened its doors to 250,000 German-speaking Jews. They were literate, many had skills, and they were hard working. Town and cities on the East Coast, the West Coast, and the vast areas in between were enriched by their contributions to the cultural and economic life of the United States. Although statistically their numbers were soon overshadowed by the influx of Eastern European Jews, the mark they left on American Jewish institutions was indelible.

Immigration to the Land of Golden Opportunities was not the only response. The even more ancient solution of returning to the Jewish homeland was also winning supporters as a solution to the so-called Jewish question. Zionism was reborn; it is the movement calling for the reestablishment of a Jewish nation in the Holy Land. Its modern origin began in Russia where the czars persecuted the Jewish people for generations. Idealistic young men and women gathered to discuss, debate, and act on the dilemma of their repression and some opted to return to the ancient homeland. The life they chose in the Jewish enclaves of Turkish Palestine and its barren and malaria-infested soil was backbreaking and dangerous. Often their efforts failed, but they were the first to believe in Aliya—the return to the land of the Israelites. In Western Europe, however, Zionism was in direct conflict with assimilationism, and its appeal was very limited, that is, until the emergence of the remarkable Theodor Herzl.

Despite the fact that relatively few German Jews actually settled in that neglected and impoverished Turkish province, the Zionist movement won considerable financial and ideological support. The ZV or *Zionistische Vereinigung* (Zionist Union) combined separate chapters into a single organization, which enhanced its strength and voice. Its members contributed monetarily to the establishment of some of the earliest Kibbutzim (collective agricultural settlements) in Palestine.

THE CV REACTION

Still, the majority of Jewish Germans remained in the Reich. They continued to anticipate and advocate their complete integration into the fabric of German life. Through their achievements and patriotism they hoped to convince the government and their fellow citizens that they constituted an asset to the nation. Every friendly gesture on the part of the politically and socially powerful was hailed as evidence of their acceptance, every setback characterized as temporary. Now the Zionists asserted that integration into the national life of the Diaspora was at best implausible. This, they claimed, played into the hands of anti-Semites. Their own union, the CV, or *Centralverein deutscher Staatsbuerger Juedisches Glaubens* (Central Union of German Citizens of the Jewish Faith), exerted pressure on the German government to end all remaining discrimination. The CV considered it a point of honor to combat anti-Semitism, not submissively, but as their right as German citizens. Its legal arm fought bias in the courts, while its educational efforts stressed the timelessness and significance of Jewish values. Although fearful of political activity, the organization represented 60,000, or 12 percent, of German Jewry. They expected that the problem of *Deutschtum* versus *Judentum* could be resolved, and soon Jews would practice their faith as comfortably as did the German Protestants and Catholics.

But anti-Semitism has no rational basis and is not open to logical remedies. Heinrich Class's book *Wenn Ich Kaiser Wer (If I Were Emperor)* made that point emphatically. Published in 1912, Class fanned the old fires of anti-Semitism and kindled some new ones. He urged the enactment of laws forbidding Jews to vote, to work in public service, join the armed forces, or own land. He further suggested that they pay double the ordinary taxes. When the Nazis came to power, they found these suggestions inspirational for their own legislative actions.

WORLD WAR I

The rift between the Zionists and the assimilationists was temporarily healed by the outbreak of World War I. In a paroxysm of patriotic fervor, all differences were buried, not only among Jews, but also among former political opponents, who rallied enthusiastically around Kaiser and flag. German socialists, for example, dropped all pretense of solidarity with workers in other nations; the fact that the soldiers facing them on the battlefield might be French socialists ceased to be important. Clearly, nationalism had overwhelmed internationalism.

German Jews donned the uniforms and fought side by side with their Christian neighbors. As long as German victories fed the national pride, anti-Semitism was given a respite, albeit a short one. When the war ended in 1918, four years of carnage had destroyed much more than lives, property, and empires. The optimistic view that human progress was the destiny of Western man had been invalidated in the trenches. The postwar generation was born to cynicism, to economic and political turmoil, and to pessimism. Alienation was the catchword, and the good old days were recalled as having been much better than they actually were. In the bitterness over a lost war and the ensuing disorder and revolutions, the familiar scapegoat was again hauled to the surface. The trauma of defeat needed justification, and once again guilt was placed at the accustomed doorstep.

THE WEIMAR YEARS

Between 1919 and 1933 Germany tried democracy. The fundamental laws had been drafted in the city of Weimar, and that city gave its name to the following 14 years of German history. The Weimar Constitution established a democratic republic that was modeled in part after the English and U.S. systems. Most German Jews, who numbered about 1 percent of total population of 60 million, supported the liberal, pro-republican parties. The Republic granted total equality to all citizens, regardless of religious affiliations. For Jews it seemed the attainment of all their hopes. Their children graduated in increasing numbers from universities, entered the professions, worked in financial institutions, and became active in politics. Their contributions to the arts and the entertainment industry made Jews more visible to the general public. Many went into their own business; 46 percent were self-employed. Intermarriage with Christians reached an extraordinary 40–50 percent.

But, as was noted in Chapter 3, the Weimar years were turbulent. The German people did not easily adapt to the uncertainties of democratic politics. The Treaty of Versailles, always referred to as the *Diktat,* continued to fester in the national consciousness. Many were incensed by the unseemly abuse of freedom that frequently resulted in violence. Fanatics on the right and the left of the political spectrum short-circuited the election process by assassinating government officials. Among the casualties was Walter Rathenau, the Jewish minister of Foreign Affairs. He was killed by men who thought his death would somehow avenge the German defeat. The comment made by Rathenau's mother reveals the extent of the delusion that gripped Jewish society: Referring to her son's murderers, she said that if only they had known him, what a fine man he was, how totally devoted to the Fatherland, they would not have killed him.

Attempts by extremists to overthrow the government shook the Republic but did not topple it. It survived for 14 years, led by coalitions of socialists and centrists, who tried to cope with mounting internal and external pressures. The Nazis on the political right and the communists on the left were as one in their hope to overthrow the young Republic.

The Weimar years were also a period of startling contrasts. Never before had Germans enjoyed such freedom of expression nor had they been subjected to such political and financial instability. It was an age of great artistic achievements in architecture (the *Bauhaus* School), in filmmaking (Marlene Dietrich's *Blue Angel*), in modern art (Dadaism), and in literature (Erich Maria Remarque's *All Quiet on the Western Front*). The seamy side of the liberated spirit was seen in the cities. License translated into licentiousness. Excesses of every sort from pornography to gross exhibition of opulence made headlines that disgusted the struggling majority of Germans. Advocates of tradition collided with these new currents and blamed the amorality of the decade on the overindulgence of artistic and personal liberties. Some Jewish artists and playwrights were in the forefront of modern expression. Not unexpectedly, some Germans chose to blame them for all the evils that had befallen the nation.

Although the Jews had complete legal equality, most of the established bureaucracy of the defunct German Empire of William II had been left in place. They were the members of the old guard who viewed the Republic with something between distaste and hostility. Their continued authority guaranteed that anti-Semitism remained in public institutions. Nor did it abate in the private sector. German Jews were represented in disproportionate numbers in areas most visible to public view, such as the entertainment industry, the press, and the legal profession and as owners of large department stores. Their achievements energized the old antipathies. Hitler was not the only politician to realize the vote-getting power of anti-Semitism; he was, however, by far the most successful.

JEWISH RESPONSES TO THE NAZI DANGER

Why didn't the German Jews see Hitler's handwriting on the wall? Why did they not flee while there was still time? These questions are often asked, but they are based on the wisdom of hindsight. For those living in the early 1930s, the choices were not so clear.

Most German Jews loved their homeland and felt emotionally and culturally tied to it. Their attachment blurred their vision. Even though the increase of Nazi delegates in the Reichstag was worrisome, emigration was viewed as unnecessary, even unpatriotic. In the years preceding 1933, many political observers believed that Nazi anti-Semitic venom was merely a vote-getting tactic. If Hitler ever came to power, so ran the argument, such rhetoric would cease and certainly would never be enacted into law. It was unthinkable that any German government would revert to such medieval absurdity. Although debates concerning the wisdom of emigrating echoed in every Jewish home, the general consensus was to sit tight, wait, and not to panic. The few who had pursued political careers and some of the highly visible stars in the entertainment business left the country. For the majority, patience was the watchword. Not even in their nightmares could they imagine the Shoah. Yes, they suffered indignities at the hands of those hooligan Brownshirts; yes, there was destruction of property and even several murders. But these were illegal acts, and the courts were bound to reestablish the rule of law. After all, this was Germany, a nation proud of its civilization.

Let us suppose that a family decided to leave Germany in 1934. Where could they go? To places with unpronounceable names that one could hardly find on a map? What would happen to parents and grandparents who would not or could not go? Or the sickly ones whom no country wanted? What about the businesses built up over many years? How can one just walk away? For the rich and famous, the doors opened wide; for families of middle-class means or the Jewish poor, the choices were few or none. The Western world had not yet recovered from the Great Depression; every nation was struggling to keep the number of its unemployed from increasing. It was not a time to take in strangers.

"Be strong, be patient, it will pass"—such was the reassuring advice offered by Jewish newspapers. The leaders of the CV urged the Jews to react with dignity and self-respect, with helpfulness toward each other, and with perseverance. Since these were the words the Jewish community wanted to hear, they were heeded. There were, however, some warning voices. Realists who carefully studied the Nazi leadership, the mood of the people, and the indifference of other nations to the rise of Nazi power tried to sound the alarm: Leave, run for your lives. But where could they go? The U.S. State Department urged its German consuls to issue visas sparingly. "Delay, delay, delay" was the admonition of the Immigration desk of the U.S. State Department to the American consul in Berlin. Other nations would only admit refugees who could support themselves without working, without depriving native citizens of their employment. Only Hitler's increasing terror tactics and the *Kristallnacht* pogrom awakened the majority of German Jews to their peril. Then, when every corner of the globe was considered a possible refuge, they waited patiently outside the gates of embassies, hoping for a visa to anywhere. More often than not, their petitions were denied. Approximately half of the German Jews waited too long or could find no nation to accept them in time to save their lives.

ORGANIZING FOR SURVIVAL

Before the implementation of the Final Solution, German Jews organized themselves for mutual aid. As their persecution accelerated, so did their need to help one another. Step by step the government robbed them of the necessities of existence. First, Jews were ousted from political life, then they were cut off from their economic bases and excluded from cultural and educational participation. With each loss, they created their own organizations to try and fill the void. They closed ranks, supported one another, and tried to provide for their spiritual and economic needs. Many rediscovered their religious heritage; the synagogues had never been so well attended. Despite great difficulties, their organizations provided entertainment by

Jewish artists, which included some first-class musical and theatrical performances. Unemployed professors gave lecture series and adult education classes offered occupational retraining that could be helpful for future emigrants. When Jewish children were expelled from public education, Jewish schools tried to close the gap. Aid for the poor, free soup kitchens, and clothing were provided until the death trains took the final remnants to the East.

As long as the Nazis deemed it to their advantage, such self-help was encouraged by the authorities. They welcomed the establishment of technical and agricultural training programs for young people hoping to settle in Palestine. The government permitted Jewish agencies to furnish counselors to aid prospective emigrants to wade through the morass of paperwork. The remarkable cooperation of Jewish parents and English families enabled thousands of Jewish children to survive through the operation of the *Kindertransports.* Starting in December 1938, the British consented to accept unaccompanied Jewish children from Germany, Austria, and Czechoslovakia. Most were welcomed into the homes of English volunteer families; some lived in hostels or training farms run by Youth Aliya, a Zionist organization. Youngsters barely out of diapers up to their early teens were handed over by their parents to the nurses and social workers who accompanied them on their journey. By 1939, when the onset of the war ended the rescue mission, 10,000 Jewish children had been surrendered to strangers; 10,000 traumatic good-byes had been said by mothers and fathers who waved their handkerchiefs long after the trains had rolled from sight. Only a small percentage of the children estimated at 10 percent saw their parents again.

Jewish self-help associations tried to find work for the growing number of unemployed, but only Jewish businesses were permitted to hire Jews, and these were closed down by government decree. The resulting idleness of so many young people was a problem without a solution. Organized sports competitions tried to create an atmosphere of normalcy. Language instruction, particularly English, was offered to the hopeful emigrants. Two Jewish newspapers kept their subscribers informed of the latest dictates of the government and urged the people to stay calm and to remain optimistic.

The local religious congregations, the *Gemeinden,* bore the burden for some of these activities, but on the national scale, the RV, the *Reichsvertretung der Deutschen Juden (National Agency for German Jews),* played the major role. Until he was arrested and sent to Theresienstadt concentration camp, the renowned liberal rabbi Leo Baeck led the struggle to preserve a semblance of German–Jewish life. By the winter of 1938, German Jews were impoverished and received financial help from overseas, particularly from Jewish organizations in the United States. Shortly after the Japanese attacked Pearl Harbor, Germany declared war on the United States, and it was no longer possible to send direct aid. At that point, the isolation of European Jewry was nearly complete.

The Nazis had welcomed the activities of the RV because it was convenient to use the organization as a conduit for their orders. The leaders were called to the offices of the Nazi officials to receive and promulgate their latest decrees. Later, as we shall see in Chapter 8, this procedure evolved into the *Judenraete,* the Jewish Ghetto Councils. A cloud hangs over these organizations, but there can be no question that for as long as it was possible, Jewish self-help associations extended material and moral assistance to their fellow victims.

THE HOLOCAUST: MASTER PLAN OR EXPEDIENCY?

The Nazi commitment to make Germany *Judenrein* (cleansed of Jews) is not questioned by students of the Holocaust. Events occurring even before Hitler launched World War II left no doubt that he wanted to purge Germany of its Jews. His later conquests extended this passion to a wider arena. A persistent question, as yet unresolved, concerns the chronology of the Shoah. Historians have debated whether genocide was always Hitler's plan or would emigration have satisfied his objectives? Some authorities, known as the Intentionalists, are convinced that the actual physical destruction of the Jews was already outlined in *Mein Kampf.* Opposing views are held by the Functionalists. Their research led them to conclude that the annihilation strategy evolved rather than followed a preset blueprint. The conquest of Poland and war against the Soviet Union provided the opportunities for the *Endloesung,* the Final Solution. In the confusion of battle, great crimes could be committed and covered up. Himmler, obedient to implied, verbal, or possibly written instructions from Hitler, ordered the mass murders because an expedient moment had presented itself.

The controversy between the Intentionalists and Functionalists remains. We do know that the conquest of Poland initiated new Nazi policies. Previously, the killing of Jews was incidental to the tactic of making their lives so wretched that they would flee to anywhere. The laws enacted between 1933 and 1939 became progressively more brutal and were always accompanied by obscene propaganda campaigns. But there were no death camps; not until the fall of Poland were the murder factories built. The sequence of events that began with "You may not work among us" led to "You may not live among us" and escalated to "You may not live at all." In the lands conquered by Germany after 1939, the speed with which the persecution was carried out increased dramatically. Confiscation of property, expulsion from homes, and physical annihilation could, and often did, occur on a single day.

It is the view of this writer that during the early years of his regime, Hitler merely wanted a Germany without Jews. Murder was not part of his first blueprint. (This point will be further explored later in this chapter.) The systematic annihilation of Jews began after the defeat of Poland. It may well have resulted from an amalgamation of three factors. First, the acquisition of Poland brought 3.5 million Jews under German authority; such a huge number could not possibly be driven out of the country. Second, the war offered the opportunity to commit great crimes under the cover of necessity. Third, and perhaps most importantly, was the progression of Hitler's neurotic hatred of the Jews into an all-encompassing obsession.

The following personal experience may serve as a support for the Functionalist view:

> In the Spring of 1939, my parents, brother and I had been promised visas to emigrate to the United States. A visa is merely a stamp placed into a passport. For his own sadistic reasons, the mayor of Winzig, our little Silesian hometown, refused to issue the necessary passport. When, in December of that year, the American consul was made aware of this fact, he telegraphed the mayor: "Your denial of passports directly opposes your own government's policy to

promote emigration. If this family is not given their passports immediately, I will notify your superiors of the fact that you are obstructing your own government's policy." The passports were ready the next day.

WHO IS A JEW?

Nazi genetic experts had great difficulty in deciding on a legal definition of who was to be considered a Jew. Serious people engaged in lengthy and weighty debates on the subject. Precisely to whom did the increasing number of anti-Jewish laws apply? Particularly perplexing was the status of the children of mixed marriages. Dr. Bernard Loesener of the Department of the Interior was recognized to be an expert on Jewish affairs, and he was instructed to clarify the issue. The Law for the Restoration of the Professional Civil Service, enacted in April of 1933, set forth the official definition: A person is a non-Aryan if his parents or grandparents were Jewish. This applied to children having one Jewish parent or one Jewish grandparent or if one parent or grandparent practiced the Jewish religion. In other words, "Jew" and "non-Aryan" were interchangeable because both religion and ethnicity determined racial status. Christians were regarded as Jews/non-Aryans if they had one or more Jewish ancestors. But this definition required further refinement. In 1935, as part of the Nuremberg Laws, the question was resolved. A new category was created, the *Mischling* (one of mixed race). The definition now maintained that

1. a full Jew had three or four Jewish grandparents;
2. a *Mischling* was a half-Jew who had two Jewish grandparents, practiced Judaism, and/or was the child of a three-fourths Jew;
3. a *Mischling* of the first degree had two Jewish grandparents, but did not practice Judaism and was not married to a Jew; and
4. a *Mischling* of the second degree had one Jewish grandparent.

It seems inconceivable to us here and now that officials and purported genetic experts spent months working out this absurdity. But there was a deadly aspect to the application of these classifications. Although *Mischlinge* were designated non-Aryans and prohibited from many activities, most German *Mischlinge* survived the Holocaust. Wilhelm Stuckart, State Secretary of the Interior, made this bizarre observation to explain his opposition to the deportation of *Mischlinge:*

> I have always considered it dangerous biologically to introduce German blood into the enemy camp. The intelligence and excellent education of the half-Jews, linked to their ancestral Germanic heritage, make them natural leaders outside Germany and therefore very dangerous. I prefer to see the *Mischlinge* die a natural death inside Germany.

It must be noted that although all Jews were non-Aryans, not all non-Aryans were Jews. For example, children of Polish–Jewish parents were treated as fully

Jewish; Poles did not belong to the Aryan race, their blood was not worthy of salvage, and they were doomed.

EARLY LEGAL RESTRICTIONS

During the period between Hitler's rise to power and the events known as *Kristallnacht*—the Night of the Broken Glass, November 9–10, 1938, anti-Jewish laws were issued in intermittent spurts. During each lull, many German Jews and their sympathizers—yes, there were some—hoped that the worst was over. That optimism lasted until the next series of decrees was promulgated. The years 1933, 1935, and 1938 were particularly prolific. Jews were legally barred from enjoying the rights of German citizenship; they were deprived of their freedom to work; and they lost the privilege of owning real estate.

In order to have an overview of the changing legal status of German Jews during the prewar years, we need to step back to 1933. April 1, of that year, was designated a day of boycott of all Jewish businesses. An action committee of the Nationalist Socialist German Workers' Party (NSDAP) coordinated the efforts "to teach the Jews a lesson." On that date and for several days thereafter, Jewish stores, institutions, industrial concerns, and offices found *Sturmabteilung* (SA) troopers stationed at the entrances. Customers or clients who tried to enter were stopped, harangued, and sometimes beaten. The message was clear: Don't deal with Jews. This measure was also useful in testing the reaction of Christian Germans and that of foreign nations. The conduct of most Germans on this occasion foreshadowed their practices throughout the regime: compliance. When prevented from entering their intended destinations, they were first confused, momentarily annoyed, and then they retreated: No sense getting into trouble with the Brownshirts. Certainly, some Christians were privately angered, perhaps even ashamed, but the nation remained quiet, and Hitler had his answer.

The foreign press, however, in editorials and news stories, demonstrated its repugnance. The Nazi leaders rather adroitly turned this criticism to their advantage. Was this negative press from abroad not proof of the existence of a Jewish international conspiracy against the Gentile world? Did this not corroborate that *The Protocols of the Elders of Zion* was based on truth? Furthermore, the leaders of German Jewry were instructed to urge their counterparts in Europe and America to stop any adverse portrayal of Germany. Unless these "misrepresentations" ceased, German Jewish interests would suffer further. Although these threats were not usually taken at face value outside of the Reich, they initiated a dilemma: Will foreign protests against the Nazi tactics harm or help the German Jews?

In 1933, Jews were ousted from the civil service and the legal professions. The Orthodox community suffered a distressing blow when kosher butchering was outlawed. The ratio of Jews permitted to attend public schools and universities was reduced. Thousands lost their livelihoods when banned from working or participating in the cultural and intellectual life of the nation, such as the press, the radio, the arts, and the sciences. Frightening scenes of terror and humiliation became commonplace, when, for example, elderly men were forced to scrub sidewalks or the beards of religious elders were cut amid the jeering laughter of the SA. Though the government frowned upon such freelance operations because they might undermine Party discipline, it was useless for Jews to seek redress through the judicial system. The courts were not interested in such cases. Nevertheless, it became clear to the government that a systematic approach to the Jewish question was needed.

THE NUREMBERG LAWS

Between September and November of 1935 a series of decrees, known as the Nuremberg Laws, stripped German Jewry of their citizenship and returned their legal position to pre-emancipation status. The enactment of the Reich Citizenship Law and decrees that followed stipulated that Jews were subjects, indeed, unwelcome subjects. Marriage and sexual relations between Jews and Gentiles were forbidden. For the Jewish partner, a breach of the law was punishable by death. Employment of Aryan female servants under the age of 45 in Jewish homes was prohibited. Jews were barred from service in the armed forces.

The realization that they no longer had any legal recourse dismayed the German–Jewish population. Many of those who had connections overseas were preparing to leave. At this point it was still possible to take some assets out of the country. The hope of the assimilationists that respect for justice would protect them was dashed. Instead, the law had been turned into an instrument of persecution. As unease turned into fear, it was time to try and send one's children out of harm's way and begin to look into the possibility of escape.

During the 1930s, Germans had no uniform policy concerning the emigration of its unwanted subjects. Officially, their policy encouraged their exodus. A flight tax of 25 percent of the emigrant's assets was imposed, and until the middle of the decade it was possible to transfer some money out of the country. Two special banks were established that shifted Jewish assets to Palestinian banks in a rather elaborate scheme designed to ease the German need for foreign currency. Local authorities throughout the Reich were advised to permit, even to assist, in the flight of the Jews.

But no golden door, nor any door, opened for them. The lines in front of foreign legations grew longer, but the number of visas issued remained scarce. In 1933 when the Nazis took power, many Jews whose public image made them vulnerable, international businessmen with foreign connections, far-sighted men and women who realized that Hitler was dangerous, and some young Zionists left the homeland. Although their number, 37,000, was larger than that of any following year, they represented a mere 6 percent of the total. Why was the number so small? After all, Germany bordered on 10 different countries. Indeed, some escaped, but they faced a new difficulty—they were not permitted to work in their host countries. Indeed, only the philanthropy of American Jews sustained many of these émigrés. In any case, their hope to have found temporary havens was short-lived. When the Nazis marched into Poland, France, Belgium, Holland, and the Balkan nations, they demanded the surrender of the Jewish residents, and the refugees were usually among the first to be handed over to the German conquerors.

Expanding the Nuremberg Laws

The Nuremberg decrees were appended many times. Eventually, over 400 provisions dealt especially with the "Jewish problem." Jews were forbidden from entering parks, zoos, hotels, theaters, sports events, or any public building. They could not sit on public benches, use public transport, own telephones, or use public phones. The early restriction of the number of Jewish children permitted to attend public schools was increased several times until a total ban was enforced. Jews could not own radios, furs, or woolen items. When food and clothing were rationed, Jews received ever-decreasing amounts of life's necessities: no milk, no eggs, no meat. Restrictions on economic activities mounted until Christians and Jews could not work side by side in any establishment.

German courts ruled that employers who had long-term contracts with Jewish workers could abrogate the agreements. The action was justified by the claim that Jews were legally dead; ergo such agreements were null and void. The Nazification of the courts guaranteed that appeals would be decided in favor of the government. For example, when the drivers' licenses of Jews were canceled, challenges brought before the courts were denied. Clearly, the decrees issued became increasingly Kafkaesque. Minor infractions by Jews were punished with long terms of incarceration in Dachau, Buchenwald, or Sachsenhausen concentration camps. Prisoners who could prove that they were about to leave Germany were freed to pursue their emigration. Eventually, the Nuremberg laws were further amended to include an array of dehumanizing and degrading prohibitions: A yellow star had to be worn when appearing outside the home; curfews kept Jews off the streets when others shopped; and food rations grew constantly smaller. How can one comprehend the ban against seeing-eye dogs and white canes used by the blind and badges identifying the deaf? The law forbidding Jews to own pets, even birds, created scenes of tearful leave-taking as beloved companions were left at designated depots.

Juden Raus (Jews Get Out)

Until the attack on Poland in September 1939, the Nazi government used every means at its disposal to force the Jews to leave. Major cities actually provided government offices to speed the exodus along. Jews, deprived of their professional and economic status, were socially ostracized; and newspapers such as Julius Streicher's pornographic *Stuermer* were unrelenting in their attacks. There were arrests without charges and beatings in the streets. Each time there was a letup, the Jews breathed easier. The year 1936 was often misinterpreted; because the Olympic Games were played in Berlin and the government wanted to make a good impression on the hundreds of thousands of visitors. Signs in stores warning that Jews would not be served disappeared temporarily; park benches no longer advertised that these seats were for Aryans only; even Goebbels and the press restrained their abusive rhetoric. But the lull merely forecast a more violent storm to come.

The persecution of German Jews shifted into high gear during 1938. A *Kennkarte* was issued and had to be carried at all times. This was an identification card, which included physical description, fingerprints, and photo. Males of all ages were required to add "Israel" as their middle name and females were ordered to affix "Sara" to their given names. The government argued that these internal passports helped the state control its enemies. Goering ("guns, not butter") had taken charge of preparing the national economy for the coming war. His control of the Four Year Plan gave him enormous power. As long as he could claim to be acting in the interest of military preparedness, he could counteract the decrees issued by every other agency of the Reich. He demanded that all present and future traitors must be neutralized before the nation could fight a foreign war. That category included all Jews.

With increasing speed, the few remaining economic opportunities were eliminated. Jewish doctors were officially designated as medical orderlies and were forbidden to treat Aryan patients. Thousands of Jews who were not born in Germany were suddenly expelled. Despite the increased pressure, the Nazis complained, the exodus of the Jews was not proceeding fast enough. The problem, of course, was not their reluctance to go but that they could not find nations willing to grant them asylum. Only between 150,000 to 170,000 German Jews, that is, one-third of the pre-Nazi number, had left by 1938. Goering decided to speed up the process by removing them completely from the national economic life.

The method was not new but was given a new name. Instead of confiscation, it was called Aryanization and entailed the forced sale of Jewish businesses and property to Aryans. Of course, members of the Nazi organizations were the favorite recipients of this boon. The price for their assets was determined by a Nazi functionary at a fraction of the actual value. But even that amount was not handed over to the sellers. The money was deposited into a special bank account and, depending on the size of the Jewish family, the head of the household was allowed to withdraw a specified sum every month. In case of emigration, the remaining money was confiscated by the government. The rationale for this theft was based on the pretext that, ipso facto, all Jewish wealth had been acquired through fraud, which the state was entitled to reclaim.

It was no coincidence that in 1938 the government had required that German and Austrian Jews submit a form that itemized their possessions (the *Anschluss,* or union with Austria, had taken place in March 1938). The questionnaire called for considerable detail describing all items valued at 5,000 marks or more. (In comparison to the dollar, the mark was circa $0.25). Grandmother's silver candlesticks, paintings, radios, furs, furniture, cut glass, heirlooms, and jewelry had to be listed. When the time came, and that was very soon, to confiscate these personal effects, the authorities knew exactly who had what; but some official justification was needed to complete the expropriation. And that was provided by a Polish teenager living in Paris who had no idea that his actions would serve as the excuse for a pogrom.

KRISTALLNACHT

If any doubt remained concerning the intentions of the Nazis to make Germany *Judenrein* (cleansed of Jews), it was removed by the events generally called *Kristallnacht,* the Night of the Broken Glass. Neither Christians nor Jews could ever again claim that they did not realize the seriousness of the Jewish plight. The terror of November 9–10, and beyond was played out in full view of the German people. The scenes of beatings, screaming women, and arrests of men took place on the

VOICES

Papa's Slippers and Crystal Night

There really was a loud knock on the door, just like in the movies. It was November 8, 1938, about nine o'clock in the evening, when two men entered. "Gestapo" said one and "Come. Now." It was a cold night and your mother ran for my coat and a pair of shoes. I was wearing an old pair of slippers. I asked the Nazi if I could put on my shoes. He answered by putting his hand on his gun. And I left in those worn-out slippers. . . .

I was taken to the county jail, already filled with Jewish men from the vicinity. The next day a truck took us to Breslau, Silesia's largest city. But this was not the Breslau I knew; it looked like a war zone: synagogues and Jewish schools burning, windows broken, merchandise strewn about, and glass, glass, glass everywhere.

As ordered, we jumped from the truck and ran between two lines of SS men with clubs and ran into a huge yard. This was the parade ground behind police headquarters with high walls, guard towers, and searchlights. Thousands of men were already there, standing shoulder to shoulder. Soon my feet got numb. Frostbite? I stomped up and down—no improvement; my slippers were too thin. I went to the wall, hoping for warmth. Groping in the dark, I felt a door behind me. It opened. Quickly I stepped inside. I was in a passage to the building. I sat down and rubbed my feet back to life. What now? I thought I had a plan.

I passed offices, Nazis were questioning Jews. I took a deep breath, walked into one, and waited by the desk of the official. He did not look up but shouted, "Dirty Jew, what do you want?" I said, "Sir, my cows need milking and my other animals will die without feed. The fatherland needs food. May I go home to look after them?" He still didn't look up; he just yelled, " Get out."

I left through a different door and found myself in the main corridor, I could see exit signs but had no idea what to do next. An SS man ran up behind me, dragging a small old man. He asked, "You dismissed?" Unable to speak, I nodded. He threw the little man into my arms. I held him up, and as we walked on he whispered, "Where is your leave warrant?" "I don't have one." Silence. Then, "You have children?" "Four." "I don't have any; take my permit." "Can't do that." We were nearly at the glass doors leading to the street. He asked, "Try using mine for both of us?" "Yes!" As he held up his paper, one SA guard said to the other, "Lucky dogs." I dragged him down the steps to the street.

Instinctively we headed for a dark alley. Strange, my companion no longer clung to me; indeed, he was running ahead of me. I stared, "Who are you?" "Only the best actor on the Jewish stage of Breslau! And tonight I played my best role." We laughed, quickly embraced, and then we parted, each to make his own way home.

This is a story told to the author by her father.

streets and in public places throughout the Reich. Spectacular fires and widespread destruction of property were inescapable confirmation that a pogrom, an outbreak of violence against Jews, was in progress.

The first scene of the drama was played out between the German and Polish borders. In October 1938, the Gestapo executed an order to expel all Jews born in Poland. Even those who had become German citizens were included. Some 7,000 men, women, and children were declared to be stateless. They were forcibly assembled and placed into sealed railroad cars. In an eerie portent of future transports to the east, they were shipped into the no-man's land between the German and Polish frontiers. The Poles, however, refused to accept them and attempted to drive them back into Germany. The misery of these exiles, living in makeshift shelters between the borders, was obvious. Eventually, under pressure and with financial support from worldwide Jewish organizations, the deportees were reluctantly admitted into Poland, and a few fortunate individuals were admitted to Sweden.

A young man, Herschel Grynzpan, knew only that the Nazis had deported his family from Hanover. He was living in Paris, hoping to emigrate to Palestine. Unable to get in touch with his parents and sister, he became distraught and resolved to exact revenge from the Germans. He managed to purchase a revolver and went to the German embassy. There he was admitted to the office of a minor functionary, a third secretary named Ernst vom Rath. Shouting that he was avenging his people, he shot the German, who died the following day, November 9.

The shooting took place during the week-long commemoration of the *Bierhall Putsch.* The Nazi leaders had gathered in Munich to celebrate the fifteenth anniversary of that fiasco when they were informed of the vom Rath murder. Goebbels, ever mindful of the sensational propaganda value of a Jew killing a German, received Hitler's approval to turn the event into a pretext for a major pogrom. Goering and Himmler, eager to participate in the operation, rushed to the telephones and ordered the *Gauleiters,* the chiefs of the SA, SS, and Gestapo to demolish all Jewish businesses and communal institutions. Furthermore, they were to arrest all Jewish men between the ages of 16 and 60 and ship them to the nearest concentration camps.

The pogrom has been called *Kristallnacht* because thousands of windows were smashed, and the broken shards glittered in the streets like crystal. Almost all of Germany's and Austria's 267 synagogues were desecrated or destroyed; those that did not burn were dynamited. Places of business owned by Jews were razed by arson, axe, club, and crowbar.

In areas where many Jewish-owned shops were clustered together, the streets resembled a combat area. The destruction was carried out by the light of burning buildings; the air was acrid from the smell and smoke of scorched cloth and wood; and the sirens and bells of police cars and fire equipment added to the hellish image. Sidewalks were impassable with goods strewn everywhere: Here, wine from the liquor store ran like a red river on which floated puffs of feathers from the bedding store. There, eyeglasses and radios, candy and typewriters, and merchandise of every sort, all looted or trampled underfoot. Regular police and firemen were under orders not to interfere except to protect the property of Aryans.

Each town and city had variations of the scenario as local commanders of the SA, the Gestapo, and the Nazi Party interpreted the orders to "teach the Jews a lesson" with their own ideas. In some cities, private homes were ransacked, furnishings thrown from windows, and Jews beaten. Where the SA was encouraged to give vent to frenzy, murders were committed—91 Jewish men were killed and an uncounted number injured. In many areas, words such as JEWS DIE were smeared on steps and doors of homes. Some Jewish schools were torched, others left alone. Placards were hung from destroyed shops, which read: THIS IS THE PEOPLE'S REVENGE FOR

THE MURDER OF VOM RATH. DEATH TO INTERNATIONAL JEWRY. The Nazis tried hard to convince the German public that this pogrom was a spontaneous riot, caused by the wrath of the people. Rarely was spontaneity so well planned and systematically organized. In 48 hours a total of 7,500 businesses were demolished. The public at large did its best not to see, hear, or know anything and rarely participated in the attacks. Looting was forbidden, and here again, local circumstances determined the observance or disregard of that order.

The *Judenaktion,* that is, anti-Jewish riot of *Kristallnacht,* was not restricted to the destruction of commercial establishments. For two days and nights the Gestapo, the internal security police known as the SD *(Sicherheitsdienst),* and regular police combed the country in search of Jewish men. With prepared lists of names and addresses, they swarmed through the villages, towns, and cities. Streets, bus stations, and railroad terminals were turned into tragic theater as men were pulled from their screaming families. Many of the arrests were accompanied by beatings, although very few of the men resisted. For the most part, they were completely bewildered. They asked, "What have I done? Where are you taking me?" but were answered with curses. Suicides reached a new peak.

There were no indictments, no trials. The crime committed by Herschel Grynzpan required retribution from all the German Jews. Thirty thousand men were shipped to concentration camps. Officially, they were removed to prevent the German people from venting their "justified revenge" upon them. The camps Goering had set up were filled to capacity; depending on the region, the men were sent to Dachau, Buchenwald, or Sachsenhausen. There the prisoners were marched in circles; they stood endlessly at attention in order to be counted, did calisthenics, and tormented themselves with fearful pictures of the fate of their families. Eight hundred of them did not survive the hardships of the beatings and the stress of their "protective custody." In contrast to later incarcerations, these prisoners were released. First to go home were men who could prove that their emigration was imminent. Later, the others were permitted to leave if they pledged to leave Germany as soon as possible.

A Case in Point: Bremen

On the fiftieth anniversary of *Kristallnacht,* the city of Bremen commissioned an investigation into the events of the pogrom. The result of this research was intended to be used as teaching material in their schools. The following are some excerpts, translated by the author, from that document:

> In Bremen . . . resided about 900 Jews, whose homes were scattered all over town. When, during the night of November 9 to the 10 the order to "let loose" arrived at SA headquarters, the first reaction was to reach for the so-called Jews list. In Bremen this had been prepared as early as 1935. The list was copied and distributed that same night to the secondary SA facilities located in various districts.
>
> . . . SA troopers were summoned. They roamed the city without giving a thought to the nature of their orders and dutifully performed their mission. The results were recorded in the police archives. For example, in seventeen Jewish

> businesses and residences, windows were demolished, and, in part, furniture and shop fittings were destroyed.
>
> . . . "With total success we completed the incineration of the Synagogue on Garten Street and we also destroyed the living quarters of the Rabbi. We were also successful in laying waste the chapel in the cemetery and in damaging the grave stones. The visitation to the old age home at . . . was carried out by particularly diligent SA men. Here windows were broken, doors splintered, mirrors shattered, and the old people were stomped on and driven from the premises."

Two women and three men were murdered that night in Bremen. When this news reached the SA commander, the killers were told that they had gone too far. However, the men were exonerated when they claimed that they were following orders. Eventually, after the war, these crimes were investigated and the surviving murderers were brought to justice and sentenced to long prison terms.

THE AFTERMATH

No matter how blatantly the Goebbels press corps tried to assure the German public that the pogrom was an impulsive reaction by an enraged nation, the public response was negative. Too many people had seen and recognized the men with the torches and axes and knew they had come from the ranks of organized Nazis. A more serious complaint concerned the terrible waste of perfectly usable merchandise. What purpose was served by the destruction of so much property? The cost of replacing the windows alone drew millions of foreign exchange marks from Germany and kept the Belgian glass factories running at full speed for many months. Were there not many Germans who could have made good use of the furniture, the clothing, and the very buildings that had been rendered useless?

Within the Party hierarchy, the nights of violence and vandalism against the Jews reverberated at the highest level. Goebbels had clearly tried to take charge of the Jewish policy and that was not to be tolerated. Goering and Hitler, still in Munich, inspected the damage in that city, and the *Reichsmarschall* convinced the Fuehrer that such outbursts must not be repeated. As a result, the conduct of Jewish affairs was assigned to Goering and Himmler, and Goebbels was not permitted to meddle again. On November 12, Goering convened a meeting to review the recent events and discuss the future management of the Jewish problem. The principal functionaries in attendance were Himmler's emissary, Reinhard Heydrich, Economics Minister Funk, Justice Minister Franz Guertner, a representative from the foreign ministry, and a member of the insurance industry. Goebbels was also invited but received no thanks for his role. In fact, when Goering was finished denouncing the pointless destruction, the propaganda minister made no rebuttal.

The representative from the insurance companies' association estimated the losses at 25 million marks (Three million marks for broken glass). Goering directed that the insurance companies must pay the claims, but since the Reich had suffered the real damage, the money was to go into the national treasury, not to the insured claimants. The immense cleanup of the streets was also the responsibility of the Jews. Goering then ordered the Minister of Economics, Walther Funk, the successor of Hjalmar Schacht, to create legislation that would once and for all drive Jews from all economic participation in Germany. The Aryanization of businesses that had been more or less voluntary was now made compulsory. In addition, as retribution for the crime committed by Grynzpan, the German Jews were fined the enormous sum of one billion marks. At the very time when the greatest demands for aid were made upon the Jewish community, when food, clothing, and housing were needed desperately, its funds were expropriated, and German Jews became paupers.

During the debate, Heydrich (see Chapter 8) was complimented on the success of his methods in driving the Jews from Austria. He replied that despite all his efforts, the exodus of the Jews was still entirely too slow. At the present rate, it would take years to get rid of them all. At the end of the meeting, Goering remarked: "I would not like to be a Jew in Germany."

The foreign press of the Western world reported the events in their respective newspapers. In headlines and editorials, Germany was condemned. Ambassadors from many nations delivered protests to the German Foreign Ministry. The law faculties of 97 foreign universities remonstrated against such racial–political terrorism. Pope Pius XI issued a rather vague statement of sympathy for the victims. Franklin D. Roosevelt recalled the American ambassador and declared that he found the actions of *Kristallnacht* to be utterly abhorrent. An attempt, however, to boycott German goods coming into the United States was not effective. Once again, and not for the last time, the Nazis were reassured that they could do as they pleased as no doors opened to admit the thousands hoping to emigrate.

Yet somehow, after the November catastrophe, 100,000 German Jews managed to escape. They fled to Shanghai, South America, Africa, Asia, and places they could hardly find on a map. Nazi officials watched as they packed their bags; their passports were stamped with a red J (*Jude,* Jew). Each emigrant could take no more than 10 marks to his destination. All other assets were confiscated. But by then they knew that although penniless, they were the lucky ones; all other considerations had lost their significance. Even before the introduction of slave labor and death camps, the Nazi government had given its answer to the question "Can a Jew be a German?"

CHAPTER 7

Hitler's War

When historians discuss the causes of wars, they often use the term "multiple causation"; only rarely is war the result of a single determining factor. But it is accurate to call World War II Hitler's war. He planned it, directed it, and worst of all, he wanted it. The theory that both world wars were really one single event, interrupted by a 20-year truce, underestimates the essential role of the Fuehrer. It was his power, his leadership, and his concept of Germany's destiny that plunged the world into its most devastating conflict. Two obsessions dominated Hitler's mental world: hatred for the Jews and a passion to dominate Europe. These two compulsions were joined into a war of aggression. German conquests provided the SS with the opportunity to annihilate Jews from the Pyrenees to the Russian steppes and from the shores of the North and Baltic Seas to the Mediterranean. The cost of Hitler's war is estimated to range between 35 and 55 million military and civilian deaths. The Holocaust accounted for six million, a figure equal to two-thirds of the Jews then living in Europe.

Hitler believed that war was a natural imperative. He based his theory on a twisted interpretation of several highly questionable hypotheses. From Social Darwinism, he concluded that life was a struggle for survival for all life-forms, including nations. Consequently, the strongest state had the right to subjugate its weaker neighbors. The battlefield was the ultimate arena where Aryan superiority would be confirmed. Concepts of meekness and mercy, of turning the other cheek, had no place in the contest for power. All conduct, no matter how abhorrent, was justified if it furthered the ultimate goal. How many adult German men and women accepted this chilling version of national purpose, so totally in contradiction to Judeo-Christian values, is impossible to say, but impressionable youths may have been attracted to these theories.

LEBENSRAUM

There was never any secrecy concerning Hitler's foreign policy aims. He outlined his intentions in 1923's *Mein Kampf* and reiterated them in many speeches. By virtue of its superior Aryan race and the fact that Germany needed space to live, the expansion of

German borders was viewed as necessary and inevitable. This need for living space, or *Lebensraum,* was not to be satisfied through colonies on foreign shores but in the broad and underpopulated regions of Eastern Europe. The farmland and natural resources of Soviet Russia were vital to bring about the Nazi hegemony in Europe and German domination. The Fuehrer asserted that the Slavic inhabitants now in possession of these lands were racially inferior and must be forced to give way to the Aryans. They would be removed from their soil, and in the process, many would be killed. The survivors would be useful as labor to toil for their German masters. Heinrich Himmler became Hitler's most ardent pupil, promoter and executioner of this *Drang nach Osten,* the thrust to the East.

To realize these goals would require armed conflict—that was a certainty, in fact, a desirable certainty. Thus, the end and the means of Hitler's foreign policy were determined from the beginning. Once that premise is understood, the vacillations of Nazi foreign affairs become comprehensible. The making and breaking of treaties that at face value appear contradictory make sense when viewed within the policy parameters set by the Fuehrer. Peace with Russia, war with Russia; peace with England and France, then war against them; a treaty with Poland, the invasion of Poland—these actions may seem inconsistent, but the actual agenda never changed.

Hitler, who seldom took any interest in the details of domestic affairs, was personally involved in the pursuit of foreign aims. During his first week in office in 1933, he summoned his top generals and told them of his vision to conquer Eastern Europe. Since the Revolution of 1917, so he asserted, the Soviet Union was ruled by mere *Untermenschen:* Jews/Bolsheviks. (In Hitler's mind, "Jews" and "Bolsheviks" were interchangeable terms.) Russia was ripe for conquest because its former czarist/Germanic leadership had been replaced by a racially inferior dictatorship. Germany's need for eastern territories would lead to war, but until Germany was ready, a period of peace was required. During that interval the military and the civilian populations must prepare and be prepared for the coming conflict. Diplomacy in foreign affairs and strengthening the popular resolve at home would buy the necessary time.

Hitler's domestic policies also become clearer when viewed as components of this strategy. Schemes such as the proposed settlement of racially perfect SS men and their families in the Ukraine, the preparation of the young to bear arms or bear children, the misnamed euthanasia killings of those deemed mentally and/or physically unfit, Dr. Mengele's bogus research in Auschwitz, which sought to increase the number of twins born to German mothers, the brutal and wasteful treatment of defeated peoples and, of course, the Holocaust—all were components of the master plan.

THE EUROPEAN CLIMATE

The United States withdrew from the center of European affairs during the decades between the two great wars. France and England should have accepted the role of international leadership, but neither was willing or able. The Great War had weakened them, and their people were disillusioned because victory had brought them no appreciable rewards. Furthermore, French and English politicians did not present a united front against the rising Fascist states of Italy and Germany. Fear of communism at home and of the Soviet Union dominated their policies, and wishful thinking colored their perception of Hitler and Mussolini.

France feared a revival of German aggression, but lacked the power and resolve to lead Europe in preventing the military resurgence by the Nazis. The Third French Republic had suffered much during World War I, and her politicians wanted a Germany economically strong enough to make reparations payments but too weak to become a threat. Obviously, these were conflicting aims. Traditionally, France had relied on diplomatic support from Russia to prevent German expansionism, but the communist revolution had created a split between democratic France and the communist Soviets. French diplomats tried to compensate by concluding alliances with the newly established eastern nations: Poland, Czechoslovakia, Romania, and Yugoslavia. These, however, were small, struggling countries that could do little to safeguard her eastern border. As a result the French built the most complete and elaborate defensive line along its German frontier—the Maginot Line. From Switzerland to Belgium, the fortifications ran north to south in Eastern France. The line consisted of a series of underground fortresses connected and serviced by railroads, power stations, elevators, food and munitions depots, hospitals, and immense defensive installations. Three hundred thousand men could be assembled below the surface, while above ground cannons sprouted from casemates that pointed toward the German border. The existence of such a modern, extensive as well as expensive, defensive system gave Frenchmen a false sense of security that would prove to be costly beyond all expectations.

The British, on the other hand, hoped to maintain control over their empire despite the increasingly independent stance of their dominions. They had no desire to enhance French ambition to play the European superpower. World War I had turned many Britons into pacifists, and military expenditures were unpopular. Unemployment figures were high, and disillusionment with the lack of spoils from victory was widespread. As long as her naval power was superior, the British lion wanted to sleep without interference from the continent.

Hitler had inherited a number of international obligations from the Weimar Republic. Most significant was the Treaty of Versailles. The 1919 convention, concluded without German participation, was humiliating to the Germans. They lost considerable territory to newly reestablished Poland in the East, and to France in the West, she lost her colonies; the Rhineland was demilitarized; and the German army was reduced to 100,000 volunteers. Of the huge reparations assessment, however, only a small portion was ever collected. Allied statesmen had not been indifferent to the protestations that the treaty provisions were unfair, a *Diktat,* coerced upon a prostrate people and agreed to several adjustments of the original terms. The Locarno Pacts of 1925 removed the French armies from the Rhineland in return for German guarantees to respect the French and Belgian frontiers. In 1926 Germany was admitted into the League of Nations, ending its international pariah status. League membership required Germany to settle disputes peacefully, and in 1928, the Weimar Republic was one of 23 nations to sign the Kellogg–Briand Pact, which outlawed war as an instrument of national policy. The Dawes Act of 1924 and Young Plan of 1929 had provided some relief of the reparations debt and eased the schedule of payments. If Hitler had been satisfied to govern Germany in peaceful coexistence with its neighbors, further revisions of the Versailles provisions would have been feasible, even likely.

NAZI DIPLOMACY

When Hitler became chancellor, the first order of business was to secure his own and his Party's internal power. Within two years all political and most overt individual opposition had been eradicated, and he became the unchallenged master of Germany. Now his foreign ambitions were given maximum attention and the German people were indoctrinated to identify their well-being, their future with goals of the Fuehrer. In order to maintain the illusion that the regime cared about them, their basic needs and expectations had to be met. Hitler frequently reminded his audiences of the promises he had kept: reduction of unemployment, restoration of law and order in the streets, rebuilding of the infrastructure, and respect from other nations.

Until Germany was militarily strong, Hitler was careful to assume a circumspect attitude in foreign affairs. He spoke of his desire for peace with great conviction, while plans to rearm Germany were progressing in secret. He claimed that all he sought was parity with other European nations. Toward this end, he retained conservative ministers in his foreign, defense, and state departments. Not until 1938 was the servile Nazi Joachim von Ribbentrop given the official title of Minister for Foreign Affairs. Hitler went so far as to offer to disarm Germany, if her neighbors did the same. This proposal was grist for Goebbels' mill but had no hope of acceptance. The appearance of peaceful intentions was maintained, and some members of the foreign services of Europe and the United States declared what a fine fellow Herr Hitler was. Fear of the Soviet Union played a considerable role in the illusion that the Nazis were not so bad. Unlike Lenin and Stalin, Hitler was not visibly exporting his political philosophy and frightening the established order; indeed the hope was expressed that this new Germany would be a bulwark against Soviet internationalism.

In Paris, London, and Washington, diplomats turned a blind eye to Hitler's domestic and foreign machinations. Even when he withdrew Germany from the League of Nations and from the Geneva Disarmament Conference, no alarm bells were sounded. After all, so ran the argument of the appeasers, Herr Hitler had to satisfy German public opinion, for such was the nature of politics.

In 1934, the Fuehrer signed a treaty with Poland that guaranteed mutual respect of their current borders and that both countries would maintain peace with one another for 10 years. The pact startled the Western world. The Weimar government, in its search for allies, had sought good relations with Russia. How could Germany befriend Poland, the nation that was created out of deep cuts into western Russia and eastern Germany? The Treaty of Versailles had separated East Prussia from the rest of Germany, and every German believed that the loss of the Polish Corridor was a scandal to be rectified in time.

Poland was wedged between two nations that resented her very existence and hoped to regain their lost provinces. Adding to her insecurity was the lack of geographic barriers along her borders, where flat terrain left the country open to invasion from east and west. Naturally, the Poles accepted the pact offered by the Germans; it appeared to safeguard her western frontier. The question why Hitler sought peace with Poland should have raised some diplomatic eyebrows. Instead, the consensus of the experts welcomed the treaty as an indication of Hitler's intentions to be a good neighbor.

Hitler, of course, had no intention of honoring the Polish agreement. He was buying time in order to advance his military and psychological preparations for the planned attack on the Soviet Union. In fact when German armies overran Poland in 1939, that unhappy country was the first victim of the Nazi obsession for eastern *Lebensraum.*

INERTIA IN FRANCE AND GREAT BRITAIN

During the period between 1933 and the outbreak of the war in 1939, Hitler tested the diplomatic waters again and again. How far could he go in ignoring the Versailles covenant before the former Allies would stop him? His foreign policy decisions required a careful reading of the resolve of France and England. Would they go to war to prevent the resurgence of a powerful Germany? Would the restoration of military conscription, ordered in 1935, cause alarm? Would the union with Austria, the *Anschluss,* specifically forbidden in the Versailles terms, lead to more than verbal complaints? Hitler's judgment was correct—the League of Nations was a toothless tiger. At this point in time, while Germany was still weak, a show of united strength by the League might have changed history. But the former allies wanted peace; indeed,

Adolf Hitler and Prime Minister Neville Chamberlain in Munich, 1938. (AP Wide World Photos.)

they needed peace to recover from their 1918 victory. So, they chose to see Hitler as a patriotic, reasonable man who demanded only justice for his people. France paraded the Maginot Line before the world, assured that its very existence would prevent another invasion from Germany. Great Britain hoped for isolation from the quarrels of continental Europe and maintain her hold over her restless Empire. She expected that a dominant navy would serve her as it had in the past. To insure that prospect, she concluded several agreements that restricted the number and size of German surface vessels to one-third of size of the English navy. German submarines, however, were permitted to constitute 60 percent of their English counterparts, a decision the English would live to regret.

Clearly, the maintenance of peace by common action, so optimistically pledged by the League of Nations, proved to be an empty promise. France and England, the backbone of the League, did not have the necessary will to prevent renewed German aggression. International cooperation collapsed in the face of domestic problems. The United States, never a member of the League, exerted only limited influence. Congress would have opposed more direct participation in European affairs even if the president had wished it. Hitler was free to advance his goals.

BLOODLESS VICTORIES

Hitler's foreign policy responded to the inertia of the nations that might have opposed him. Each victory he achieved without resorting to war encouraged him to pursue further adventures. Germany's neighbors were unwilling to read the danger signs, and today, with the advantage of hindsight, we are disconcerted by this blindness. In the 1930s, however, the opinion was widely held that the German people would not support a war if some of their reasonable objectives were realized. If that meant the abrogation of some provisions of the Versailles treaty, that seemed a fair price to pay for peace.

The Treaty of Versailles barred any German military presence in the Rhineland and in the highly industrialized Ruhr region near the French border. Most Germans found that prohibition insulting to their national honor. When Hitler moved troops into the forbidden zone in 1936, the League of Nations protested with words, not action. Predictably, Hitler's popularity increased greatly. In the same year, Germany officially withdrew from the League and from the Locarno Pacts in which Germany, France, Czechoslovakia, and Poland had pledged peaceful adjudication of disputes. Italy and England had agreed to act as guarantors of these decisions, but again, German conduct, so clearly in contrast with Hitler's peace-loving oratory, did not arouse serious concern in Paris or London.

In 1936, the leftist republican government of Spain was under attack by the followers of the Fascist general Francisco Franco. Mussolini and Hitler concluded a military alliance with the Spanish Fascist and sent massive aid to Franco's forces. The Spanish Civil War served as a proving ground for Hitler's soldiers, tactics, and weaponry. The Soviet Union, in turn, sent support to the opposition until the losses sustained by the Republican army caused Stalin to withdraw his aid in 1939. England and France declared their neutrality, but thousands of young men from the Western democracies, including the United States, volunteered to join the anti-Fascist army. Their efforts, however, could not turn the tide, and Franco was victorious. The joint

Spanish venture of Hitler and Mussolini strengthened the relationship of the two dictators. In 1939, the Rome–Berlin Axis framed a formal alliance of aid and friendship that allowed both men to proceed with new confidence in pursuit of their grandiose plans.

AUSTRIA—FIASCO AND VICTORY

Hitler, who was Austrian by birth, was bent upon the unification of his actual and adopted homelands. The annexation, specifically forbidden by the treaties ending the Great War, was known as the *Anschluss.*

Hitler first attempted to gain control over Austria in 1934. The German Nazi Party supported a growing number of Austrian Nazis and incited them to attempt a coup d'état against the government of Chancellor Engelbert Dollfuss. When the Austrian SS employed political terror tactics against Dollfuss, a right-wing dictator in his own right, he responded with mayhem and murder. In retaliation, the Austrian supporters of Hitler broke into the chancellor's office and shot him in the throat. In the style of a gangster movie, the Nazis refused him any medical attention, and Dollfuss bled to death on the sofa. Nevertheless, the plot to topple the government failed because the Austrian army, under the leadership of Justice Minister Dr. Kurt von Schuschnigg, routed the Nazis. In an interesting byplay, Mussolini mobilized his army on the Italian–Austrian border to prevent the fall of the legitimate Austrian government. Hitler had to acknowledge that the *Anschluss* would have to wait.

Schuschnigg became chancellor and remained in office until 1938 when German troops marched into Austria and consummated the annexation with a show of military might. By then Mussolini had given his guarantee of neutrality, while the politicians of France and England continued to delude themselves that this breach of the Versailles Treaty would finally satisfy Germany's demands. After the fall of the Third Reich, the Austrians claimed to be Hitler's first victims, but the pictures of Austrians greeting the Fuehrer in an ecstasy of jubilation as he entered Vienna told a different story. Schuschnigg was sent to a concentration camp where, astonishingly, he survived and outlived Hitler by more than 30 years.

THE SUDETEN GERMANS

Pan-Germanism, the policy that justified the gathering of all German-speaking people within the borders of the Reich, was one of Hitler's consistent themes. The *Anschluss* had kept that promise, but ethnic Germans resided also in Poland and Czechoslovakia. The success of the bloodless annexation of his homeland emboldened Hitler to step up the pace—union with Sudeten Germans.

The pre–World War I Austro-Hungarian Empire had been composed of many different nationalities—several had long hoped for independence. When the Central Powers were defeated in 1918, the victors changed the map of Europe. Hungary, Yugoslavia, and Czechoslovakia were given independence, while Austria was left as a small, landlocked German-speaking country. Among the newly established nations, Czechoslovakia was the showpiece of success. Its parliamentary democracy functioned well; Czech industry was balanced with Slovak agriculture, and the solid leadership of its president, Thomas Masaryk, enabled the young Republic to thrive. But, echoing the problems of the once great Austrian Empire, Czechoslovakia was confronted with ethnic diversity within its borders. Her population of 14 million was composed of Czechs, Slovaks, Germans, Moravians, Hungarians, Austrians, Poles, and Ruthenians. Among these, the German minority caused the most severe problems. More than three million so-called Sudeten Germans lived mainly in the Bohemian northwestern mountainous regions. They would have preferred incorporation into the German Reich. Although the government in Prague tried to accommodate their grievances, they remained dissatisfied.

A Bohemian politician named Konrad Henlein founded the *Sudeten Deutsche Partei.* The stated aim of the Party was regional autonomy. Henlein was actually a Nazi in Sudeten clothing. His ideology mirrored Hitler's, and his relationship with Berlin was mutually beneficial. Henlein accepted substantial financial support and in return provided Hitler with the excuse to demand the annexation of the Sudetenland. Henlein's organization represented 60 percent of the Sudeten Germans, and his deputies in the legislature in Prague were instructed to be totally uncooperative. On orders from Hitler, they demanded virtual independence for their region, expecting, perhaps hoping, to be refused; a refusal could become an excuse for a German invasion.

The annexation of Austria had created a mere ripple on the international scene, and Hitler expected that the incorporation of the Sudetenland would be met with another slap on the wrist. In February of 1938, he tested international reaction by sending troops to the border. The Czechoslovakian government, however, responded by massing a well-trained, well-equipped army of 400,000 along the disputed area. When France and the Soviet Union indicated their willingness to uphold their treaty obligations and support Czechoslovakia in case of attack, the German troops were withdrawn. But not for long, no, not for long.

Henlein was ordered to step up his agitation, to demand nothing less than autonomy of the Sudetenland. The Prague government led by Eduard Beněs desperately to prevent the dismemberment of the nation and offered Henlein a semi-independent state, modeled after the Swiss cantons. But Hitler did not want concessions, he wanted dismemberment. For the Beneš government, the loss of the northwestern region would be a disaster; its mountains provided a natural defense line, and much of Czech industry would be exposed without that barrier. The survival of the Republic had been guaranteed by treaties with France, the Soviet Union, and England; now the question was this: Would these promises be kept in the face of German demands? The ambivalence of the British government under Prime Minister Neville Chamberlain was a bad omen; France and the Soviet Union would not act alone to protect Czechoslovakia. As Henlein and his Nazis created chaos, the Beneš government tried to cope with the disorders by invoking martial law. On September 12, Hitler made a speech in which he accused the Beneš government of atrocities against the German minority. Germany, he shouted, would not stand by while such crimes were committed. Europe was faced with a full-blown diplomatic crisis.

APPEASEMENT AT MUNICH

The dread of war impelled Prime Minister Chamberlain to approach Hitler directly. As an English gentleman, he was going to speak to his German counterpart and with a shake of hands secure tranquillity in Europe. He made the first airplane trip of his life to meet with Hitler in his mountain retreat at Berchtesgaden. Hitler's demand remained unaltered: immediate possession of the Sudetenland or there would be war. Chamberlain, after consultation with his divided cabinet in London and French Premier Edouard Daladier (but not with Beneš), informed the Prague government that it must cede the areas inhabited by the German-speaking majority. The Czechs had no choice but to accept the ultimatum. Believing he was the bearer of good news, Chamberlain returned to Hitler with the Czech reply. But instead of gratitude, Hitler was furious. He had decided to raise the stakes; he now presented the British Prime Minister with a map that indicated new territorial demands. Chamberlain agreed to submit the map to the Beneš government. The French responded with equivocation, but Beneš replied with an explicit NO. Millions of people all over Europe remained glued to their radios, hoping for peace but fearing war.

Benito Mussolini suggested the convening of a four-power conference to ease the tension. Chamberlain, Daladier, Hitler, and Mussolini met on September 29, 1938, in Munich. Neither Czechoslovakia nor the Soviet Union was invited despite the fact that any decision would affect their vital interests. In the long run they may well have been grateful for that affront; future generations could not blame them for participating in the ensuing shameful events.

The Munich Conference has become a metaphor for appeasement. It was there that Czech independence was handed to Hitler in the vain hope that this sacrifice would prevent war. Once again, Hitler raised the prospect of peace, so ardently hoped for, when he declared that the Sudetenland was his final demand. Whether or not this fiction was actually believed hardly matters. The impotence of European powers was revealed for all to see: First, it was obvious that the League of Nations was ineffective; second, France and England were militarily and psychologically unprepared to fight; and third, Hitler, the man and his aims, had been utterly misjudged.

The Munich Pact stipulated the Czechoslovak government cede to Germany an area large enough to leave Czechoslovakia defenseless. Slovakia was given virtual self-government cloaked as federated status, while Poland and Hungary were permitted to annex small border districts. Beneš resigned, and the proud achievement of Versailles, a prosperous, democratic Czechoslovakia, was doomed. Nonetheless, upon his return to England, Chamberlain waved a copy of the agreement and told his countrymen that he had brought them "peace in our time." The gift of prophecy, however, belonged to Winston Churchill, who warned that this was not the end but only the beginning of the reckoning, the first sip of the bitter cup to come.

Munich was a great success for Hitler and encouraged him to proceed toward further adventures. His generals had been fearful of military confrontations, but he had judged the irresolution of the West correctly. It is possible that at this time he began to be convinced of his own infallibility. An ironic footnote to these events was the fact that a group of German officers under the leadership of the chief of the general staff, General Franz Halder, had plotted to remove Hitler by a coup d'état.

When Chamberlain appeared in Munich, hat in hand, the planned resistance within the officer corps, which included several of its highest-ranking members, was aborted.

THE CZECH FINALE

The dismemberment of the Czechs' territorial remnant was accomplished in the following spring. Hitler ordered the president of the truncated republic, Emil Hacha, to Berlin. The scenes enacted at that meeting concluded the Czech tragedy. Hacha begged Hitler to allow his people to retain their national life. Hitler responded with

Map 7-1 ***Germany's Expansion, 1933–1939.*** (From Jackson J. Spielvogel, *Hitler and Nazi Germany: A History, 2E.* Upper Saddle River, NJ: Prentice Hall, 1996.)

threats that for every Czech battalion, there was a German division ready to march. The Czech nation, he warned, was about to be invaded, with or without Hacha's consent. How much blood it would cost the Czech people was entirely in his, the president's hands. Unless his signature was affixed to the prepared document, inviting the German troops to cross the border and restore order, squadrons of bombers would raze Prague. Hacha, who suffered from a heart ailment, fainted. Hitler's doctor revived him. Hacha pleaded for permission to telephone his cabinet but was refused. Finally, at 4:00 in the morning, physically and emotionally exhausted, he signed the document permitting German troops to enter his homeland, which ceased to exist on March 15, 1939 (see Map 7-1).

Czechoslovakia was Hitler's last bloodless victory; from here on, the German people would have to pay a price for his foreign exploits. France and England, even the Soviet Union, began to make military preparations. No longer was it doubtful whether Hitler would strike again; the question was merely where and when. During the summer of 1939, the world had its answer. The German propaganda ministry directed its full attention to the alleged suffering of the German minority living in Poland. There was an ominously familiar ring to the claims of atrocities committed against hapless fellow nationals. The next victim of Hitler's aggression had been identified.

THE STARTLING HITLER–STALIN PACT

From its inception, Nazi doctrine had emphasized its total opposition to communism. The Goebbels press spared no adjective to reduce the Soviet leadership to the level of brutes. Often they were characterized as Jews/Bolsheviks, *Untermenschen* (subhumans), and Mongols. The Nazi *Weltanshauung* consistenly dramatized the inherent evil of communism and the racial defectiveness of Jews. Defeat of Russia would rid the world of two threats at the same time and give the vaunted Aryans access to the vast lands of the European east. Thus the annihilation of a hated regime and a hated people was neatly dovetailed with the conquest of coveted territory. No wonder the political world was astonished when unexpectedly it was announced on August 23, 1939, that Germany and the Soviet Union had signed a nonaggression pact.

The two foreign ministers, Joachim von Ribbentrop and Vyacheslav Molotov, had worked out an accord that stipulated that for 10 years neither country would support any third country if it attacked either Germany or the Soviet Union. That much, at any rate, was revealed to the public. There was also a secret protocol providing for the division of Poland and giving Stalin a free hand in the Baltic States. These arrangements became clear when Soviet armies marched into eastern Poland after the Polish defeat by Germany. In light of the fact that neither dictator had any scruples, the astounding Berlin–Moscow entente was not nearly as bizarre as it seemed at first glance.

Stalin's intentions were probably twofold. The Munich appeasement of the previous year had caused consternation in Moscow. Was it possible that the four signatories in Munich might combine their forces against the Soviets? Stalin had been diplomatically rebuffed by the Western democracies, and his nation's isolation caused much concern. The treaty with Germany relieved the fear of a combined Western assault. A second reason for the alliance was Russia's need for time to build up its military power. Stalin probably expected that sooner or later Germany would launch an attack, but the communist regime was not ready. Hitler's agenda, on the other hand, included avoiding at all cost a two-front war. With Russia neutralized, he could conquer Poland easily and—if it became necessary—then turn his attention to the western front, without intervention from Stalin. He was hoping, though not certain, that the appeasement mentality of Munich would continue and that he could wage "a little war" against Poland. Should France and England wish to spill their blood for the Poles, however, he would teach them a lesson in warfare, but on one front at a time. His basic aim remained unaltered; Russia, with its vast farmlands, its wealth in oil, and other natural resources, was the proper place for the expansion of the Thousand Year Reich.

Once again, as anti-Polish propaganda grew more strident by the hour, the world held its breath. Hitler did not keep the anxious millions waiting very long. As always, he sought a justification for his actions. As a preface to the attack on Poland, a piece of absurd drama was staged in order to depict Poland the aggressor. Himmler's most valued aide, Reinhard Heydrich, chief of the Gestapo, wrote the script. SS men dressed in Polish army uniforms pretended to attack a small radio station in the German border town of Gleiwitz. The fictitious attack was given a realistic touch when the dead body of a German civilian was left at the scene. Cameras clicked, and the Nazis had "proof" of Polish treachery. Actually, the dead man had been an inmate of a concentration camp. Hitler, whose armies were already massed at the border, marched into Poland on September 1, 1939. Within two days, France and England honored their defensive treaties with Poland and declared war on Germany. Thus, World War II began with a farce, but it ended in a tragedy of momentous dimensions.

THE WAR AT A GLANCE

This brief account cannot detail the complicated ebb and flow of battles fought on four continents. A few generalities have to suffice in order to explain the international composition of the six million Jewish Holocaust victims. Our interest, therefore, is confined to the European arena of the conflict. The Pacific and African operations, although vital in the defeat of the Germans and their Japanese ally, require only passing attention here.

The two coalitions of belligerents became known as the Axis and the Allied powers. Germany and its original Axis partner, Italy, were more or less reluctantly joined by Hungary, Romania, Bulgaria, and Finland and, in 1941, by Japan (the Rome–Berlin–Tokyo Axis). In Europe, the military aspects of the Fascist partners were completely dominated by Germany. The alliance of Poland, France, and England devolved into the Allies, which eventually included the Soviet Union, the United States, Canada, Australia, New Zealand, and most of the remaining Western world. Spain maintained its official neutrality but had close ties to Germany. Sweden, Switzerland, Portugal, Ireland, and Turkey were able to stay out of the conflict probably because Hitler decided they were more useful to him as neutrals.

During the first two years of the war, Germany was astonishingly successful. Its military tactics, the *Blitzkrieg* (lightning war), utilized mobility to an extent hitherto unknown in the manuals of any general staff. Hitler recognized that in manpower and resources his enemies were superior, and if the war lasted too long, their superiority might result in his defeat. Thus, speed was the essential factor; armies had to move like lightning. German mobile columns appeared deep in enemy territory, often days before their opponents thought it possible. The German offensives were usually initiated by heavy bombing aimed at the destruction of the enemy's air force and communication and transportation systems. These attacks were followed by dive bombers hitting hostile troop concentrations to inflict heavy casualties and create chaos. Before recovery was possible, assaults by all types of mobile artillery, from light tanks to motorcycle companies, caused further losses and heightened the confusion. Heavy tanks secured the rear and prevented escape and reorganization. Aerial assaults on fleeing civilians produced panic and frenzy.

The war lasted six years. It ended in the European theater of operations on VE Day, May 8, 1945. It had been fought with new weaponry and new tactics on land, at sea, and in the air. Civilians were involved in every aspect as bombs maimed and killed them, incendiaries burned their homes, invading armies put them to flight, and food shortages left them undernourished. Worldwide, the dead numbered between 35 and 55 million. The devastation and military expenditures have been estimated to cost the incomprehensible figure of $2 trillion. To an even greater degree than World War I, this was a global war and a total war. Aerial bombardments brought unparalleled destruction to cities, and the introduction of atomic weapons in the Pacific theater of operations threatened the very existence of life on earth.

During the war, the Nazis had expanded their dwindling workforce by compelling men and women from the conquered territories to work in German fields and factories. At the end of the war, some seven million foreign workers were left in the Reich. Most labeled DPs (displaced persons) went to their home countries, while some refused because their native lands were now under Russian domination. As the Soviet armies marched westward, they established communist puppet regimes in eastern Europe and the Balkans. Many of the slave laborers from these regions did not want to live under communism. Some sought refuge in temporary internment camps, others roamed across Europe wondering where and how to rebuild their lives (see Chapter 12).

At the end of the war, the United States and the Soviet Union emerged as rival superpowers. Their competition for political and economic predominance, the Cold War, lasted for 45 years. Their conflicting aims boiled over into military confrontations at several junctures. The division of Germany into democratic and communist regions, West Germany and East Germany, was part of this struggle of the giants. Not until 1990 was Germany reunified into a single nation. A new peacekeeping organization was created, and since hope does spring eternal, the world prays that the United Nations may eventually accomplish its mission.

Of the fate of the Jews under the Nazis, little was known as certainty until the fighting stopped. When Allied soldiers liberated the death and concentration camps, battle-weary combat soldiers cried. All speculation, all rumors, and all denials came to a halt. A Shoah, a genocide of six million Jews, had been carried out during chaotic war conditions. German conquests had enabled the Nazis to identify, round up, isolate, transport, and kill their victims. Even in areas where German occupation was of short duration, such as in Italy and Hungary, Nazi organizational skills and fanaticism had assured the annihilation of hundreds of thousands of Jews. It seems absurd to call killers dedicated, but the designation does apply.

THE DEFEAT OF POLAND

Half of the six million Holocaust victims had lived in Poland; all death camps were located in Poland; and the greatest percentage of nationals killed by the Nazis were Poles. It is appropriate that we examine these unhappy circumstances more closely.

The conquest of Poland was completed in one month. Hitler's *Blitzkrieg* strategies caught the Polish army in a huge vise between the Baltic States and Slovakia. The Poles, whose forces still included horse cavalry, tried bravely and pathetically to defend their country against tank units and aerial attacks. Warsaw was bombarded relentlessly and held out for four weeks. The Soviets invaded Poland from the east to claim their share of territory as stipulated in a secret clause of the Molotov–Ribbentrop pact. The statistics of men killed in action in this campaign speak for themselves: German losses were 11,000 compared to Polish losses of 120,000. Seventy thousand of these casualties occurred in battles against the Germans and 50,000 against the invading Russians. Although the French and English governments honored their treaty obligations and declared war on Germany, military aid was not, perhaps could not be, sent in time to prevent the fall of Poland.

The Nazis occupied western and central Poland, a region that in 1939 had a population of 20 million. The eastern territories and its 12 million people were occupied by the Soviet Union in 1939. When Germany declared war on the Soviet Union in 1941, these provinces were quickly overrun by German armies (Map 7-2). Thus, many Polish refugees who had fled eastward to escape the Nazis were overwhelmed two years later. Among these, a fortunate minority made its way deeper into Russian territory, some traveling as far east as Siberia. The hardships they endured were grim but most survived, whereas life under Nazi occupation was a nightmare from which 5,600,000 Poles never awoke.

Hitler had resolved to destroy Polish national life. He considered its Slavic inhabitants racially undesirable and its farmlands suitable for Aryan expansion. To secure their subjugation, the annihilation of the entire Polish elite was ordered. With stunning ruthlessness, most members of the Polish aristocracy, military officers, political leaders, priests, and the intelligentsia were murdered. Prewar prominence in any field of the nation's political, economic, or cultural life was a death sentence. Like the proscriptions of ancient times, these murders were carried out to eliminate the possibility of organizing any anti-German resistance. (Actually, such Nazi brutality motivated opposition.) The SS and Gestapo followed the German armies and executed hundreds of thousands who might—or might not—have posed a threat to German occupation. The people of Poland, more fearful of their Russian neighbors than the Germans, were totally unprepared for such savagery. Those members of their government who eluded the Nazi murderers and escaped to England left behind a people in chaos and despair. Although the Poles did not expect a merciful occupation, the slaughter of men and women whose very accomplishments condemned them to death was without modern precedent.

Map 7-2 ***The German Partition of Poland, 1939/41–1945.*** (From *The War Against the Jews 1933–1945,* by Lucy S. Davidowicz. Text copyright © 1975 by Lucy S. Davidowicz, maps by Vincent Kotschar, copyright © 1975 by Henry Holt and Co., Inc. Reprinted by permission of Henry Holt and Co., Inc.)

Poland was cut in two. The western provinces, which the Germans called the *Ostgaue,* were annexed to the Reich. Largest within that region was the *Warthegau.* South-central Poland, renamed *General Gouvernment,* became the private kingdom of Hans Frank, Hitler's friend and lawyer. Frank had risen rapidly in the Nazi hierarchy and held several important legal appointments before he was chosen to be the czar of occupied Poland: He combined the avarice of a Goering (stole a Leonardo da Vinci and a Rembrandt for his own home in Germany) with the ruthlessness of a Himmler (condemned to hanging by the postwar Nuremberg Tribunal). Unhampered by moral or political restrictions, he wanted to reduce the Polish people to ignorant toilers for the Reich. A sampling of his directives makes the point: He ordered German to be the official language of his realm, confiscated and appropriated great art treasures, and executed countless innocent people. He did not restore civic order, and refused to permit restoration of even minimal services to the public. He described his function as that of a lord in charge over so many slaves, whose value was proportionate to their usefulness to Germany. His own lifestyle was royal, and his residence in his administrative capital of Cracow was palatial.

Three major death camps were located in his territory. He frequently complained that the constant influx of Jews interfered with his administrative duties, words which actually meant: "This is my dominion, SS meddling with my authority must stop." That never happened.

HIMMLER'S VISION OF POLAND

Hans Frank, to his regret, did not own the Jews; Himmler and the SS did. With yet another title to fit his extended authority, Himmler was named Reich Commissar for the Consolidation of German Nationhood. In this role, he was charged with three mandates: first, reduce the number of biologically undesirable Jewish and Slavic people; second, identify and preserve any Aryan elements in the population; and third, plant Germans in regions usurped from the native population. To accomplish these goals, he promoted settling SS men and their families on confiscated land, thus joining Polish soil to the Reich forever. Like warrior knights from the Middle Ages, he envisioned a new nobility to secure German *Lebensraum* in the East by the labor of Slavic serfs.

The people of Poland did not assume the German occupiers to be compassionate, but their severity, soon turned into brutality, was not expected. Polish misery, deliberately inflicted, has been thoroughly documented. Hitler's orders were simple enough: Germanize Poland in 10 years. The cost to the native people was irrelevant; they were consigned to a life of service and submission. It is important to acknowledge the scale of Polish suffering, particularly in view of the oft-repeated charge that most Poles cared nothing about the fate of the Jews. While anti-Semitism was widespread, it is also true that many Poles risked their own lives to save their Jewish neighbors. Himmler, much to Gauleiter Frank's discomfiture, had been granted by the Fuehrer a free hand to do whatever he thought necessary to keep Poland secure. For the *treue Heinrich* that spelled a reign of terror in the East.

During the years of occupation, ordinary Polish men and women were at the mercy of many, often competing masters. There were Himmler's minions, Frank's appointees charged with the civil administration, as well as collaborating Polish officials, who heiled Hitler to retain their positions. Under specific circumstances, officers of the German army ordered them about. But none of the authorities alleviated hunger or provided fuel to heat even one room. Indeed the authorities vied with one another to loot their victims' food, goods, and treasures. The confusion of conflicting orders created continuous anxiety and frustration. For example, a Pole seeking to obtain a driver's license could not be certain where to apply; he was sent from one office to another and had to wait many hours in long lines until the weeks of interrogation and intimidation made him quit the effort. The Nazis had no wish to resolve this anarchy; a rudderless, frightened, and impoverished people were, in their view, more likely to be docile and compliant.

It is not an exaggeration to speak of the enslavement of Polish workers. Men and women were treated as renewable commodities, shipped here or there, to work on farms, in mines, or in factories. Almost a million farmers were uprooted to make way for the Germanization of their land. Lack of nutrition, cold, disease, and punishment for real or imagined acts of sabotage took an appalling toll on civilians. The fact that some of the Poles joined together in secret, usually in the forests, and formed resistance groups is testimony to their tenacity and courage.

The people of Poland were also severely afflicted by a particularly vicious aspect of Himmler's *Lebensborn* (fountain of life) program. The major thrust of this scheme was the encouragement of German girls to bear racially desirable children, preferably fathered by SS men. A less-known component of *Lebensborn* was the kidnapping of blond, blue-eyed children from occupied Poland. Babies and young children were snatched from their parents and sent to German couples for adoption. Their exact numbers are not known, but it has been estimated that several hundred thousand children "disappeared." If the Nazis kept records indicating the fate of specific *Lebensborn* children, they have not been found.

When the bloodletting was over, after six years of German occupation, Poland lay prostrate. Statistics give their own horrific account: In 1939, the population was roughly 35,000,000; in 1945, that number was reduced by 5,600,000. In other words, the Poles lost 16 percent of their people. More than half, approximately 3,000,000 of these, were Jews. No other country, not even the Soviet Union with its war time dead and missing individuals of 23,100,000 (or 13.7 percent), suffered greater per capita losses. By comparison, the Germans, subjected to years of carpet bombing and enormous military casualties, rank third in this sad litany, with the death of 10.47 percent of its population.

THE WAR IN THE WEST

The period from the fall of Poland in October 1939 until the following spring has been dubbed the "phony war," or *Sitzkrieg* (sit-down war), because there was no activity on the western front. Hitler hoped but failed to drive a wedge between the French–English alliance, and his generals advised against a winter campaign. In the spring, the Germans struck again, without the formality of a declaration of war. Denmark was overrun in a single day. The German admiralty had urged the occupation of Norway in order to secure submarine bases in the war against England. The Norwegians held out for a month. On May 10, the *Blitzkrieg* armies marched into France. By invading the poorly prepared Low Countries, they outflanked the Maginot Line. Holland asked for an armistice in five days; Belgium lasted three weeks. The combined armies of Britain and France were unable to stop the German advance. Only the "miracle of Dunkirk" saved the Allies from complete disaster. This miracle was actually a retreat. British ships rescued 215,000 of their own men and 120,000 French soldiers from the northern beaches of France. In June, Paris was surrendered to prevent its destruction. A demoralized, defeatist French government under Marshall Henri Pétain wanted peace at whatever cost. The official capitulation of France was consummated on June 22, 1940. On that day, at the exact spot in the forest of Compiègne, where, on November 11, 1918, Germany had acknowledged its defeat, an ecstatic Hitler turned the tables on France. It was probably the moment of his greatest triumph. At this point, Mussolini added a tainted jewel to Hitler's crown; with France prostrate, he opted to join Hitler's war. Franklin Delano Roosevelt called this action a stab in the back, and the phrase has stuck.

Hitler's terms were harsh. Alsace and Lorraine were annexed to the Reich. The large northern sector, including Paris, was placed under military administration, although Nazi politicians could not keep their hands in their pockets and frequently interfered. The French, like all the occupied peoples, were compelled to pay for the cost of the occupation. German aims, quite simply, were to exploit the conquered people and their products to the fullest. By implied and direct terror, the possibility of any opposition to the occupation forces was to be prevented. German determination to wipe out the French underground resistance organizations cost thousands of French men and women their lives.

The central and southern two-fifths of France were permitted to form a puppet state. Marshall Pétain, hero of the Battle of Verdun in World War I, now became a German pawn. He always claimed that his compliant attitude toward the Germans saved many lives; however, the problem of cooperation with the enemy continues to haunt the French. When the war ended, Pétain was tried, and he spent the rest of his life in prison. His Vice Premier, Pierre Laval, was an outright collaborator of the Nazis. He allowed his country to be looted, made no objection when French slave laborers were forced to work in the Reich, and even tried to raise a French army to fight alongside the Germans. In his desire to please his Nazi masters, he not only complied with, but tried to anticipate their wishes. His role in the deportation of French Jews was shameful (see Chapter 9). Laval, too, was tried by his countrymen and met his death by firing squad in 1945.

Not all the Jews living in France were French. Tens of thousands were refugees from other Nazi-occupied lands. Many were illegal residents; thus their number cannot be precisely determined. The prewar native Jewish population was about 300,000, with perhaps an equal number of émigrés. Paris was the magnet; in 1940, it is estimated that more than half of its Jews were from Poland, Czechoslovakia, and Germany. The conquest of Holland and Belgium caused a renewed influx. The possibility of a sudden and disastrous French defeat was totally unforeseen. As in all the conquered countries, foreign Jews were the first to be sacrificed to Nazi demands.

GOVERNING THE CONQUERED NATIONS

The Nazis had no master plan for the administration of their conquests. None of the defeated peoples were given a systematic, businesslike government. All were exploited, all had quotas of food and other goods to be shipped to Germany, and all supplied man and woman power for Germany's war needs. And certainly all were afflicted, though the degree of severity differed from region to region. The racial characteristics of northern and western Europeans were valued as Aryan or nearly Aryan; therefore, their blood was not as expendable as Slavic or Jewish blood, and their survival rates were greater.

In Norway, a native Nazi, Vidkun Quisling (his name is now synonymous with traitor), served as the puppet prime minister. He shared power with the equally hated Gauleiter Josef Terboven. Denmark was permitted to keep its democratic institutions as long as the government and people cooperated with the Germans. When that cooperation was sabotaged by an active Danish resistance organization, Reich Commissioner Werner Best and the German army appeared in Copenhagen. Although the German administration of Holland and Belgium differed in theory, the reality of daily life varied little. Belgium was governed as a military district, and an Austrian lawyer, Arthur Seyss-Inquart, was appointed Reich Commissioner of the Netherlands. He had been deputy to Hans Frank in Poland, and with such tutelage, his reign among the Dutch was brutal. When he stood at the dock during the Nuremberg Tribunal, he admitted to "fearful excesses" of his rule. He had hoped to impress Hitler with his diligence in sending Dutch Jews to their death; among them was a girl named Ann Frank.

Everywhere, native resources, food, as well as manpower were diverted to benefit Germany; art treasures were plundered from public and private collections. The small size of the Low Countries and their terrain made it very difficult to escape from German surveillance; nonetheless, underground fighters organized and harassed the despised conquerors. Members of resistance groups faced not only the danger of German capture but also the treachery of their own countrymen, who collaborated with the enemy in order to gain some advantage for themselves (Map 7-3).

GREAT BRITAIN ALONE

After the German conquests on the continent, only the English remained to deprive Hitler of total victory. That stubborn island people, led by Winston Churchill, refused to see the futility of resistance. Did they not realize that fate had ordained that Nazism must triumph? Although the English stood alone, they spurned Hitler's peace feelers. Hitler believed that the English people would demand that their government enter into a rapprochement with Germany if they suffered heavy losses at sea. However, even though German submarines inflicted much damage, they could not stop all of the vitally needed shipments from reaching the island. The British Commonwealth nations and the United States provided the essentials, and the English could not be starved into submission. Hitler needed a quick victory; a

VOICES

Excerpts from Windmills, War, and Water

For my children, from mother:

Your father was born in 1918 to a well-to-do German-Jewish family. His childhood in a small Prussian town was pleasant and peaceful. Papa Steinhardt farmed and operated a mill, a bakery, and other enterprises. Even as a boy, Josef ("Jup" in Dutch) learned about growing crops and raising animals. But after Hitler came to power in 1933, he had no future in Germany. He was 18 when his parents sent him to Camp Wieringen in Holland. This was an agricultural school that prepared young Zionists for life in Palestine. There he met and befriended former university students who widened his interrupted education. But, in 1940, before the group could emigrate, the Germans invaded my country. They brought the Holocaust to the Netherlands, and we lost over 70 percent of our Jewish population.

I too grew up in the countryside, in the village of Westgrafdyk. My father was the postmaster/mailman and made his rounds on his bicycle. I was in high school when the Germans overran my country. My two brothers were conscripted to do slave labor in German factories; food was rationed; and although we rarely saw any Germans, the villagers hated the invaders.

One day I was helping in the post office when a handsome young man came in to use the telephone. This was, of course, your father. His accent was strange, and gradually, on later visits, he told me about himself. The Nazis had arrested the students of Camp Wieringen, and most were shipped to concentration camps. He and a few others were selected for farm work, and now he was working on a nearby farm. I looked forward to seeing him, but suddenly he stopped coming. Later I learned that he had run away to join the anti-Nazi resistance group organized by Mr. Manshold, who owned a large estate in the Polder—land reclaimed from the Zuidersee.

When Jup returned to me after the war, he told me of his work in the Resistance. His hair was dyed red or blond, depending on his false identity papers. He divided his time between farm work and underground missions. Mr. Manshold's hayloft served as a watchtower over the flat landscape. When Germans approached, the lookout imitated a bird's whistle to warn the resisters to disappear into the false ceiling space over the barn.

This is one story I never tired of hearing:

"One night my assignment was to collect guns dropped for us by English planes. I was on my bicycle when two German soldiers stopped me—it was past curfew time. One soldier said to the other, 'Another disgusting Dutch slob.' I did not let on that I understood him and in Dutch kept repeating 'sick cow, cow sick, need vet.' He had called me a slob, so I became a slob. I spit on the ground, I wiped my nose on my sleeve, I scratched myself in unmentionable places. The soldiers looked at me in disgust. They took me to the town jail and next morning, wanting nothing more to do with me, they threw me out. When I returned to the farm, Mr. Manshold said, 'Glad you're back.' But not as glad as I was!"

By permission courtesy of Nellie Humphreys.

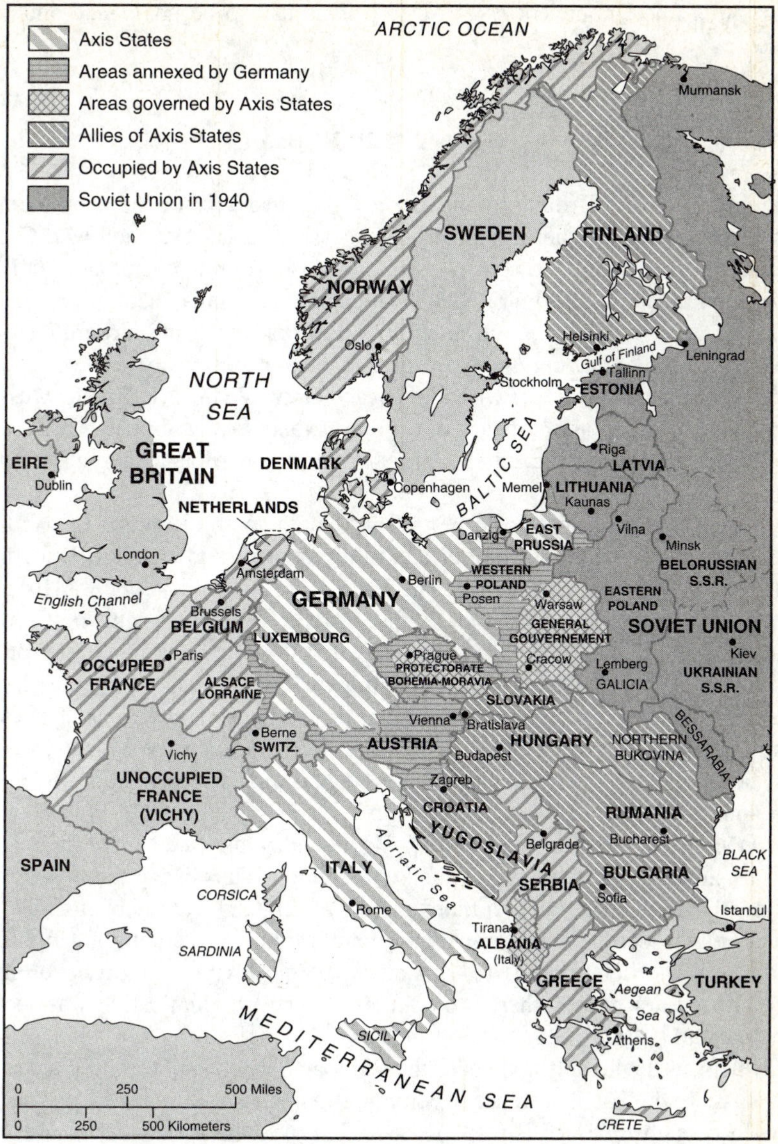

Map 7-3 ***Europe under Nazi occupation before June 22, 1941.***

prolonged war might bring Russia and the United States into the conflict. The Fuehrer decided to invade Great Britain (Operation Sea Lion) as soon as the German air force established its superiority over the skies. Goering promised that his *Luftwaffe* was equal to the task, but the RAF (Royal Air Force) continued to hold its own and eventually dominated in the air. The persistent aerial bombing of English cities strengthened rather than weakened English resolve. This, in Churchill's words, was Britain's finest hour. Hitler's invasion plans had to be postponed and finally canceled.

THE BALKANS AND OPERATION BARBAROSSA

The failure to force Britain to the peace table had created new problems for Hitler. Germany lacked the raw materials necessary for an extended war. Gasoline propelled the *Blitzkrieg,* and Germany had none. Oil-rich Romania and its Balkan neighbors, Hungary and Bulgaria, had been cajoled and threatened into cooperating with Nazi interests. Hitler would have preferred not to expend any military manpower in the Balkans and continue to dominate the area politically and economically. But there he came into conflict with his ally and erstwhile mentor, Benito Mussolini. The Italians looked upon Southeastern Europe as their sphere of influence. They had invaded and conquered the small Adriatic nation of Albania and now coveted Greece.

Greece, however, was not Ethiopia or Albania. With the aid of British forces, the Greeks routed the Italians. Hitler had to divert armies to rescue Il Duce from a humiliating defeat and also to safeguard the Romanian oil supplies. His armies defeated the combined Greek and English forces; even the island of Crete was occupied by Germans. It became necessary for the Germans to secure Bulgaria and Yugoslavia as well. The cost of controlling the Balkans was an ongoing liability, particularly due to the persistent harassment from Yugoslav guerrillas. This change in plans caused a fateful two-month delay in the attack on the Soviets; just how fateful became clear when German soldiers found themselves fighting the Russian winter and the Soviet armies at the same time.

On June 22, 1941, two years after Hitler and Stalin had signed their 10-year nonaggression pact, Hitler attacked the Soviet Union. Thus began the two-front war he so greatly feared. The Fuehrer maintained that England was unable to land troops on the shores of continental Europe, and therefore he was actually not fighting on two fronts. The official pretext for the attack on the Soviet Union was so thin that Goebbels need not have bothered to contrive it. The true motivation was rooted in past hatred and present needs.

Hitler was unalterably convinced that German *Lebensraum* was destined to be on Polish/Russian soil. His abhorrence of communism had never diminished, and he feared that given enough time, British troops might link up with the Soviet Union. It was essential to defeat Russia before this could happen. Furthermore, Mussolini's attack on Greece had brought the English to the Balkans, threatening Germany's oil supply. The time was ripe to activate *Fall Barbarossa,* the code name for the Russian invasion. He anticipated victory before the onset of winter. The Soviet armies, Hitler claimed, were dominated by Jews and Bolsheviks and would offer little resistance (Map 7-4).

Hitler was well aware that Japan and the United States were on a collision course. He encouraged the Japanese to attack the United States because he believed that a war in the Pacific would prevent American forces from playing a significant role in Europe. Russia, according to this plan, would be crushed in a few months, and at that point, even with some aid from overseas, England would be forced to surrender. The

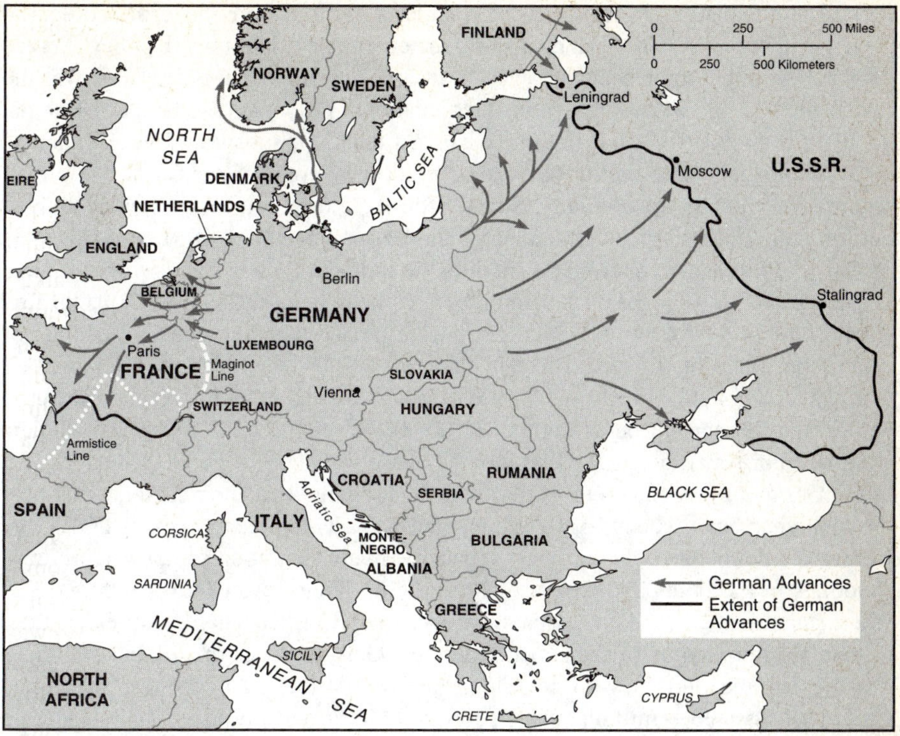

Map 7-4 ***Military Operations of World War II: The German Offensives, 1939–1942.*** (From Jackson J. Spielvogel, *Hitler and Nazi Germany: A History, 2E.* Upper Saddle River, NJ: Prentice Hall, 1996.)

motherland would have it all: raw materials, *Lebensraum,* and slave workers, to fulfill the destiny of Hitler's vision of the New Order—German domination of Europe.

Hitler miscalculated fatally. Although German divisions penetrated deep into the Soviet Union, they were unable to take either Leningrad (now St. Petersburg) or Moscow. Unprepared, often without winter clothing, the cold took a terrible toll among the German soldiers. The eastern front bogged down along a line reaching from the outskirts of Leningrad to the fringes of Moscow and stretched south to the gates of Stalingrad (now Volgograd). The Battle of Stalingrad, considered a turning point of the war, stopped the German offensive, and by the fall of 1942, German troops were on the defensive. Hitler, who had convinced himself that he was a military genius, now took personal command of the armed forces. No doubt, he had some military talent; however, when his strategies failed, he insisted that cowardice and treachery among the generals, not his orders, were to blame. His refusal to permit troops to retreat, even when in an untenable position, was particularly costly. At this time, however, Allied victory was still far from certain. The Germans had taken the entire Crimean Peninsula; General Erwin Rommel, the Desert Fox, campaigned successfully in Africa; and the German U-boat fleet inflicted heavy losses on Allied shipping.

The population of these areas of conquests had to endure the terrible ordeal of Nazi occupation. As in Poland, absurd racial theories determined policy. Where cooperation might have been achieved, resistance was fostered. Surely, this was the case in the Ukraine where the arriving Germans were welcomed as liberators. But that goodwill evaporated when it became clear that the Germans viewed the Ukrainians with utter disdain. The Baltic States, too, might have collaborated; instead, German severity nullified that potentiality. Soviet officers, and of course Jews, were singled out for the infamous "special treatment." The German treatment of Russian prisoners of war (POWs) is a chapter that dishonors the military code of any civilized nation. During the first onslaught of the Barbarossa campaign, an estimated 5,700,000 Red Army soldiers were taken prisoner. They were herded together, deprived of food or water, shot outright, forced to live in their own filth—all under the eyes of their German captors. Minimally 2,000,000 of them died, although some researches believe that number to be as high as 3,500,000. Over 3.5 million Russian soldiers were taken prisoner during the first months of the war. They were labeled subhuman in the German press and were treated with such cruelty that their captors must bear the subhuman label. The Nazis were unprepared to accommodate so many POWs and instituted a deliberate policy of mass starvation in concentration camps and arbitrary shootings in the fields and woods of Russia. Surviving Soviet POWs reported that when starvation drove them to cannibalism, their German guards expressed utter disdain for the victims of their own atrocities. Only when German labor shortages became extreme were they used as slave laborers. At the end of the war, the Soviet Union had lost 23.1 million of its people, military and civilian. This staggering number is greater than the losses of all the other belligerents in Europe combined.

The German administration of the conquered Russian regions was a botched operation. The authority of different Nazi officials, the military, the SS, and the private empires carved out by Goering, Himmler, and Albert Speer of the Armaments Ministry collided amid bewildering confusion. Disregard for the needs of the native population was the only point of unanimity.

THE TURNING POINT

It is impossible to know with certainty why Hitler declared war on the United States just after the Japanese attacked Pearl Harbor on December 7, 1941. The fact that he had concluded a tripartite agreement of mutual aid with Italy and Japan was not a decisive issue; Hitler honored his signature quite selectively. Perhaps he believed that President Roosevelt was bound to enter the conflict in any case or that the United States presented little danger because the Americans would be unable to fight in the Pacific as well as in the Atlantic arenas. He may have believed that Europe would be prostrate at his feet before the hated Roosevelt could interfere. How little he understood the Americans; obviously, he did not grasp that such a declaration rallied the American people to a resolute, unified stand against the Germans.

Hitler had been correct when he stated that Germany could not win a long war. When his quick successes of the earlier campaigns could not be duplicated after 1942, Allied victory was simply a matter of time. The courage and perseverance of Britain and the Soviet Union afforded the United States the necessary breathing space to draw upon its great human and material resources. On the seas, in the air, and on the ground the combined effort of the Allies overwhelmed the Germans. The contributions of the United States were essential, in providing armies, ships, weaponry, and medical supplies as well as vitally needed quantities of food. The psychological effect of the American commitment is difficult to measure, but surely it inspired renewed courage to the weary, embattled people throughout Europe. Nonetheless, victory was dearly won. To the last day of the war, Hitler's armies, still 10,000,000 strong, inflicted heavy losses, even when the final outcome was no longer in doubt.

The British began the rout of the Axis powers in 1942 in North Africa, and together with American troops, they defeated Hitler's and Mussolini's African divisions. The Allies then crossed the Mediterranean to invade Italy, and although the Fascist government of Mussolini collapsed and Italy surrendered, the Germans rushed south to face the Allies. The Italian campaign was hard fought and lasted until the end of the war.

The Soviets had pleaded for a second front to divert Germans from her battle fronts, and on June 6, 1944, the long awaited landing on the coast of Normandy began. While Russian armies advanced toward the German heartland, Anglo-American forces fought their way eastward across France. Most German cities were rubble when the western and eastern Allied armies met near Berlin. On May 8, 1945, President Harry S. Truman (Franklin Delano Roosevelt had died in April 1945) and Prime Minister Winston Churchill declared victory in Europe.

Air raid on Berlin during WWII. (Corbis/Bettmann.)

Until the end, Hitler directed operations from one of his several underground bunkers. He was still obeyed, despite the fact that in defeat, his destructive impulses reached new heights. In July 1944, a group of German army and civilian anti-Nazis attempted to assassinate him. Hitler's fury and revenge were maniacal; accusations, some true, some false, condemned men to death by methods of execution that Spanish Inquisitors would have envied. As Russian soldiers entered Berlin, Hitler, in his bunker beneath the Chancellery garden, directed armies that no longer existed. His scorn for the German people was evident when he ordered the destruction of everything the enemy might find useful. Had these orders had been carried out, the ruin of the Reich would have been total. Hitler, irrational, perhaps insane, saw treason everywhere; he condemned his generals, even Goering and Himmler, and expressed nothing but disdain for the suffering German people. It was their weakness, he raged, which caused him to lose the war, their shame to prefer peace to death. Afraid of falling into Russian hands, he shot himself on April 30, 1945. According to his instructions, his body was burned. Goebbels had never wavered in his loyalty and with his family also remained in the Berlin bunker. He poisoned his six children and then he and his wife committed suicide, "A Germany without Hitler was not fit to live in."

The legacy of the 12 years of Hitler's dictatorship cannot be evaluated in the context of this text. Suffice it to say that from the ashes of the Third Reich, a vastly different world was wrought. Every aspect of human life, psychological, military, economic, political, religious, and philosophical, was permanently and deeply affected. There was so much suffering, so many losses, and such upheaval that even the balm of time cannot erase the scars. And yet, veterans of many battles, men well versed in the cruelty of war, testified that nothing in their experience equaled the horror they felt upon entering a concentration camp. There they saw the absolute evil that man can do to man.

CHAPTER 8

From Ideology to Isolation

The killing fields of European Jewry were Poland and Western Russia. The trains rolling in from all the regions conquered by the Germans terminated at the ghettos, at slave labor camps, and at the death camps of Poland. The Soviet's western provinces were the prime hunting grounds of the mobile killing units of the SS, *Einsatzgruppen.* The major ghettos were cut from the slum sections of Polish towns and cities, and all the death camps were located in Poland. Here, far from the German heartland, the ordinary Aryan civilian could not see the pits of barely covered corpses, could not hear the cries of those starving behind the walls and fences. The chaos of war, so the murderers believed, would cover every depravity; soon the Jews would be extinct, and no one who mattered would know the truth.

The history of annihilation began with the reestablishment of that medieval institution, the ghetto. After the conquest of Poland, the Nazis abandoned their efforts to terrorize the Jews into emigration; the process was hopelessly slow. The decision was made to commit genocide. Whether mass murder had always been the intention of Hitler or was determined after 1939 matters little. The official protocol that condemned every Jewish person within German control was signed in January of 1942, but actually the killings had begun earlier. The annihilation of millions presents logistical difficulties on many levels, and the first efforts belie the German reputation for efficiency; they were messy, botched, emotionally hard on the SS executioners. The answer was Zyklon B and the gas chambers. It is, however, important to realize that shooting and gassing were not the only methods used to make the world *Judenrein;* terror, imprisonment, slave labor, transports in overcrowded railroad cars, enclosure in the ghettos, starvation, mass shooting by the *Einsatzgruppen* and their auxiliary troops, deprivation of every imaginable necessity of civilized life, epidemics, suicide, and medical experiments—all contributed to the death toll. Often several techniques were employed concurrently, which overlapped at a specific time or place. The *Endloesung* of the Jewish question does not lend itself to a chronological presentation because the Shoah was often frenzied and chaotic.

AN OVERVIEW

A time frame is nonetheless useful, even indispensable for historical accuracy, and may be helpful at this juncture: At the conclusion of the brief Polish campaign in October 1939, the Nazis began to force Jews into labor battalions. Men as well as women were quite literally snatched off the streets of cities and towns and impressed to work without wages. During the spring of 1940, the formation of ghettos began; Lodz was the first large city to experience the upheaval of dislocation in February of that year. At the same time, German victories on the western front resulted in the expulsion of Jews from the occupied areas. Sometimes immediately, sometimes after brief stays in transfer camps in their native countries, they were shipped to Polish ghettos and camps. The trains with their human cargo began to roll in 1940 and continued throughout the war. The transports, usually in freight and cattle cars, without food or water, sealed without fresh air, caused many thousands of deaths.

Beginning in July of 1941, the Final Solution, the *Endloesung* of the Jewish question, moved from "natural attrition" to outright mass killings. Following the German army into the Soviet Union, mobile SS units and their auxiliaries shot between 1,500,000 and 2,000,000 Jews. The concentration camps too were given new functions. Their proclaimed original purpose, political reeducation, was never developed, and the camps became slave labor and death camps. The introduction of poison gas in specially built facilities started in 1941 and ended in the winter of 1944. And finally, as the German armies were retreating before the Red Army during that last winter of the war, the remnant of concentration camps' victims were forced to march to Germany. Many thousands died on the roads. The number of Holocaust survivors is estimated at 300,000. The ideological basis, that is, the paranoid hatred of Jews, had been government policy since 1933. The agents to carry out the genocide, the SS, had the training, the will, the arms, and the official instructions to turn ideology into annihilation. The Fuehrer needed no approval for his actions. No parliament, no court of justice, and no political opposition had survived to challenge the crimes of the state. The voice of the people was stilled; the churches, with minor exceptions, were submissive to secular authority; and the killing techniques either already existed or were adapted without difficulty. Members of the medical and the judicial professions, though sworn to support life and justice, in their official posture supported the actions of their government.

TRACKING THE JEWS

The first step toward annihilation was to ascertain how many Jews lived in a designated region. Americans who are accustomed to keeping religious affiliations private are often puzzled about the ability of the Nazis to identify their victims. During the 1940s, it was not difficult to discover the religious membership of Europeans. Not only did most official statistics indicate faith, but also ordinary documents, such as licenses, insurance policies, passports, applications for jobs, school records, and membership in organizations, commonly recorded religion. The registers of Jewish congregations and associations were confiscated as a matter of course by the

Germans. Thus, it was not difficult to determine the number of Jews, their addresses, their occupations, and even the status of their bank accounts. The knock on the door at midnight was no euphemism to the Jews living under the Nazis.

Several thousand intended victims survived by hiding, but that stratagem usually depended on the willingness of others to take great risks. Some Jewish women who looked Aryan, blue-eyed blondes in particular, "passed" as Christians. Their chances to survive improved if they made their way to a new neighborhood, a place where no one recognized them. The Nazi offered favors—even a chance to stay alive—to Jews and Gentiles who denounced Jewish "passers." Jewish men, nearly always circumcised, obviously were in constant danger of discovery.

THE MISCHLINGE

Hitler's policy vis-á-vis the *Mischlinge,* the half and quarter Jews whose parentage was Aryan and German, was much debated but never resolved. Categorized as non-Aryans, they were not deported or sterilized. Some areas of employment were closed to them, but usually they were left alone. This special consideration afforded to German *Mischlinge* was not given to those living in conquered areas, where they shared the fate of the Jews.

In the Reich, the Aryan partners of existing mixed marriages were under enormous pressure from the Nazi government to divorce their Jewish partners. The choices made by couples under such conditions were often heartbreaking.

DESPOILING THE VICTIMS

Identification of the Jews preceded their economic exclusion. In Germany, this procedure took several years, but it was accomplished rapidly in the occupied territories. There, Jews were deprived of their citizenship, their jobs, their businesses, and the practice of their professions as quickly as possible. Their possessions were looted and their assets confiscated. For millions of Jewish families in the occupied lands, expulsion from their homes accompanied their economic ruin. Confinement in ghettos, forced slave labor, imprisonment in concentration camps, and death followed rapidly. In the eastern regions, where the *Einsatzgruppen* roamed, the Jewish inhabitants could be stripped of every possession and every right, including the right to live, in one single day.

The final phase of the Holocaust was the outright killing process. At first, the SS squads, the *Einsatzgruppen,* used guns. When shooting was deemed too slow and such direct contact with the victims regarded as psychologically undesirable (for the shooters), new methods had to be found. After a brief experiment using carbon monoxide gas generated from the exhaust of vehicles and diesel motors, the death factory was initiated. Instead of the killers rounding up the victims, the victims were brought to the killers. Within three years, all the ghettos were emptied; some hundreds of thousands were used as slave laborers, but most were killed in the gas chambers. Invariably, whatever the victims had brought with them, even the hair on women's heads and the gold fillings in their teeth, became the property of the Nazi state.

TYPES OF CONCENTRATION CAMPS

The location of concentration camps was determined by two main criteria: they had to be on or near a railroad junction, and they had to be hidden from German eyes. The isolation of the victims would make escape more difficult and insure against the possibility of assistance from outsiders. The eastern camps were usually built by prisoners, thus placing them on unhealthy, swampy sites was irrelevant to the German planners.

The term "concentration camp" has several definitions and requires clarification. The original, official German explanation that the camps were installations for the reeducation of political opponents, antisocial individuals, and troublemakers was bogus. The earliest major camps, Dachau, Buchenwald, and Sachsenhausen, detained actual and suspected dissidents such as labor union leaders, communists, socialists, members of the clergy, pacifists, and others. Jews were always among them, but in the early months after Hitler came to power, they did not comprise the majority.

Concentration camps were huge prisons, where so-called enemies of the state served sentences at the pleasure of several agencies entrusted with the security of the regime. The camp system expanded rapidly and developed three distinguishable types. Some sites combined several functions within the same compound. Best known are the death camps of Treblinka, Chelmno, Maidanek, Belzec, and Auschwitz-Birkenau. These were the killing centers. The second group of concentration camps was designed to serve the killing process as well. Here, death came more slowly as the result of catastrophic living conditions. These installations were attached to work sites, where starving prisoners were forced to perform heavy labor. Most of the victims survived for a few weeks, some for a few months. The number of work-related camps was constantly expanded; largest among these were Gross-Rosen, Ravensbrueck, Stutthof, Bergen-Belsen, and Theresienstadt in Czechoslovakia. Jews predominated among the prisoners in most of these camps. The third type was designated as labor camp. The inmates were, for the most part, non-Jewish men and women who had been rounded up in the conquered nations. Their work was usually connected to military needs. Some of the factories and mines exploited the skills of both Jews and Gentiles. In such facilities, the Jews were quartered separately, received less food, and suffered greater brutality. A vast network of hundreds of satellite installations was created that enslaved millions. Buchenwald alone had 134 sub-camps. The Germans treated their slave workers as a resource, whose survival was of no concern to the state. Often, toiling in factories and mines below the surface of the earth, men and women saw no daylight, lacked even the most rudimentary hygienic facilities, and received starvation rations. Inevitably, the death toll was high. As noted earlier, upon the collapse of the Reich, they became the displaced persons of Europe. Destitute and bewildered, they roamed about as they looked for loved ones. Many were afraid to return to their communist-dominated homelands, and most suffered ill health and deep psychological scars. Their number, estimated at seven million, presented serious problems to the Allied occupying forces at the end of the war (see Chapter 12).

HIMMLER'S EMPIRE

The SS was Hitler's elite political army. Since no equivalent force exists in this country, it is not possible to compare it to anything familiar to Americans. In its discipline, the SS imitated the military; in ideology, it was trained to follow the Fuehrer with fanatical loyalty. Depending on the specialty of the unit, the SS was empowered to act as police, as judge, jury, and executioner, as spy and counterspy, as future Aryan settlers in the eastern *Lebensraum* conquests, as enforcers of political correctness, and as liquidators of all people deemed unworthy of life. The man who built this powerful force was Heinrich Himmler. He derived his authority directly from Hitler, but no clear table of organization connected the *treue Heinrich* to his own group commanders. Himmler imitated his Fuehrer's formula and gave his subordinates ambiguous, often overlapping, areas of control. As his command doubled and redoubled, the most aggressive of his department chiefs amassed the greatest power. To the sorrow of millions, they competed enthusiastically to impress Himmler with the fierceness of their hunt for supposed enemies of the Reich.

SS stands for *Schutzstaffel,* or Defense Echelon; its black-uniformed troops were also called the Black Order. From the small band of handsome men, Hitler's bodyguards numbering a mere 289 in 1929, Himmler carved out an empire of force and fear. As the circles of SS responsibilities widened, so did the number of collateral organizations. Eventually, all of the Reich's policing power was concentrated in his office of the Reich Security Main Office (RSHA). The parent organization, the general SS, was constantly culled of men to serve in one or another of the spun off groups. One of the early tasks of the SS was to protect the Nazi Party organization. The original function of the SD (*Sicherheitsdienst,* or Security Service) was to ferret out its enemies. These units under Reinhard Heydrich were enlarged until they numbered 100,000 and were responsible for total internal security. Heydrich was a technocrat par excellence. A man without friends, he had been cashiered from the navy for womanizing—an insult he never forgot. His raw ambition and cold-blooded pragmatism were exactly what was needed by the SS. Himmler relied on him to find the practical means to implement his vague visions of an Aryan-dominated Europe. Although Heydrich had no particular hatred for the Jews, this indifference did not diminish his effectiveness in the management of their destruction. A specialist in terror with an insatiable hunger for power, he had the bearing, the blond appearance, and the arrogance of the very model Aryan superman. His meteoric career ended in 1942 when Czech resistance fighters killed him with grenades thrown under his car. Hitler and Himmler reacted to that assassination with a fury that cost 860 Czechs their lives. The entire Czech village of Lidice was destroyed on the unproven charge that the assassins had been sheltered there.

The *Totenkopfverbaende* (Deathshead Units) were SS specialists empowered to guard and administer the concentration camps. The name was derived from the symbol on their uniforms, a human skull. In 1934, Himmler appointed a convicted political terrorist, Theodor Eicke, to the post of inspector of concentration camps. Eicke had served as a commander at Dachau and went about his task with uncompromising hatred for the inmates. He scrapped the pretense that the camps were rehabilitation centers and changed their function to penal institutions. Eicke's directives were clear, brutal, and detailed. For example, he wrote the barbaric rules governing solitary confinement, the method of administering beatings, and instructed his men that pity for the enemy was an emotion unworthy of an SS man.

In 1936, after a successful power struggle with Goering, Himmler acquired control over the regular German police, called Orpo *(Ordnungspolizei).* Its members were uniformed and did such ordinary police work as regulating traffic and patrolling the streets. However, when the need arose, Himmler did not hesitate to simply incorporate entire squads into the SS. The same sort of unwelcome adoption coerced the Equestrian Association into the SS. In fact, Hitler awarded honorary SS command titles to men who had no connection to the SS. Thus, the notion that all of Himmler's men were totally imbued with Nazi ideology is open to question.

The secret state police (*Geheime Staatspolizei,* or Gestapo) had been spun off from the SD and became the Nazis' most powerful tool for apprehending political dissenters. Its very name was whispered with dread. The use of torture in the interrogation of suspects was well known; escape was all but impossible, and appeals from its verdicts were futile. The normal limits of common law or common humanity did not apply to Gestapo operations. A network of informers called *Spitzels* tattled on their neighbors, even minor infractions. Wherever German conquests brought Nazi rule, the Gestapo followed to investigate, sometimes to conduct show trials in its own courts, to imprison, to torture, and to execute. Fear was intentionally fostered as an effective weapon to discourage potential opposition. The Kripo *(Kriminalpolizei),* or criminal police, was also attached to Himmler's security forces. Its units often participated in the annihilation of Jews. Their role in executing the Final Solution was rationalized by a fine legal point: Being a Jew was in itself a crime, and all property owned by Jews was the result of criminal activity; thus the criminal police were rightfully involved in the elimination of Jews.

The *Einsatzgruppen* (Special Mobile Task Forces) played a particularly dreadful role in the *Endloesung,* the Final Solution to the Jewish problem. Himmler's trusted disciple Heydrich selected the shooters from his SD units. Originally used as political counterintelligence in Austria, they followed the armies into Russia. Their mission was the immediate liquidation of the Jews in the occupied provinces. Before the men were dispatched to the East, they received some weeks of indoctrination. They were told that their task would be difficult but essential to the Fuehrer. No further details were revealed. Their numbers never exceeded 3,000, and how so few men were able to murder between 1.5 and 2 million human beings will be discussed in the next chapter.

The largest branch of the SS was the *Waffen SS,* or military arm of the SS. It expanded until it numbered a million men and became the largest of the SS organizations. Hitler was never convinced that the officers of the regular army were completely loyal to him, whereas the *Waffen SS* could be trusted. The early recruits were thoroughly indoctrinated with Nazi ideology and also received the training of regular soldiers. The Allies found them a formidable foe that combined military ability with the fanaticism of the true believer in Hitler's vision. First used in the Russian campaign and later in France, they earned a reputation for courage and loyalty to Hitler. They served under their own officers but were attached to regiments of the regular army. As might be expected, animosity between their units and the *Wehrmacht* was a common problem.

The *Waffen SS* attracted large numbers of so-called non-German Aryans into its ranks. At the end of the war, half of its soldiers were foreigners designated as ethnic or racial Germans and foreign Aryans. As the war dragged on, the requirements of total commitment to Hitler and ideological training were often cut back. Men who hoped for military glory and quick advancement, which was not easily available to them in the regular army, were also drawn to these units. After the war, they may well have regretted that the runic SS symbol had been tattooed in their armpits; it was impossible for them to deny their membership in the SS.

SS Membership and Training

Himmler's armies were fluid, commanders were changed, functions were altered, methods of recruitment and training were adjusted to fit new circumstances, and rival leaders of the various subgroups rose and fell in power. Only Himmler's authority remained intact and unchallenged. Considering his and Hitler's personality, it is reasonable to assume that Himmler agreed with the Fuehrer's final aim concerning the Jews but devised his own approaches and methods of annihilation. To achieve the task of killing so many millions, Himmler was forced to incorporate entire organizations outside the Nazi Party system into his ranks. As a result, the psychological and physical membership qualifications became less stringent. With the caveat that the internal gyrations of the SS cannot be addressed in the limited space of this text, they will be outlined in the following section.

Not until Germany was defeated did the world (and that includes most Germans) discover the full design of the secret realm of the SS. Himmler had adamantly refused to share with anyone, including other Reich ministries, any information about his Black Order. Even the methods used in his training schools, the so-called Adolf Hitler Schools, were wrapped in secrecy. The criteria for enlistment, however, had to be made common knowledge in order to attract the desired types.

It would be comforting to say that the SS was composed of sadists, misfits, and assorted flotsam and jetsam of human society. If that were true, we could separate the rest of us from the killers and be consoled that these were not normal men. But the facts reveal a different truth. Himmler's men, no doubt, included a small percentage of psychological misfits, neurotics, and even psychotics, but it has been estimated that these numbered approximately 5 percent of the total. The great majority were so ordinary, they could be anyone. Researchers have not found any common distinguishing personality traits. Yes, many were very ambitious, eager for advancement and recognition, but such generalizations fit most careerists. The Blackshirts had ordinary families, varied in their educational and economic backgrounds, and came from Protestant as well as Catholic homes. Yes, they had been exposed to propaganda manipulation; yes, they had been taught that a show of mercy was a sign of cowardice; yes, their heads had been filled with grandiose assurances about their sacred mission, but nothing, nothing at all, can explain their willingness to become mass executioners of the innocents.

Essentially, though not completely, the SS was a volunteer organization. The qualifications required for its officers resembled those of the *Wehrmacht.* Among Himmler's most cherished recruits were the sons of the old aristocracy. Their upbringing had accustomed them to taking command and expecting obedience. They carried themselves with the proud bearing, some might say overbearing demeanor, that Himmler demanded and believed the carefully fostered notion that the SS represented Germany's new elite. Among the Black Order's senior officers, more than half came from families whose surnames began with the vaunted aristocratic "von."

The sons of the upper middle class, that is, successful professional, industrial, and business families, also contributed to the SS leader. These young men were not ne'er-do-wells; indeed the number of academic degrees among this group is high. Many were lawyers, some were physicians, and others were economic and technical specialists. Their recruitment often began in the Hitler Youth movement and was based on recommendations from their troop leaders. Many of them were the technocrats who saw career opportunities no other service could offer. In the *Wehrmacht*, family background *and* tradition played an important role in the selection of officer candidates, while the SS promoted all qualified candidates.

Most of the noncommissioned SS volunteers came from the farms. The revival of primogeniture left younger sons of small landowners free to seek their fortune in the prestigious Black Order. If they performed exceptionally well, they might have the opportunity to become officers. The respect, even awe, afforded to the smart black uniform and the secrecy surrounding many of their functions created an aura hard to resist. It was, of course, necessary to meet the physical requirements: a well-proportioned body, Nordic features and coloring, excellent physical condition, and a hard-to-define authoritative bearing. Certificates, such as baptismal and marriage records, had to prove the candidates' Aryan ancestry going back to the year 1800. The future German lords who would colonize the eastern *Lebensraum* must look splendid and act masterful.

An applicant's minimum age was 18. His initial training lasted six months. The rigorous physical demands were equaled by psychological requirements. Rituals were imperative: midnight oath-taking; a mess hall decked out in medieval flags, swords, and daggers; torch-lit parades; and other imagery of a cult. Upon completion of the initial phase, the novice swore personal loyalty to Hitler unto death. Next, he was obliged to fulfill his *Landjahr,* or six months' labor service. At the end of that duty, the hopeful SS recruit owed yet another duty to the state, his military service. If his record in the army was good, he was now ready for his inauguration into the SS brotherhood. In another electrifying ceremony, he swore that he would not marry without the approval of the SS *Reichsfuehrer* Himmler. In other words, his future wife had to pass the racial purity muster, and her appearance was to be judged worthy to bear an SS man's children. As might have been noted, there were no intellectual requirements at all. These were the men who brought European Jewry to the brink of destruction—pushed them into ghettos, shot them, poisoned them, and burned their remains.

Organizing the Shoah

As was noted earlier, the Germans had incorporated three districts in Western Poland into the Reich. Hitler ordered that these newly created *Gaue* of greater Germany were to be cleared of Jews at once. Also, Wartheland, the enlarged territories of the

East Prussian and Silesian provinces and greater Danzig (now Gdansk), was to become *Judenrein* as soon as possible. Himmler gave instructions for the uprooting of hundreds of communities to be completed within three months, a goal that even his best effort could not effect.

The new eastern boundary of Poland, established by the Ribbentrop–Molotov treaty with the Soviet Union, was along the river Bug. The first expulsions from that region consisted of forcing the Jewish families across the river into Soviet territory. The brutality of this action was exemplified by the fate of the Jews of Chelm. Of the 1,800 deportees, 400 survived. Hundreds were gunned down, and many drowned when forced to swim across the Bug. In some areas, Soviet soldiers on the east bank would not permit them to come ashore, causing the hapless victims to run that gauntlet twice.

Six months after the defeat of Poland, 78,000 Polish Jews had been driven eastward. Although their experiences were horrifying, those who made their way to the Russian interior comprised the largest number of Polish Jews to survive the war.

The Deportations

Himmler had charged Heydrich with the overall responsibility of the Jewish problem, and he, in turn, turned to Eichmann to solve the logistics of Jewish deportations. It was decided to use trains instead of trucks because it would be easier to guard them. Each convoy would carry one thousand evacuees. At first they were permitted to bring food for the journey, but that privilege was quickly withdrawn. Short-distance trial runs within Poland prepared the SS staff for the main task, the mass shipment of Jews from Southern, Central, and Western Europe to Hans Frank's General Government. In effect, most Jews experienced two expulsions, first from small Polish towns to the ghettos in larger cities and then from the ghettos to the concentration and death camps.

The forced evacuations carried out during the winter of 1939–1940 served to instruct the Germans on such matters as how to procure the rolling stock from the railway authority, how to set up intermediate camps, and how to coordinate the various authorities involved in the mass exodus. Timetables had to be devised and assembly points selected for further transport. Eichmann found that negotiation with the Ministry of Transport required considerable skill. It was never a simple matter to secure the necessary trains and prevail over contradicting demands of the military. The SS was compelled to pay the railroad for transporting the Jews, and the cost was passed on to the Jewish elders and their communities. The fees were based on the number of "pieces" a train carried; how the "pieces" arrived did not matter. The same charge was paid whether they reached their destination dead or alive.

As early as September 19, 1939, Reinhard Heydrich met with *Wehrmacht* personnel to explain the policy of cleansing Poland of its Jews, its intelligentsia, clergy, and aristocracy. He claimed that such actions were necessary to secure the conquered areas from forming anti-German opposition. With a few exceptions, the army was content to have the rear secured by the SS by whatever methods they wished to use. Heydrich explained that there was to be an end to the amateurish improvisations by the SS. Activities by single or small groups of Nazis, such as beatings, shootings, kidnapping, forced labor, arson, collections of ransom for release of prominent men in the community, public humiliations, and tortures—all such unofficial conduct was to end.

Instead, a unified, properly organized approach was instituted. Since the army hoped to stay aloof—brutality against civilians was bad for morale and discipline—the SS was free to carry out the Fuehrer's wishes.

During the early stages of the deportations, lists of the expellees were prepared, but as their numbers grew, compiling these rosters was often neglected. A great deal of paperwork was required to catalogue the goods and properties the Jews had to leave behind; declared abandoned, they became Reich property. The amount and sort of possessions the deportees could take with them was strictly controlled, and they were searched for forbidden items. It should be noted that while the "passengers" could bring very few of their belongings, they were instructed to take all valuables, such as jewelry.

Eichmann wanted the deportations to progress with a minimum of strain on the SS. The use of deceptive stratagems duped many victims to gather willingly at or near railroad stations. Over and over the Germans assured the Jews that they were about to be resettled further east, that no harm would come to them, that families would be permitted to stay together, and that the early arrivals would be in the best positions to establish their new lives. The local Jewish elders were persuaded to encourage their charges to make their exodus as trouble-free as possible; resistance to German orders would endanger everyone.

Survivors of the Holocaust shudder as they remember their transport to the camps. The trains were made up of freight and cattle cars, and filling the cars was accomplished by violent pushing until every inch was occupied, and there was no room to sit down. The single pail in the corner soon overflowed with human waste. The humiliation of men and women attending to their bodily needs in public was a foretaste of the dehumanization process intentionally designed by the Nazis. People who died on the trains had no space to fall down. There were cases of mothers giving birth in cars so packed they had to squat. Thirst made people delirious, while hunger caused fainting and madness. Worst of all was the overwhelming need for a breath of air. The trains were sealed, and many cars had no ventilation.

Families who had traveled just a few days barely recognized each other when they tumbled from the cars upon arrival. Dirty, disoriented, physically weakened, and trembling with fear for themselves and loved ones, they were often incapable of absorbing the events that had engulfed them so suddenly. Their confusion seemed to infuriate the SS, and they were met with blows and curses. Those who died during the journey were tossed onto the siding by prisoners in striped uniforms, who emptied the cars. The trains became adjuncts to the killing process.

GHETTOS

Why Ghettos?

The German public was never told the truth why the medieval institution of the ghetto was reintroduced. The official explanations ranged from the need to protect the Jews from the wrath of the Poles, to the necessity to prevent the spread of epidemics that the Jews were prone to do, to the convenience of centralizing them in preparation for their permanent resettlement. After the war, the majority of German civilians claimed they may have heard some rumors but actually knew nothing about the ghettos. It is far from clear whether these disclaimers deserve our credence.

The actual purposes for isolating the Jews were not so benign. Ghettos were useful to the Nazis in several ways:

1. The so-called natural attrition of the Jews was accelerated because the Germans controlled the flow of all goods into the ghettos.
2. The confiscation of Jewish assets was facilitated when the owners were no longer on the premises.
3. Ghettoes were sources of concentrated and expendable manpower; workers were "sold" to enterprises serving the German economy.
4. Ghettos made the final disposal of the Jews—whatever form that might take—an easier task.
5. The appointment of Jewish councils of elders, *the Judenraete,* minimized the need for Germans to administer the ghettos.

Besides freeing Nazi personnel for other duties, the *Judenraete* gave the SS a psychological advantage: The confined population was likely to blame their suffering on the elders, on the Jewish police within the ghetto, on the bureaucrat who refused to issue a ration card, or the request for medicines for the sick, or food for the starving, then on the rarely seen Germans. It was better to divert the wrath of the thousands away from the few SS and direct it toward their own people.

Establishing Ghettos

As noted earlier, the ghetto was an intermediate step between the Jews expulsion from their homes and the Final Solution. It was Himmler's responsibility to set up ghettos in conquered Poland, mainly in Hans Frank's General Government. The physical separation of Jews from the rest of the population had been underway in Germany, Austria, and Czechoslovakia, before the invasion of Poland. Evictions of Jews from their residences had been legalized by the imaginative stratagem that since Jews were not members of the German people's community, the *Volksgemeinschaft,* they could not be members of the residential community, the *Hausgemeinschaft.* The ejection of Jewish families from their homes and relocation to assigned buildings was the responsibility of the Gestapo.

Walled or fenced ghettos were instituted in Poland but not within the Reich. German Jews, including those who lived in villages or small towns, were allocated specific houses within larger cities. The doors of apartments into which the Jews were forced to move were marked with a star, black print on white paper. In 1942, it was decided that German Jews over six years of age must wear on their chests a six-pointed star, the size of the palm of a hand, with the word JUDE written in black on yellow background. It is difficult to conceive of serious bureaucrats attending meetings to decide on the size of the lettering and the age of the youngest children to be labeled.

Confinement within the Reich was short-lived. Expulsion from the sacred soil of the Fatherland was never in doubt; only the method and timing had to be chosen. Mass deportations from Berlin began in 1941. Shipped in freight cars to the Lodz ghetto, they shared the life and death of its inhabitants. The German example gave the Nazis a model for their actions in the East; these small-scale deportations provided the procedural guidelines and legal rationalizations. In the future, however, the pace of removal would be much faster and number of victims much greater.

The control of the ghetto Jews through their own elders also imitated a model first used within Germany. Traditionally, German Jewry had regulated its own religious, educational, and welfare needs. Under the stress of Nazi attacks, they had formed a centralized umbrella organization, which eventually was known as the RV, the *Reichsvertretung* (the National Representative Agency). Its leader was the renowned Reform Rabbi Leo Baeck, a man with outstanding credentials. He was a scholar, World War I army chaplain, and head of Berlin's Jewish community. We can glimpse his character by his refusal to leave Germany in order to remain at his post. When he was arrested in 1943 and sent to the Theresienstadt concentration camp, he served there as the head of the council of elders. He survived the camp, and until his death in 1956, he continued to play a prominent role in Jewish affairs. Although his stature was extraordinary, his role as chief of the *Judenrat* was mirrored in all the ghettos. Rabbi Baeck shared with his Polish counterparts the hopeless task of trying to balance the needs of his people with the increasingly brutal orders of the Nazi masters. His moral courage, his dedication, and his presumption that a Jewish administration was preferable to a German one cannot be doubted. But the results were such that in future grave doubts were raised concerning the role of the *Judenraete*. The SS used them to do their work, and it can be said that they contributed to their own destruction.

The five major ghettos were located in Warsaw, Lodz, Cracow, Lublin, and Lvov. Initially, only Polish Jews were confined, but the process was soon extended to include other nationals. German Jews were added in 1941. During the same year, the conquests in the West expanded Himmler's responsibilities to include France, Holland, Belgium, Denmark, and Norway. All areas were ordered to be made *Judenrein*. Hitler's later campaigns in Southern and Southeastern Europe brought additional trainloads from the Balkan countries and Italy. The great majority of these victims, however, did not interrupt their final journey by a stay in Polish ghettos but went directly to the concentration and death camps.

Reinhard Heydrich, Himmler's most valued adjutant, was an efficient administrator. Even before the Poles surrendered, he began to expel Jews from Western Poland. As a rule, they were given no time to prepare for their final exodus from the villages and small towns where their ancestors had lived for hundreds of years. In some instances, they were permitted 15 minutes to pack some belongings. Those who had relatives in the territories not scheduled for annexation to the Reich were urged to join them. The rest were forced to depart on foot or by train to ghettos in cities designated by the Germans. Usually they were permitted to take one or two suitcases per person. The bulk of their possessions had to be left behind and was immediately confiscated. Goering, personally and as the chief of the Four Year economic plan, was the designated benefactor of this plunder. Because the majority of Polish Jews were poor, the booty was disappointing.

The Star of David attached to the top of this street car indicates it is in use for residents of Warsaw's Ghetto. (Corbis/Bettmann.)

Life in the Ghettos

Why did relatively few of the ghetto inhabitants escape? There are several reasons. Only the young and the strong could attempt such a feat, and many were unwilling to leave their parents and siblings behind. But a greater obstacle to flight was the knowledge that German revenge on their families would be swift and deadly. The SS commander demanded daily reports on the number of inhabitants and counted the workforce within the ghetto regularly. The family and sometimes friends and relatives of the missing individual were held responsible for escape. They were executed at once. Furthermore, if someone had been able to get over the wall or through the fence, then what? Once on the Gentile side, one needed papers, food, and money. Only with the aid of friends could an escapee hope to survive. Denunciations of Jews to the Nazis were a constant danger. To hide or help a fleeing Jew was also a matter of life and death; a good Samaritan risked his own life and that of his family as well.

Ghetto inhabitants were totally dependent on supplies from the outside. Food and water, electricity and waste disposal, medicines and telephones, postal service, even cemetery space were supplied or withheld at whim by the Germans. The dimensions of the ghettos, the number of blocks, houses, and available rooms, were decided by SS decree. Frequent reductions in the size of the ghettos created overcrowding. Occupancy of seven persons per room was common. The situation was exacerbated by the continuous influx of new refugees from all over Europe. The death rate from starvation was in direct proportion to the insufficient food rations and lack of medical supplies. No matter how well-meaning the *Judenrat* administrators, nothing could change the fact that the fate of the Jews was in the hands of their enemies.

Several factors influenced life and death in more than 20 ghettos. Geographic location was important; the presence or absence of swamps, woods, and nearby villages related directly to the feasibility of escape. The rivalry between the SS and the military commander in the region could work for or against the survival of the Jews. The military commanders usually demanded workers for the manufacture of war materiel and their influence on the SS could shorten or prolong survival within the walls. Always of immediate impact on the degree of misery were two other variables, namely, the personality of the Nazi commander and the makeup of the specific *Judenrat.*

At one extreme were the deluded Jewish leaders with messianic complexes, who claimed that God had willed them to save their communities. At the opposite end were the ghettos, which were organized to represent, as much as circumstances permitted, the will of the majority of its inhabitants. Some of the elders knew or guessed that their labors mattered little and all would soon be dead no matter what their efforts to appease the Germans. Ghetto elders ran the entire gamut, from weakness to heroism, from practicality to flights of fancy, and from humanitarian to selfish concerns. Perhaps the most common complaint against the leadership was favoritism. Council members often were able to spare their own families and friends some particular degradation, provide them with better quarters, perhaps allot them an extra ration, save them from the heaviest labor, or delay their boarding the train that eventually took them all to no man's land. The bitterness engendered by unfair practices of Jews toward other Jews ranged from fury to resignation.

The traditional respect for one's elders confounded many of the young Jews, whose efforts to organize for resistance and revolt directly opposed the hope of the *Judenraete* that obedience and compliance would save lives.

Despite the differences among ghettos, a number of similar characteristics were discernible. The German policy of holding many people, even the entire community responsible for the actions of individuals, proved to be very effective. For example, a child went over the wall to try to get some food on the other side. He was caught by the guards and now his entire family, or perhaps all the people living in his house or the entire street on which it was located, was found guilty. The SS regarded death as the fitting penalty for nearly all infractions. Fear of the wrath of collective guilt and collective punishment enabled the Germans to maintain control with few SS men until it became clear to their prisoners that they were doomed no matter what they did.

Ghetto Jews were subjected to curfews; all were compelled to wear identifying markings, a star on an armband or pinned to the chest or back. All men and women were obliged to report for forced labor in accordance with the quotas set by the Germans each day. Every ghetto was overcrowded and, inevitably, prone to the spread of communicable diseases. Typhus was the most recurrent plague, but various illnesses induced by malnutrition and poor sanitation decimated the population. The greatest suffering was caused by hunger. Each month starvation killed an increasing number of people. Children and the elderly died first, but lack of food felled even the once strong and hale. In winter, the shortage of fuel contributed to death by hypothermia; people froze in their beds, in the street, and at the workplace.

Terror permeated the air of the ghetto. A Jew could be shot or beaten to death by a German without any cause whatever, and the killer went about his business without fear of any rebuke from his superiors. No one knew with certainty what the Nazis planned to do, and rumors substituted for information. Each day created another cycle of hope and despair: Jews with skills could work and live; no, the SS was enraged at *Wehrmacht* interference and for spite would kill everyone; resettlement in the East would begin soon; no, a fiery death awaited those who left the ghetto; the war was going badly for the Germans and the Jews would be liberated; oh, no, defeat at the front would merely incite the SS to further outrages. In this atmosphere, every emotion, envy, selfishness, and animosity as well as generosity, sacrifice, and altruism, was magnified. There were quarrels about food, water, and coal, about medicines, and about the best place to wait in line at the soup kitchens. Endless discussions concerning the value of work permits and the price of anything available on the black market occupied the idle hours. The wildest rumors found acceptance as people were desperate to get through just one more day.

The heroism of the children in the ghettos must be recalled; they added significantly to the food supply. Even little ones, as young as five years old, managed to get to the Gentile side. They brought back vegetables bought or foraged from Polish farmers. Some German guards opted not to see or hear these nightly shadows; others beat them terribly or shot them for a couple of beets or potatoes.

FUNCTIONS OF THE *JUDENRAETE*

For as long as possible, and that meant four years at most, the councils of elders attempted to give ghetto life a semblance of normalcy. Bureaucracies were established to provide for schools, hospitals, and orphanages. Officials in charge of sanitation faced the impossible task of preventing human waste from causing deadly contamination. Fire brigades were organized to keep the slum dwellings from burning to the ground. During the early months, when it was still possible to receive packages or money (mainly from American Jewish institutions), the *Raete* confiscated these donations and then distributed the contents to the most needy in the ghetto. The elders were forced to tax everything imaginable to raise the money required to carry out their functions. In ghettos where the Germans permitted the production of goods needed by their army, a small portion of their value might be made available to the councils.

A Jewish police force kept public order and was used to carry out the most hateful of German commands. They lined up the columns of slave laborers who worked in various installations outside the wall; they met the incoming trains and pushed the new arrivals into the worst housing; and during the final stages of ghetto existence, they forced the victims into the cattle cars leaving for the death camps. Survivors have testified that the ghetto police usually attracted the worst elements in a community. Their brutality earned them a loathing that often exceeded hatred for the Germans.

Men and women hoped to get factory work; their survival rates were higher compared with those digging antitank ditches and carrying rocks to repair roads. Holding a work permit usually entitled the bearer to larger food rations; thus that blue or pink piece of paper provided the worker with a chance of survival. The hope that those who contributed to the German war effort would be allowed to live lingered on until the dissolution of the ghettos. But there was never enough work, particularly when the SS forbade laborers to leave the ghetto. Without a source of supplies from the outside, no large-scale manufacturing was possible. Those who still had something to sell stood on street corners, hoping for buyers. The greatest demand was for food, followed by the need for warm clothing and heating materials. After the Nazis requisitioned furs, woolens, leather goods, and bedding, the harsh Polish winters continued to cause acute suffering. Even when the

Jews in front of a well in the Ghetto of Lublin. (AP Wide World Photos.)

Judenraete made an effort to parcel out available supplies with fairness, there was never enough and cries of partiality were inevitable. Eventually, the councils established soup kitchens to feed their starving people.

The population within the ghettos changed constantly because of decimation by deaths and increases due to the arrival of non-Polish Jews. The newcomers were not always gracefully accepted. When the ghettos were first established, there were considerable differences in the economic standing of the population. In the end, nearly all were paupers, although a gap between the "haves" and the "have-nots" remained. When the Nazis decided to reduce the number of Jews by starvation, those families that had been able to hide something of value found a flourishing black market where a pearl might buy a piece of smuggled horse meat.

The councils as well as individual ghetto dwellers made every attempt to imitate the world that had been left behind. Although suicide rates increased, and some people were driven to insanity by the sight of unburied bodies in the streets, by the pleas of beggars in rags and of children too weak to cry, the great majority fought to retain their humanity. They sought and found solace through participation in a variety of cultural and religious activities. Actors performed in makeshift theaters; political parties continued to argue about Zionist, socialist, and other issues; debating societies disputed philosophy and religion; and musicians gathered to play and sing for their own pleasure and that of others. The devout prayed to God and asked for his merciful intervention. Although the Germans forbade the establishment of schools, many teachers gathered pupils in their rooms and hoped to give the children some hours of normalcy. Newspapers were secretly authored, copied, and avidly read. Books had never been more precious. Men, women, and children kept diaries to bear witness to their suffering. In prose, poetry, and with pictures, they described what they saw and felt and hoped that the world would remember them. Some of their manuscripts and a number of drawings and photographs survived the liquidation of the ghettos and allow us to marvel at the vigor of the intellectual energy of ghetto life. Indeed, many of the "people of the book" were sustained by their ancient heritage until death overtook them.

THE LODZ GHETTO: A CASE IN POINT

In 1941 the process of confining Polish Jewry in ghettos was well underway, and in August of 1944, the last major ghetto, Lodz—which had been the first, was emptied. At the Wannsee Conference of January 20, 1942, the Nazi hierarchy in charge of the Jewish question had confirmed an earlier decision to solve the Jewish question through mass murder. The fact that most of European Jewry was already concentrated in ghettos simplified the execution of the final step. The Jews themselves provided much of the required paperwork as well as the personnel to collect the victims and load the trains. The period of ghettoization was brief, but it was important as a link to the Final Solution. It is estimated that one-fifth of Polish Jewry died as a result of ghetto conditions before the Final Solution was implemented. The fact that so many of the victims were already assembled in Poland, site of the death camps, allowed the *Endloesung* to proceed with momentous speed.

The city of Lodz in Southwestern Poland illustrates the life and death of a Nazi ghetto. The chief of the council of elders was named Mordekhai Chaim Rumkowski. He was a childless widower, formerly the director of an orphanage. One can sum up his dictatorial administration as well-intentioned at best, self-serving at worst, and bizarre for sure. He may have developed megalomania, for he was certain only he could save "his" Jews. His eagerness to lead the community during the trauma of Nazi occupation was explicable only in terms of his faith in his mission: God had appointed him to do His work. The original members of his council who might have been unwilling to accept his authoritarian style had been murdered following a summons by the Germans. Thereafter, the council was composed of men who had no previous standing in the community and were unable to curb Rumkowski's excesses.

The Lodz ghetto existed for four years and four months, longer than any other. It was sealed off in April 1940, and its 160,000 people endured the same misery of starvation, illness, and helpless anxiety suffered by all the other ghetto Jews. Compared with others, however, Lodz had several, albeit temporary, advantages. The enclosed area contained some farmland, where a little food could be grown; the overcrowding reached 5.8 persons per room, not over seven as in other ghettos. Rumkowski preached the doctrine that hard work for the Germans would keep the Jews alive. That shred of hope was as vital as food, until, in the end, the truth of their impending death could no longer be denied.

Surely Rumkowski realized the impossibility of serving two contradictory purposes: saving his people on the one hand and obeying the Germans who planned to kill them on the other. His authority was always a gift from his Nazi masters, to be granted or withdrawn at will. The SS chief charged with the supervision of the Lodz ghetto was named Hans Biebow. It suited his objectives to have a strong administration within the ghetto, to have one man responsible for carrying out his orders. Biebow and the SS profited from the manufacturing carried on in the ghetto, where men and women produced clothing at a feverish pace. He wanted calm and orderliness and never even hinted at the eventual dissolution of the ghetto.

Rumkowski, the "king of the Lodz Jews," had almost no previous organizational experience, yet he managed ghetto life with ruthlessness and skill. He not only developed police, welfare, hospital, judicial, educational, and religious departments but also turned the ghetto into a giant workshop. Among the Jews of Lodz were a large number of skilled workers, many of whom had been involved in the once flourishing textile industry of the region. There were also cabinet makers, tailors, shoemakers, tinsmiths, and other proficient artisans. Food rations and work production were linked, and Rumkowski permitted no interference with his design: Work and we shall live. He issued ghetto money imprinted with his picture, wrote orders above his personal seal. He appeared at public functions with his retinue and bestowed regal favors upon petitioners. Many of the Lodz workforce had been unionized and continued to identify with their associations. When they organized a strike in order to win some concessions to ease their terrible working conditions, Rumkowski refused to back down. He brooked no tampering with his authority, and hunger drove the workers back to their 10-hour workdays at starvation rations.

During the 1941–1942 winter, the ragged thousands were stunned to receive their first order of expulsion. This was merely the beginning; the last such demand came in August of 1944. The Nazis told Rumkowski to have 10,000 men, women, and children ready for "resettlement." At that time, the Jews did not know that this was a death warrant for the gas chambers of Chelmno. Rumkowski decreed that this consignment should be selected from among the "undesirables" of the ghetto residents. In effect, that meant people who had run afoul of his administration (perhaps for the theft of a potato) along with their families. Those who refused to present themselves for deportation received no food rations. If Rumkowski had any illusions that the Germans would be satisfied with one trainload, he learned the truth within a month. Nearly 1,000 Jews per day made the heart-wrenching trip to the rail station. As Germans repeated their demands to reduce the ghetto population, the next group to be pushed out consisted of the people who were unable to do productive work. The unemployed from age 10 and up were shoved into the waiting freight cars. When that category had been exhausted, non-Polish Jews who had been shipped in from other parts of Europe were placed on the death list.

A new order for selections coincided with the arrival of a group of Jews from Wartheland. They knew about the installations of mass murder and removed any doubt that "resettlement" was the euphemism for death. When the Nazis instructed Rumkowski to transport the sick, the 10,000 children under age 10, and all men and women over 65, the terror experienced by the population cannot be described. Now that the truth could no longer be denied, who would be willing to shove the victims into their freight cars? For a promise that their own children would be saved, amid screams and curses of helpless parents and children, the police tried to complete their dreadful task, but Germans, aided by collaborators from the Baltic states and the Ukraine, had to finish the savage roundup.

Rumkowski's authority disappeared along with his Jews. He kept a few of his welfare programs operating and hoped the worst was over. Perhaps he thought he had saved the remnant. During the summer of 1944, some 76,000 Jews continued to work and survive in the Lodz ghetto. But as the German armies retreated across Russia, the total eradication of Poland's second largest ghetto was ordered. The remnant of the men and women who had endured for so long and hoped so fervently to live until Germany's defeat were consigned to die at Auschwitz-Birkenau. Among the last to go was Mordekhai Rumkowski.

THE WARSAW GHETTO: ANOTHER CASE IN POINT

The Warsaw ghetto was the largest. For a time, about a half million Jews from Warsaw, from the surrounding countryside, and from Germany and Austria were imprisoned within its 10-foot-high walls. It was organized in October of 1940, about a year after the defeat of Poland. One month later it was sealed off from the outside world. Five hundred thousand people had been crammed into an area of approximately three and one-half square miles. Only by realizing that between 7 and 13 people lived in every single room of the approximately 1,500 buildings is it possible to comprehend the overcrowding. Whatever the suffering in other ghettos, it was duplicated and intensified in Warsaw. It must also be remembered that the Polish capital had undergone extensive bombardments, and much of it lay in rubble.

As was true in all ghettos, only those who worked as slave laborers were issued food rations. The allotment was so meager, less than 200 calories per day, that only smuggling prevented immediate mass starvation. The Germans did not permit any nutritious foods such as fruits, fresh vegetables, meat, milk, or fish into the ghetto. Packages sent from the outside were confiscated, and safe drinking water was at a premium. Malnutrition made the population susceptible to epidemics, which raged within the city with regularity.

The Warsaw ghetto was under the internal administration of 24 members of a council of elders headed by the widely respected engineer, Adam Czerniakow. His meticulous diary survived the war and gives convincing evidence of his earnest desire to provide a fair administration. He hoped to preserve Jewish lives and act as a buffer between the SS and his people. From the onset, these goals were unattainable. To the Nazis, he was merely a useful instrument of management and who would eventually aid in the genocide. If he hoped that his people would understand his dilemma, he was largely disappointed. He was blamed for every shortage, every cruelty ordered by his masters. The venality of the Jewish policemen who enforced German demands was placed at his door. Occasionally, he stood up to the SS, even winning some minor points; but in reality, he was unable to alter German intentions, not even delay them for a day.

Czerniakow tried to be impartial in the distribution of allotments of food, fuel, and services; but there was never enough, and the afflicted people reproached him angrily. Just as the Nazis predicted, the *Judenrat* was held accountable for the misery of ghetto life. The elders, well aware of the Nazi policy of communal guilt, struggled to keep the Warsaw ghetto calm. They supported various institutions designed to alleviate some of the suffering by sponsoring intellectual, educational, and recreational activities. Clandestine organizations were equally important in easing the stress of such an unnatural existence. Among the self-help activities were attempts to make the ghetto valued and valuable in the eyes of the Nazis. All types of merchandise were in short supply in Poland, and the Jews turned to manufacturing. Ghetto craftsmen literally made something from almost nothing; rags and junk were transformed into useful items. They produced clothing, bed linens, shoes, cutlery, pots and pans, paper, and toys. The vitality necessary to forge such enterprises under such circumstances was in itself a triumph. The workers hoped that the German army would realize that it was to their advantage to authorize ghetto production. For nearly a year, some raw materials flowed through the gates of the wall. During the exchange of goods from the Jewish to the Polish part of Warsaw, it was possible to smuggle in some food. Aside from this quasi-legal trade, an illegal underground system of manufacture and exchange developed. With luck or pluck, by means of black market ventures or corruption, some Jews actually, though only momentarily, became rich. They lived with reckless abandon, ate in ghetto restaurants, and smoked cigarettes in cafes. The gap between these few and the starving masses added to the unbearable tension.

In 1942, Himmler ordered the liquidation of all ghettos; liquidation was the SS euphemism for mass murder. The entire process was to be completed by the end of the year, though it was not done until the summer of 1944. At that time, the Warsaw ghetto imprisoned an estimated 350,000 people. They were among the first to hear the requiem dirge. In July 1942, the Nazis began to demand that the *Judenrat* provide "settlers" for the journey to the East. The death camp Treblinka was the usual destination of the Warsaw Jews. The weak and helpless were the first to be dragged to the *Umschlagplatz,* the place of assembly for the deportees. The SS promised that volunteers for the "resettlement" would find better conditions; they distributed precious rations of bread and jam to those who willingly reported to the train station. When the supply of volunteers ran out, ghetto police forced their fellow Jews into the freight cars. The Warsaw ghetto police force numbered about 1,700 and was under the command of a hated apostate, Jozef Szerynski. His men handled the roundups with brutal competence, with the assurance that their own families would be exempt from deportation. In fact, nearly all of the police and their families were sent to Treblinka in September 1942, on Yom Kippur, the Day of Atonement.

On July 23, 1942, Adam Czerniakow shot himself. He had been asked to hand over the children and could not do it. He knew where the trains were going, and he could do nothing to stop them. The debate, whether he should have used his gun to kill Germans, whether he should have rallied the people into rebellion, is pointless. His note said that he "could no longer bear all this." We do not know, nor can we ever know, his true state of mind when he made his decision. His death changed nothing. The expulsions continued. The Nazis called in auxiliary forces composed of some 800 Ukranians, Lithuanians, and Letts who were eager to participate in the *Aktion.* Polish historian Emanuel Ringelblum, whose chronicles were discovered after the war, recorded events with laconic accuracy: Yesterday so many disappeared, today, so many more. He lamented the fact that the Jews had not offered active resistance when the number of potential fighters was greater. In his estimation, a mere 50 SS men directed the entire evacuation of the ghetto.

One week after the liquidation order was issued, about 65,000 Warsaw Jews had been sent to their deaths. Each train was loaded with a cargo of 7,000 screaming, crying, silent, praying people. Amid the chaos, the march of Korczak's orphans was an unforgettable sight. The internationally renowned educator and pediatrician Janusz Korczak had cared for many foundlings in his orphanage. When he was offered the opportunity to escape, he refused. With two little ones in his arms, he and his staff led their charges, dressed in their Sabbath best, singing and carrying banners, to the *Umschlagplatz.* Even the Germans were stunned. When people refused to leave their rooms, the Germans and their accomplices encircled specific streets, stormed the houses, and drove out the inhabitants. By the end of the summer, 300,000 men, women, and children had been forced out of the ghetto.

The remnant of the Warsaw ghetto population, approximately 65,000, was largely made up of young people who continued to work in several factories. Perhaps because their more cautious elders were no longer among them, the idea of forcibly resisting the Nazis became a movement, a reality, a declaration of war against the murderers of their family and friends. Here, the most significant of the armed struggles between Nazis and Jews was fought. But, inevitably, when the Warsaw ghetto uprising reached its inevitable conclusion, the ghetto was razed, turned into rubble and ashes, and its inhabitants lost to the world (see Chapter 10).

CHAPTER 9

Annihilation: Theory and Practice

Could the Holocaust have happened without Hitler? The debate over the specific role of the Fuehrer in the annihilation of the six million continues. Whatever conclusion historians may reach, it is clear that Hitler's hatred for Jews was central to the policy of their destruction. That one man can command such power over others, that he is able to call to the surface every evil instinct in the minds and souls of his followers, is a terrifying admission. Perhaps psychologists will someday discover why the highest ranked species among the mammals destroys its own kind more savagely than any other. For now—an answer eludes us.

Hitler's compulsion to destroy the Jewish people was transformed from his mind to the reality of genocide by means of a compliant and dutiful bureaucracy, by modern technology, and by echelons of highly disciplined killers. The process required a totalitarian government and a silent or obedient or irresolute population, who believed that they were not responsible for their government's crimes. The abnormalities of war provided the cover, which, at least in part, obscured the truth from the general public of every continent.

The Shoah, so fully and so precisely documented, so enormous in its scope, remains at the center of the study of man's inhumanity to his fellow man. Deniers of the Holocaust are irrational because the documentation available from German sources alone is too concrete, too huge, and too thoroughly scrutinized to leave a shred of doubt. Although the number of six million Jews killed is generally accepted, not all researchers agree on a final total. Probably an exact accounting can never be made, even when all the tons of Third Reich papers have been catalogued. Whether we speak of five and a half or six or six and a half million, such discrepancies have no bearing on the fundamental facts of Holocaust history.

Nazis rounding up Jewish men, women, and children during the destruction of the Jewish Ghetto in Warsaw, 1943. (AP Wide World Photos.)

MOBILE KILLING SQUADS

The original concept of mobile terror units dated back to the annexation of Austria and Czechoslovakia, where they played a minor role in the "pacification" of the region. During and after the Polish conquest, murder squads were used to decimate the Polish elite, and, in a rather haphazard way, kill Jews. In the western theater of operations, namely France, the Low Countries, Denmark, and Norway, the army did not permit SS intrusion, much to Himmler's distress. During the campaign against the Soviet Union, however, he was given nearly complete freedom to conduct waves of organized massacres that have no counterparts in history.

Reinhard Heydrich, Himmler's most valued second in command, had begun to prepare for major *Aktionen* in May 1941. He assembled 3,000 men, picked from every organization under Himmler's authority, and told them that "real men" were needed for a task of special difficulty but of enormous importance. This special duty was to be performed in the East, not a place to which volunteers were likely to flock. No specifics regarding their mission were revealed until after weeks of intensive indoctrination. Even then, references to their actual objectives were oblique, cloaked in euphemisms like "political criminals" requiring "special treatment," "eradication of typhus carriers," and "elimination of the Bolshevik menace."

The official wording of the assignment of the *Einsatzgruppen* was to follow the German army into the Soviet Union and protect its rear from attack by partisans and saboteurs. In actuality, their mission was the slaughter of innocent civilians on a hitherto unprecedented scale. The *Einsatzgruppen* shot between one and a half and two million Jews, as well as many hundreds of thousands of non-Jews within a period of less than two years. Among the Gentile victims, the number of Russian prisoners of war was particularly high. The standard legal cover for these executions was the small hyphen Hitler placed between two words so that they became one: Jew-Bolshevik. All Jews, per se, were indicted as communists; consequently, they were dangerous subversives. Since Jewish children, even the unborn, were genetically destined to become mortal enemies of Germany, they, too, were under a death sentence. When that accusation wore thin, several commanders of the mobile squads told their men that the killings were necessary to prevent typhus, or some other epidemic. These incredible rationalizations seemed to satisfy the perpetual need for a legal cloak for the commission of heinous crimes.

Nearly all the German generals of the regular army accepted the presence of the *Einsatzgruppen* as long as they did not interfere with regular army activities. After the war, the military claimed that it had no hand in the dreadful work of the mobile killing units, but the facts do not bear out those assertions (see Chapter 12). The records show that in some regions there was considerable cooperation between the terror squads and the *Wehrmacht* in rounding up victims, even in the actual shootings. The military, as a matter of policy, turned all captured Jewish prisoners of war over to the SS for immediate execution. When Colonel General Johannes Blaskowitz and Admiral Wilhelm Canaris, the chief of the *Abwehr,* the German military counterintelligence, protested to their superiors in Berlin about the savagery of the SS, they were told not to interject themselves into an area outside their competence.

Common Men with Uncommon Duties

The commanders of the mobile killing squads came from the German middle class. Most were professional men, lawyers, doctors, intellectuals, and even a minister of the Protestant church. The *Einsatzgruppen* were organized into four units: Group A, the largest with 990 men, went north to the Baltic states; B operated in the north-central region of Russia; C worked in the south in the vicinity of Kiev; and D, the smallest with a strength of 500, advanced behind the southernmost German army in the Crimea (see Map 9-1). Each battalion was augmented by auxiliary troops of native Eastern Europeans. Among these were ethnic Germans who lived in Poland; another large contingent came from the Baltic States, with additional men from Romania and the Ukraine. The murder of 60,000 Jews in Odessa, which shocked even the Germans, was the grisly work of Romanians. These volunteers knew exactly what their functions would be when they signed on, and their deliberate, often enthusiastic, participation in these crimes defies rational analysis.

The killing squads were also augmented by several reserve police units, generally composed of men who were too old or too young to be inducted into the general military. Many had joined the Order Police in the hope of avoiding service far from their homes. Their training in police work, however, hardly prepared them for their duties in the Soviet Union. Since Himmler was the chief of all police enforcement, he was empowered to order them to participate in *Aktionen* against civilians. The inexplicable

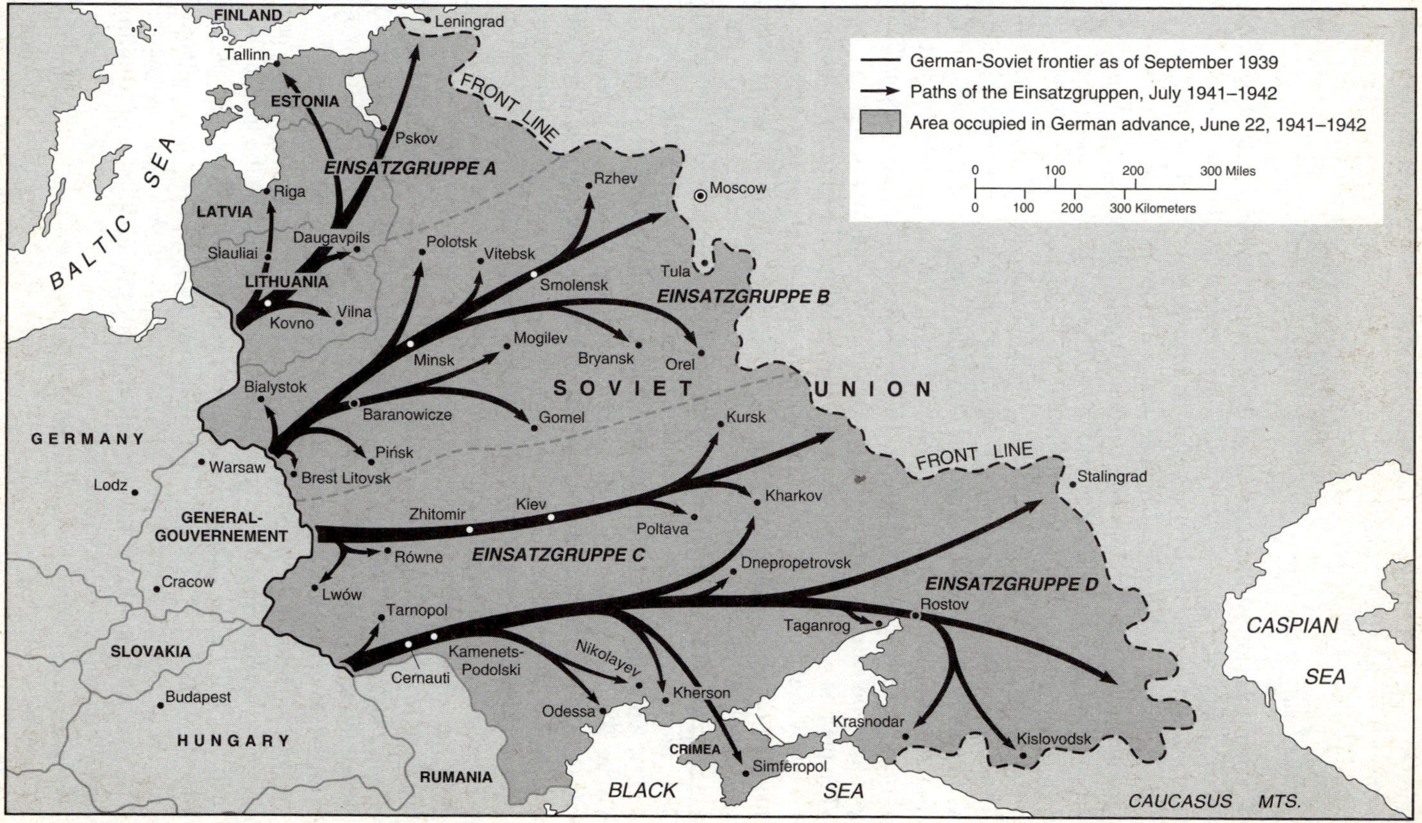

Map 9-1 ***The Einsatzgruppen, 1941–1942.*** (From *The War Against the Jews 1933–1945,* by Lucy S. Davidowicz. Text copyright © 1975 by Lucy S. Davidowicz, maps by Vincent Kotschar, copyright © 1975 by Henry Holt and Co., Inc. Reprinted by permission of Henry Holt and Co., Inc.)

participation of ordinary Germans in such butchery was the topic of an excellent book by Christopher Browning (see the Bibliography).

Bolts from the Blue

As the German invasion in the summer of 1941 penetrated deep into Russia, the people in the conquered regions were totally unprepared for the fate that awaited them. They had no idea that Hitler was poised to wage another war, a war that had no bearing on military combat aimed against many Slavic and all Jewish civilians. Marked for immediate annihilation were communist party functionaries, the political leaders of captured towns and villages, and Jews. The Soviet government had failed to warn its people that this invasion was not to be compared with the Kaiser's in 1914. In fact, some Soviet citizens, particularly Ukrainians who despised Stalin and had suffered under the harshness of his regime, actually welcomed the invading troops as liberators. Even the Jews had no idea what to expect at the hands of the Nazis. But the illusion that the Germans were civilized and would respect the accepted rules of warfare did not last long. The ruthlessness of the invaders and their contempt for the defeated population became evident very quickly.

When the first wave of killers swept into Russia behind the German armies, the Jews were easily deceived. They had no reason to question the Germans who spoke of resettlement, or temporary relocation to move civilians away from the battle zones. The imposing Nazis in their black uniforms, often on horseback, issued orders through the native rabbis and prominent elders, and they were obeyed. When told to assemble in the town square, Jews assembled; instructed to march to the outskirts, they marched; and directed to climb aboard trucks, up they clambered. When the vehicles were filled, some Jews ran after them, hands outstretched, pleading to be lifted on board and join their parents or children. Had anyone told them that they were about to be shot, they would not have believed such an outrageous idea. In many rural areas, the Jews were the only skilled artisans, and was it not a well-known fact that the Germans appreciated good workers? It was impossible to envision the madness of a government that would destroy its assets.

After the first wave of killings, rumors of the mass shootings flew ahead of the *Einsatzgruppen.* The roundup of the victims became more difficult and more brutal. Many Jews, perhaps one and a half million, fled eastward, deeper into the vastness of the Soviet Union, even to Siberia. In the final accounting, they comprised the bulk of Holocaust survivors from Nazi-occupied areas. The Jewish population in the conquered Soviet regions was estimated at three and a half million, which included Jews from Eastern Poland, refugees from the Baltic States, and two million Soviet Jews. Despite the fact that over 40 percent of these intended victims escaped, the numbers killed by the *Einsatzgruppen* were staggering. During the first five months of the operation, it is estimated that half a million men, women, and children were executed.

A second wave of killings was ordered against those who had evaded the first *Aktion.* When this was halted in the fall of 1942, one and a half million had already been shot. It must be remembered that these murders were not the result of bombs delivered from planes high above, or barrages of cannons fired in the heat of battle;

these victims stood naked and helpless in front of their killers who shot them, one by one, by one, by one. . . .

Methods of Murder

Although each commander of the *Einsatzgruppen* performed the executions with his own style, some generalities can be noted. To make the task easier, the victims must remain calm. That required skillful lying to the assembled groups. Often the SS used the local Jewish leaders to convince their neighbors that no harm would come to them. The killing sites, usually facing newly dug ditches, were outside of the towns and villages. Once the victims were loaded into trucks, escape was nearly impossible. Screaming their incessant *"Schnell, schnell"* (quickly, quickly), the killers lined up their prey in assembly line fashion. Some commanders ordered the Jews to kneel in front of their open graves; others shot them standing. A *Gruppen* captain could demand that the Jews hand over their valuables, or he might choose to leave any assets intact until requisitioned by SS economic personnel. None of the killers were permitted to profit in any way from the death of the Jews. All property became the possession of the SS organization. The description that follows is a composite of the testimonies given at the Nuremberg War Crimes Trial and other trials. These accounts were given under oath by survivors and dovetailed with reports from members of the *Einsatzgruppen.* There are also German documents and corroboration from onlookers to attest that the killers usually proceeded in the following sequence:

A Case in Point

After the German army had rolled through a small Russian town, the inhabitants who had fled into nearby woods filtered back to their homes. Even under German occupation, life took on a degree of normalcy since the front had moved eastward. Depending on the region, within days or weeks or months, a new and different enemy suddenly appeared. These Germans were dressed in black, not in the army gray, *Einsatzgruppen.* They fanned across the countryside, often in smaller squads, the *Einsatzkommandos*, which may again be subdivided into *Sonderkommandos* composed of fewer than 50 men. The commanding officer asked for the rabbi or the head of the town's Jewish council. Having no idea what to expect, the community leaders hurried into the presence of the Germans. Depending on his personality, the officer might use a casual manner to soothe the fears of his victims or speak with authority, to make certain that he would be obeyed. All the Jews must assemble at once in the village square. Within 10 minutes, he would conduct a roll call in preparation of their resettlement further away from the scenes of battle. This will be done for your own safety; a mere formality, a temporary measure. Leave everything in your homes and make certain that everyone, even babies, were brought to the town square. Anyone failing to follow orders will be shot.

News of the SS's command spread very quickly. Some of the Jews had heard terrible rumors concerning such roll calls and were frightened. A few of the young people decided to hide despite parental admonition that it was best to comply. They slipped away, hoping to reach some of the partisan groups forming in the woods. The majority suspended their individual judgment and followed the advice of their leaders: Authority must be obeyed. Clusters of families gathered in the marketplace. In minutes, several hundred Jews stood quietly before the Germans.

The black-shirted, black-booted commander appeared. He was on horseback and looked very imposing. He told the Jews that there was a slight change in his plan; he would explain later. Everyone was to go to a hillside a few kilometers outside the town. Groups of 100 must leave every 10 minutes; some of his soldiers would go along. Those who were too weak to walk could go on the truck. The rabbi wanted to ask why this was necessary, but when he stepped forward, the soldiers pointed their guns at him, and he stepped back. While some of the very old, the sick, and the very young were helped onto the truck, the first group left. Gentile neighbors watched them disappear from view. They wondered why the Germans had requisitioned a bulldozer. The noise of its motor could be heard, coming from beyond the hill. What could the Germans be digging?

When the Jewish families arrived at the knoll, they were met by another small squad of SS men, possibly 10 or 20. Their leader shouted at the families to hurry and get undressed. Get undressed? Surely, they did not understand. But when one of the soldiers began to tear the dress and underclothes off one of the women, there could be no doubt. The children were the first to become panic-stricken; some ran about wildly, others clung to their parents. The Germans were shouting, ordering the naked men, women, and children to line up in front of them, on the ridge atop the hill. When several children ran toward the woods, one of the soldiers raised his rifle, and they fell dead. The Jews gasped, the mothers screamed, but the shooter merely reloaded. At that moment, many Jews realized that they were about to be killed. But even though their eyes told them the truth, their brains and hearts could not accept such a verdict. A shocked numbness seemed to roll across the crowd. Many faces lost all expression as they stood naked, with children in their arms, in a row in front of their killers. A beautiful young girl broke away, ran toward the Nazis. In Yiddish, she cried, "Look at me, look at me, I am only sixteen. . . ." She never finished her sentence and fell in a heap. That bullet animated the group. Old men tried to bless their children, mothers clutched their own and other people's babies, wives and husbands attempted one last embrace, and some called upon God to help them. The men from the *Einsatzkommando* cursed and then the whole squad opened fire, and the Jews plunged into the mass grave below.

Some people were shot but not immediately killed. They lay among the dead and dying, trying to climb out of their grave. But a fresh truckload of victims had arrived. They could hear the cries and terrible moans coming from below and quickly understood their fate. That glazed look of disbelief swept across many faces, unable to comprehend an incomprehensible cataclysm. Some of the children and young people recovered their will to live and made for the woods. Rarely was such an escape successful. An old man with a flowing beard refused to take off his underwear. Religious Jews will not appear naked before their children. He was the first to be killed in his group.

The newly dead and wounded fell upon those already in the ditch. There was a horrible clutching and grabbing among the injured to get to the top, to get air to breathe. Blood, so much blood, mixed with the bladder and bowel contents of the dead and dying. The ditch was heaving with bodies pushing and pulling. And the bodies kept piling up. Only a few, very few, escaped from such mass graves. Even if a victim had the strength to climb out of the pit, it required extraordinary survival instincts to hide when the Nazis brought back the bulldozers to cover up their gruesome work.

The Killers

No matter how thoroughly the brains of the killers had been washed, like Lady Macbeth's damned spot, it was never enough. Their officers repeatedly reminded them that they were instruments in a great historic mission, but the words could not cancel the deeds. These were men with families; how could they separate their own cherished children from the ones they tossed into mass graves, some dead, some still living? Could they accept the burdens of savagery that Himmler placed upon them and remain sane? Even with an unlimited liquor supply at their disposal, could they ever return to a society in which murder is a punishable crime? One also has to wonder why so few of the men requested other duties. Such transfers were possible without penalty. Was fear of reassignment to the dreaded Russian front an overriding concern? Perhaps the sense of accountability blurs after 10, or a 100, or a 1000 murders.

Himmler was aware of the problem, and he was concerned. He toured the quarters of the *Einsatzgruppen* often and tried to lift the morale of his men. He told them that he knew that theirs was a heavy task and somehow they must "overcome themselves." Did he mean that they must suspend their humanness? Their feelings of pity and morality? Even their ordinary intelligence? After all, how great a menace were the Jews? It was known that not a single member of any mobile unit was killed by a Jew. In August 1941, Himmler finally witnessed an *Aktion.* It was a small massacre, merely 200 Jews. The commander of the squad noted that Himmler was extremely nervous when the executions began. By the time they were over, the chief of the SS was near collapse. He gathered himself enough to make one of his speeches, but the men had seen his reaction. The officer of the unit told Himmler that his men were finished as normal members of society. "What kind of fellows are we training here? Either neurotics or savages!"

A better, faster method for killing Jews was urgently needed. The gas chambers were the result of the search to spare emotional anguish, not of those about to be killed, but of the killers.

THE WANNSEE DECISION

This infamous meeting took place on January 20, 1942, in a lovely lakeside villa outside of Berlin. Six months earlier Goering had ordered Reinhard Heydrich, the chief of the SD, the Security Forces, to consult with various members of the government and devise a comprehensive plan to solve the Jewish problem. Invitations to the meeting had been accepted by 15 officials who had an interest in the outcome of the deliberation. They included delegates from the Eastern Occupied Territories, from the Department of Justice, from the Four Year Economic Plan, from several agencies involved with the occupation of Poland, as well as from an undersecretary of the Foreign Office and some from the Ministry of the Interior. The SS was represented by a general and, of course, by Heydrich and Eichmann, both experts on the Jewish question.

The stated purpose of the gathering was to discuss the fate of the Jews, but there was little discussion. Actually, the annihilation was already under way, but it had not yet been given official sanction. No matter what crimes the Nazis committed, they sought an official policy statement to legitimize their conduct. The delegates quickly learned that Himmler's SS was in charge of the Jewish question; a fact established by Heydrich in his opening statement. Eichmann took the Minutes which have survived and reveal that the group merely sanctioned a policy already under way. As noted above, mobile murder squads, the *Einsatzgruppen,* had followed the German armies into the Soviet Union and were systematically shooting hundreds of thousands of Jews.

Seven of the fifteen delegates attending the Wannsee meeting were academics who held doctoral degrees. They adapted the euphemism *Endloesung,* Final Solution, to refer to the annihilation of all Jews within the grasp of the Germans. But Chairman Heydrich did not confine his plans to the regions already occupied. He distributed a chart that enumerated the final total of intended victims. According to his data, 11 million were left in Europe, a miscalculation of approximately two million. His number included the Jews of neutral nations, Turkey, Switzerland, Sweden, Spain, and as yet undefeated England in his projection.

There was some discussion concerning the logistics of transporting so many people from one end of the continent to the other. The fate of the *Mischlinge,* the children of mixed marriages, engendered a longer debate than the projected murder of 11 million people, but no solution was reached concerning their fate.

Heydrich reviewed the various measures that had been tried but failed to make German-dominated territories *Judenrein.* He informed the conferees that the Fuehrer had authorized the evacuation of all Jews to Poland, where they would be used as slave laborers. With barely concealed double talk, he stated that it was expected that many would die of natural causes. In the event that the survivors should attempt to rebuild their lives, they would be dealt with subsequently. Decades later, when Eichmann was tried for his crimes in Jerusalem in 1962, he testified that the men sitting around the table at Wannsee openly discussed various methods of murdering the Jews. No doubt, the assembled delegates knew the true meaning of the Final Solution and agreed to make it the official policy of the German government. Not one of the officials rose from his chair to ask: "Why? Why are we condemning millions of Jews to die? Aside from the moral implications, how do these deaths benefit our country?" After some 90 minutes, the meeting adjourned for an excellent lunch.

Postwar Germany turned the lovely villa overlooking the expanse of the Wannsee into a museum that memorializes the Conference. This is significant not only because it is uncommon for a nation to display its past ignominy to the world, but also because the many documents exhibited there deny every presumption of the Holocaust deniers.

SOME GERMAN REACTIONS

Some of the German witnesses to the killings were revolted by the savagery of the SS. The disgust stemmed from two sources. First, the murder of Jewish craftsmen ruined the very industries from which the German war effort could have benefited. The army, in need of everything from winter clothing to bullets, tried, and in the long run failed, to prevent the destruction of needed manpower. This was particularly urgent in the textile industry, which was dependent on Jewish craftsmen. Second, such massacres could not be kept secret. Even the special squads combing the sites of the killings, digging up the bodies, burning them, and using special bone crushers to disguise the evidence could not erase the crimes. There had been onlookers who whispered about the sights they had seen. And was it reasonable to expect that all the killers would go to their own graves without revealing their past? What reaction could they expect, from their families, from the world outside Germany? A case in point was *Gauleiter* Wilhelm Kube, the political head of the occupied territory of White Russia (Ruthenia). Like many other dedicated Nazis, he despised the Jews but disapproved violently of the SS and its atrocities. He was furious that the *Einsatzgruppen* destroyed his workforce and shamed the name of Germans. Furthermore, they crisscrossed his domain without consulting him. In the strange world of Nazism, *Gauleiter* Kube, the anti-Semite, worked hard to save Jews. When he heard of planned shootings, he warned the potential victims; he protested to his superiors and found a sympathetic ear in the *Reichskommissar* for the *Ostland,* Heinrich Lohse. Not only were the SS inflicting unnecessary savagery upon the Jews, the mass killings of ordinary Russian peasants were equally self-destructive for the orderly governing of Soviet lands. Kube had become a thorn in Himmler's side, and while the *Reichsfuehrer* was considering ways to neutralize him, Soviet partisans solved his problem. In September of 1943, Kube's maid placed a lethal bomb under his bed. Himmler was delighted and called the assassination a blessing.

The use of the mobile killing units was coming to an end in any case. Himmler decided that gas would replace precious bullets, and a more impersonal method of ridding Europe of its Jews would cause less trauma for his SS. Furthermore, it was not possible to restrict the number of witnesses when the executions took place in the open. It was time to move the killings from the eyes of the public.

THE GAS VAN EXPERIMENT

The *Einsatzgruppen* had trapped the Jews where they lived; the next procedure reversed the arrangement, and the victims were transported to the killing centers. Midway between these methods was a third course of action, a transitional one, using diesel-powered gas vans. This practice was relatively brief because it failed in two important respects: The numbers killed were too small compared to the effort expended, and it did not alleviate the distress of the executioners.

The diesel vans were introduced in Chelmno, a camp the Nazis had established north of Lodz. An old, isolated mansion had been converted into an execution site. Its commander started out with three vehicles, which were specially equipped to asphyxiate the Jews of Lodz. Always reluctant to let anything of potential value escape them, the prisoners were told to undress because it was necessary to disinfect them to prevent the outbreak of infectious diseases. No need to get upset; this was a matter of hygiene. The naked Jews were ordered to board the vans that supposedly would take them to the delousing quarters. Actually their clothing was stored for possible use by Germans, although at the end of the war, mountains of garments had accumulated.

Fifty or more men, women, and children climbed into each vehicle. They had no inkling that a hose had been attached to the exhaust pipe so that the deadly carbon monoxide fumes emptied into the sealed interior. If all went according to plan, it took 15 minutes to poison a "cargo." Then the driver stopped near a pit, where a group of Jewish prisoners emptied the van. They removed any valuables not discovered earlier and covered the corpses with earth. Only the promise that their lives would be spared could induce some Jews into a *Sonderkommando,* the ghastly special work detail. The bodies they handled were covered with bodily discharges, horribly distorted by the gas, and yet strangely flexible, as if still alive. The Nazis, of course, did not keep their word; sooner or later the members of the special work units joined the other corpses in the pit.

At the height of their use, some 30 gas vans were in operation, but their utility was problematic. The locked-in victims realized what was happening and screamed, banged on the doors, pleaded, and caused the drivers great discomfort. Sometimes it took longer than the prescribed quarter hour to complete the process. Also, gasoline was in short supply and needed for military purposes. And finally, with so many Jews to be killed, 50 or 60 at a time was simply too slow. At that rate it could take years to finish the process of annihilation.

FACTORIES OF DEATH

The solution to Himmler's problem of how to expedite the Final Solution was found in the expertise of Criminal Police Inspector Christian Wirth. Since the abandonment of the so-called euthanasia killings in Germany, Wirth was at loose ends. He had been responsible for the installation of the ostensible bathhouses in which "undesirables," handicapped Germans, had been murdered by carbon monoxide. Himmler commissioned Wirth to oversee the construction of gas chambers in most of the killing centers in Poland. But the Wirth method, which used carbon monoxide gas from fixed diesel engines, was often inefficient. A vermin-killing poison, hydrogen cyanide, patented by IG Farben and known as Zyklon B, created fumes that were more effective. The blue crystals killed more quickly and were easily dispensed from the roof into openings in the ceilings above the deadly shower rooms. Contact between the SS and their victims was thus reduced to be minimal, and Himmler's men would be spared the trauma associated with earlier methods.

The "production quotas" at the death camps of Chelmno, Belzec, Sobibor, Majdanek, Treblinka, and Auschwitz–Birkenau were measured in the numbers put to death. In the language of the reports submitted to SS headquarters in Berlin, certain criminals had received "special treatment." In a monstrous imitation of the world of ordinary manufacturers, there was competition among the death factories to see which facility could produce the highest number per day. Auschwitz–Birkenau, the largest of the facilities, could kill 12,000 prisoners a day; a record achievement no other camp commander could challenge. But then, no other facility could accommodate 2,000 victims at one time and kill them in 15 minutes or less. Indeed, the name Auschwitz well deserves to be a symbol of the Holocaust.

When the equipment was ready, the ghettos were emptied and trains from Nazi-occupied Europe began to roll toward the Polish countryside. Himmler had found in SS Major-General Odilo Globocnik, chief of the police of occupied Lublin, the right instrument to oversee all the death camps. Odilo supervised the construction of four of the six death camps, Belzec, Majdanek, Sobibor, and Treblinka; only Auschwitz–Birkenau and Chelmno were not his work.

In the strange world of Nazi bookkeeping, the names of the prisoners who went directly to their deaths were not recorded, but detailed files were kept on the concentration and slave labor camp inmates. Documentation from the fees the German railroad received for transporting Jews to the death camps as well as other sources allow an approximate count of the victims whose names were not registered. Present research suggests the following numbers and killing sites:

Chelmno	152,000
Belzec	600,000
Sobibor	250,000
Treblinka	70,000
Majdanek	125,000
Auschwitz–Birkenau	2,000,000
	3,197,000

The number given for Auschwitz–Birkenau is a minimal figure; other estimates that include non-Jewish victims range as high as four million. In the judgment of some historians, the total of Jewish victims for all of the death factories was approximately four million. The victims of the *Einsatzgruppen* and additional hundreds of thousands killed in the ghettos, in concentration and slave labor camps, on the trains, and during death marches result in the aggregate assessment of six million.

In the minds of many students of the Holocaust, the words "concentration camp" evoke a single image, namely Auschwitz. Because it was the largest camp and its killing center, Birkenau, was a part of the complex installation, such a metaphor is understandable, but it is also misleading. The Nazi commissioned several types of camps to suit differing needs. The transit or internment camps, such as Westerbork in Holland, Drancy in France, and Malines in Belgium, were assemblage points from which detainees were moved eastward. Theresienstadt located in the Czech Protectorate was called a ghetto but was also used as a transit facility for the shipment of Jews to death camps. The numerous slave labor camps and their even more numerous satellites dotted the Nazi-occupied landscape like hundreds of pustules. Mauthausen in Austria was one of the worst of these; Neuengamme and Stutthof in Northern Germany were other examples. Ravensbrueck, also in Northern Germany, imprisoned mostly Christian women, many from France and Poland, and only during the last few months were

Jewish women pushed into its overcrowded barracks. Ordinary concentration camps, if one may use that term, were detention compounds in which prisoners languished for indeterminate periods of time. From there they might be transferred to work sites or to death factories. Dachau, Bergen-Belsen, and Buchenwald, all in Germany, fit into this category. Often the functions of camps changed and overlapped. The Auschwitz network, for example, was utilized as a slave labor facility; its death chambers had the largest capacity, and many prisoners were transferred to other facilities. Because all camps had high death rates, it could be said that all were accessories to the annihilation process. (*The Macmillan Atlas of the Holocaust* by Martin Gilbert contains excellent maps on the geography of the Holocaust.)

GAS CHAMBERS

Christian Wirth, who had been in charge of Hitler's "euthanasia" killings, supervised the installation of the first gas chambers at Belzec. This camp was located on the railway line between Lublin and Lvov, and considerable effort was made to conceal the true purpose of the structure. Signs, such as THIS WAY TO THE DISINFECTION ROOM, and arrows, pointing TO THE SHOWER BATH, were designed to prevent panic. The diesel engine that fed the gas into a sealed chamber was activated as soon as the prisoners were locked in. Roughly 30 minutes later, the "special treatment" had been administered. Thus, mass murder had been made easier for the killers, as direct contact with the victims was minimal.

The men of the special *Totenkopfverbaende,* the SS Deathshead Formations, who constituted the concentration camps' guard units, found it reassuring to regard themselves as good civil servants. Himmler visited often to tell them so; they were merely following orders and doing a very difficult but necessary job of destroying a dangerous pestilence. The guards at Chelmno, where many sick Jews were gassed, actually received bonus pay as if they were really killing people with infectious diseases. Although every concentration camp survivor witnessed and/or suffered many incidents of sadistic treatment by guards, the SS's official position discouraged private acts of degenerate behavior. A Nazi Commission of Special Inquiry investigated some of the most flagrant cases of abuse. Two hundred complaints (of course, none from the victims) resulted in convictions for corruption and unauthorized murder. Most infamous among the condemned was Karl Koch, commandant of Buchenwald and Lublin. He was given the death sentence for pursuing private wealth and for indulging his sadistic cravings. In the world of Nazism, only the state had the right to loot, torture, maim, and kill. It is safe to assume that an unknown number of guards who were never indicted would have been judged criminally insane or guilty of heinous crimes in any court of law.

THE MANY FORMS OF DECEPTION

The question "Why did nearly all the condemned Jews go so quietly to their deaths?" is raised in every Holocaust history class. No precise answer can be given, but a response should be attempted.

First, it is necessary to understand the prevailing conservative and paternalistic society of Eastern European Jewry during the first half of the twentieth century. This is a difficult leap into a past wherein the word of the father was unquestioned law. And fathers were unwilling to urge their children to endanger themselves, their family, and the community by disobedience to the Germans. The desire to keep the family together was compelling beyond logic; there was the hope that the ordeals to be endured could be eased by a comforting word, a gesture of love. Permitting one's children to escape the ghetto and face cold, hunger, and an unknown fate without their support terrified most parents. Even so, some children, even babies, were left in the care of Gentiles by desperate mothers and fathers. Most, however, clung to one another until the end. As we will note in the following chapter, when no illusions of survival were left, the young people in several ghettos defied their elders and resisted the Nazis.

Nothing in the history of the last thousand years had prepared Jews to fight for their lives with weapons. As strangers, more or less tolerated by reluctant host countries, they had relied on petitions, on the goodwill of a few friendly officials or kings, and on bribery as a means of survival. The past had taught them to absorb the blows of their enemies because striking back, even in self-defense, resulted in catastrophic retaliation against the entire community. The nightmare of Russian pogroms had not faded from the collective memory. Jewish boys were taught to bring honor to their families by virtue of scholarship, not through physical strength and skill. And always, after each assault, the remnant had rebuilt Jewish life. This had been their formula for survival in the Diaspora.

As we study the Holocaust from a distance of more than 60 years, we find the deliberate murder of people who broke no laws and posed no danger to the Germans very difficult to comprehend. We know the facts, have met survivors, read the admissions of guilt by perpetrators, but still cannot grasp the death factories. How much harder it must have been for the Jews who had lined up in front of the false showers to understand their fate. Human intelligence has limits of comprehension, and the human spirit has limits of endurance. Self-deception or denial of reality relieves the mind of its suffering when all else fails. It was easier to deny the truth about the strange, acrid smell in the air and the meaning of the ashes coming from the chimney than to face the reality of impending death. Some of the victims, so completely and suddenly deprived of every aspect of their former lives, turned into automatons, robots, empty shells, going here, standing there, bereft of their reasoning ability. The tattered ones who had come from starvation-plagued ghettos or other concentration camps resembled the walking dead. Unable to absorb the losses of the past, they could not comprehend the present, and surely it was a blessing that they could not see their future.

The commanders of various death camps devised their own methods of deception to keep their installations running smoothly. In Auschwitz–Birkenau, the arriving trains were met by music from an orchestra; in Treblinka, flowers bloomed at the railway depot, and the SS guards grouped them according to their skills, carpenters here, tailors there, to create the impression that after resettlement they would work in their trades. In the entry of the "showers," prisoners were told to tie their shoes together to prevent later mix-ups and to remember the number of the peg on which they hung their clothing. The women were reassured that their hair would grow back; the shaving of heads was a sanitary measure, lice cause typhus. And mothers were urged to hold their babies close so none would get lost in the confusion.

The Jews complied. What could they have done—these rows of naked men and women, facing the SS with their loaded guns, their dogs, and whips? Had the Germans not proven time and again that disobedience by one would cause the death of many? Who would dare to lift a hand, or try to run away, when the retaliation would be so swift and so terrible and fall on so many? And finally, who among them had the energy of mind and body to resist? Many who knew that death was a certainty had but one wish: Let it be over with; let it end.

Sonderkommandos

All the death camps were located on or near railroad lines. The first arrivals came from Poland and Slovakia, then from Germany, the Low Countries, France, Greece, the Balkans, the Soviet Union, and, finally, Italy and Hungary. The SS was in charge, their numbers augmented by auxiliary troops made up of volunteers from the local population. Jewish prisoners, organized into *Sonderkommandos,* were employed for some of the most repugnant work. When the rail cars were unlocked, a putrid stench escaped from the interior. Depending on the length of the journey, the severity of the crowding, the degree of cold or heat endured, and the number of days spent without food and water, prisoners were in a state of partial or complete shock. They had no idea where they were; the usually windowless cars had not allowed them to see the terrain through which they had passed. Rumors, fear, and often darkness had added to the trauma of the journey.

Those who were able jumped from the train; the others were pushed or beaten into an orderly procession, destined either for work or the gas chambers. Every car had a number of dead propped up among the living. Members of the *Sonderkommandos* hauled them away and then hosed down the filthy wagons. They worked hard and fast, screaming at the prisoners, sometimes hitting them, in order to impress the SS with their usefulness. Some dared to whisper a word of advice to a new arrival: "Don't carry the baby," "Stand up straight," or "Say you know how to sew." They labored because they knew how easily they could be replaced and forced to join the line to the deadly showers. Death camps, as opposed to the slave labor camps, required only small workforces. That meant that nearly all, and in many instances every single person, coming off a train was immediately dispatched to die. Women and children had virtually no chance of surviving death camp selections.

In some death camps, *Sonderkommandos* were replaced frequently; in others, they lived for several months. The Nazis made use of these prisoners before and after the gassing. With German orderliness, barbers shaved the hair of the women, others cleaned and sorted the belongings of the dead, piling up eyeglasses, tons of hair, baby shoes, and crutches. The most fortunate inmates worked in the offices, preparing reams of paperwork and keeping accounts for Himmler's comptrollers in Berlin. The most harrowing duty entailed the handling of corpses. First, the dead had to be removed from the gas chambers, which then had to be cleaned of human waste. Disposal of the corpses, however, could not take place until a final act of robbery and desecration was committed. Members of the *Sonderkommando* were required to pry

Communal grave at the Bergen-Belsen concentration camp. (Corbis/Bettmann.)

open the jaws of the dead and remove any gold from their teeth; others searched for jewels that might have been hidden in any bodily orifices. Depending on the facilities of the camp, the corpses were turned into ashes in the ovens of the crematoria or buried in mass graves or soaked with gasoline and burned in pits.

Most of the camps had cremation facilities as a solution to the problem of disposing of so many hundreds of thousands of bodies. This method was also useful in destroying the evidence of the crimes, an issue that became more important when the Soviet armies began to push back the Germans. During the last few months of the war, a frantic attempt was made to incinerate bodies that earlier had been thrown into mass graves. But time ran out. It took six hours to burn 100 paraffin-soaked bodies. There was never enough gasoline to speed up the process. Advancing Russian troops encountered evidence of heaps of partially burnt bodies as they fought their way westward.

AUSCHWITZ'S ORGANIZATION

Some 160 miles southwest of Warsaw, in a swampy marsh near the German border of upper Silesia, the Nazis established the largest and most complex of their many concentration camps. The demented world of Auschwitz gave full expression to the worst betrayal of humanity found in the annals of history. Because of its size and the completeness of its facilities, this camp merits a closer look. Its name is rightfully placed at the center of the genocide of European Jewry.

The original camp was established in 1940 as a place to imprison a variety of people declared dangerous by the Nazis. The wrought-iron legend over its main gate, *Arbeit macht frei* (Work gives freedom), encapsulated the irony of a place where only death brought freedom. The barbed wire fences were electrified; sentries with machine guns looked down upon the hapless masses day and night. From time to time, shots were fired by members of the SS, simply to raise the level of anxiety by killing a few prisoners. Two hundred dogs trained in tracking and killing were kenneled just behind the SS barracks. Auschwitz was the only camp where prisoners who survived their immediate destruction were branded with a number tattooed inside their left forearm. Even before the addition of the slave labor and death camp facilities, the entire installation was designed to speed the "natural" reduction of prisoners through hunger, cold, disease, terror tactics, and executions.

The Nazis adopted the techniques first established in the older camps such as Dachau, Buchenwald, and Sachsenhausen. To keep SS personnel at a minimum, they used inmates to supervise other inmates. As the camp expanded, a hierarchy of ranks developed among the inmates. The Camp Elders, Block Elders, and Room Orderlies appointed to carry out SS orders greatly reduced the number of Nazis needed to run their prisons. The term "Elders," however, belies the type of inmates who held these posts. The SS preferred non-Jewish convicted criminals, mostly from Germany and some from the conquered countries for these assignments. There were also a number of Jewish Kapos (from the Italian word meaning *head*) in the camps. Since it was their function to maintain rigid discipline, the most vicious among them were apt to be chosen. A Kapo, that is, a prisoner in charge of other prisoners, held the power of life and death over his charges even though the SS could execute him as indifferently as any other inmate. If he struck an inmate and marked his face by the blow, that man would not survive the next selection for the gas chambers. The Kapo's authority to make work assignments was equivalent to deciding if an already weak or ill man would or would not live another day. On the other hand, a choice job in the kitchen or in any enclosed structure extended some inmates' chance of survival. Obviously, many prisoners lived in constant fear and secret rage. Mastering these emotions, however, was vital in a place where an average prisoner remained alive for three months.

Although Jews made up the majority of men and women who died in Auschwitz, many Gentiles, particularly Poles who had run afoul of the Nazis, were among the imprisoned. Also, there were Germans convicted of crimes ranging from robbery to antisocial behavior (such as unwillingness to work); Gypsies, whose fate was not decided for years; pacifists such as Seventh Day Adventists; and homosexuals. After June 1941, Soviet prisoners of war, hundreds of thousands of them, were deliberately starved to death in complete disregard of the international conventions regarding the treatment of POWs. Russian soldiers were the first victims of the Zyklon B gas experiments. Jews began to arrive en masse after the Wannsee Conference, first from nearby Poland and Silesia, later from the entire European continent. The great majority were immediately led to the gassing facilities at Birkenau.

Auschwitz grew constantly between 1941 and 1944 until the map was dotted with names like *Auschwitz I* (the main camp); *Auschwitz II* (the Birkenau killing factory); and *Auschwitz III* (Monowitz, the slave labor camp for Buna, the IG Farben oil and rubber plants). Many other factories, including Siemens-Schuckert and Krupp, clustered nearby. Few Jewish arrivals, about 10 percent of the men, considerably fewer women, and none of the children and older generation, were permitted to live and work. The imprisoned non-Jews fared better and comprised the majority of the slave workers until 1944 when the Hungarian Jews filled their thinning ranks.

CHEAPER THAN SLAVES

The industrial complex at Auschwitz encompassed several square miles. The IG Farben cartel, Germany's largest industrial enterprise, had established an extensive compound, which included the Buna Werke for the manufacture of synthetic rubber, and a coal-based oil refinery. To save the workmen some strength, they were no longer marched the several miles from the main camp, but were housed and fed in barracks near the factories. In fact, they were leased chattels, easily replaced when worn out, for whom the SS received payment. Only toward the end of the war, when the need for workers became acute and the SS Economic and Administrative Department under Oswald Pohl was given authority over the inmates, did conditions improve slightly.

The workday usually started at three or four in the morning and lasted until late evening. In addition to laboring in the factories, quarries, and various road construction projects surrounding the camp, prisoners processed the by-products of death. At the huge storage structures called "Canada" (a place of riches), they counted, cleaned, sorted, and readied for shipment to Germany the enormous quantities of goods left behind by the murdered Jews. The dead were robbed of everything from the ribbon in a child's hair to diamonds sewn into the hem of a coat. Inmate accountants recorded every item, for as the Germans so often said: *"Ordnung muss sein"* (There must be order). Members of the SS took personal advantage of the pool of talent at their disposal. Jewish tailors fashioned suits, coats, and uniforms for the SS and their families; former cobblers made them shoes and fine boots; and jewelers created lovely pieces from the abundant gold and precious stones. During most of Auschwitz's existence, Rudolf Hoess was its commander. Whenever he wanted to impress visiting dignitaries, or amuse himself and his staff, he could count on the availability of talented musicians and actors to brighten their dreary life in the Polish wasteland.

HUNGER

The inmates of Auschwitz had less value than slaves. They cost nothing because the *Judenraete* had paid the price of their transportation to the camp. They were doomed at any rate and could be replaced at will. Inmates were deliberately given starvation rations. Hunger, the sort one cannot even imagine, gnawed at the men and women relentlessly. While there was no general formula for survival in Auschwitz, and while every individual had to find his and her own strength to live another day, their one common memory is hunger. Enduring terror, dehumanization, deprivation of the simplest human sanitary needs and fear for missing

VOICES

Jolie's Soup

When Jolie, a Holocaust survivor, entered my classroom, the students fell silent. She had a presence, a beautiful face and figure, and an elegant style. Her voice was soft. Her audience leaned forward to catch every word. After she had left, I asked the group which of Jolie's wartime recollections made the deepest impression. This was their choice:

In 1944, the Nazis put us on a train bound for Auschwitz. I lived in Hungary, and at age 16, I was lucky that I could ride together with my parents in the same boxcar. When we arrived, guards separated us into two lines. My parents were separated from me. My mother, who looked young for her age, argued with the guard to let her be with me. He kicked her and said "go with the others, you dog," and so we were together. When our heads were shaved and we were herded into a shower, we could still see each other, and fortunately, we were housed in the same bunk. Whatever misery each day brought, hoping that we would see each other at night gave us the strength to live. I was lucky to have my mother with me, which was most unusual.

I was in a work gang that left the camp at dawn and returned at dusk. Our group moved stones from one place to another. My mother worked elsewhere. We were guarded by Germans who were too old to serve in the armed forces. One day, to keep my mind off of my hunger pains, I hummed one of Beethoven's sonatas. One of the German guards heard me and said "I recognize that melody; do you play an instrument?" "Yes, the piano," I said. "*Lieber Gott* (dear God)," he said angrily, "You are ruining your hands." My jaw dropped as I stared at him. Of course, my hands were a mess. To my amazement, he brought me some gloves.

At the end of one day, he brought me some real soup, not the watery ersatz we were usually fed. I hid it under my blouse and brought it to my mother. "Mama, the guard gave me this soup; it's for you." I said. "I'm not hungry my love," she whispered. I was so proud to offer her this sustenance, and was crushed by her refusal. We argued back and forth about who should eat it. We decided to eat it together, each dipping into the precious soup. I took tiny sips, determined to give mama the best of it but she saw what I was doing and became angry. She threatened to spill the soup on the ground and then said "I will feed you and you will feed me." I agreed and so we fed one another, filling each spoon with all it could hold.

Risking his life, the German guard brought me food occasionally, which helped sustain us until we were liberated.

When Jolie finished, the room fell silent until one student asked "Don't you hate the Germans?"

"We each have the capacity for hate and the power to make that choice. The German guard who helped save me had a choice. I hate what the Nazis did." she said, "There is a difference."

By permission courtesy of Rolland Zeleny.

loved ones—each prisoner dealt with such suffering in ways unique to his and her personality. But hunger was the universal dimension, the single most unforgettable agony.

A thin soup with a few grams of black bread made from some substitute for grain was the main meal at midday. Mornings and evenings, a liquid called coffee and

Jewish women selected for slave labor in Auschwitz–Birkenau. (Photo by Bernhard Walter; Source: National Archives and Records Administration.)

another piece of bread were doled out. Naturally, a forbidden trade developed. Prisoners who had the energy and will bought and sold any item that could eventually be turned into food. That required access to "Canada," where everything could be obtained, or to the machine shops or any place at all where theft might go unnoticed. A homemade tin cup for a cigarette, a cigarette for a vest, a vest for a piece of chocolate, a piece of chocolate for an apple. . . .

These were the "organizers"; they risked punishment, even death, with their trades and smuggling. Some became experts, bartering item for item, but at the end of the chain was something edible. The "organizers" were akin to the *Prominenten,* the men and their female counterparts who by virtue of their luck and pluck maintained the outward aspects of their humanity. Often they bore low numbers on their arms, indicative of their early arrival and amazingly long survival in the camp. These men shaved, using the precious hot liquid at breakfast and dull knives; the women exchanged a meal for a comb or a toothbrush. They washed their clothes and, without a place to hang them to dry, put them on wet, even in winter. Sooner or later, the SS noticed them and considered them useful. Sometimes they were rewarded with positions of some authority or were permitted to work indoors, or given a Red Cross package. Such gifts were life-giving. Unlike most of the Kapos, the *Prominenten* were generally respected and often helpful to others. They set an example of how to remain civilized in a savage and brutal environment.

Not only the death camps in Poland, but all concentration camps were intended to reduce the number of inmates by "natural" attrition. There was, of course, nothing natural about 500-calorie-a-day diets, lack of proper clothing, long hours of exhausting labor, beatings, or overcrowded barracks, where two or three slept in the space for one. There was nothing natural about the institutionalized dehumanization designed to break their spirit. The SS knew that the will to live was essential to survival, and to speed up the genocide, they routinely did not permit prisoners to wash or use the latrine, and kept them standing at roll call for hours. The inmates were cursed, kicked, and beaten without cause. They were forbidden to raise their eyes in the presence of their tormentors—they must witness all punitive executions. Without names, reduced to numbers, they could not own a scrap of paper or the stub of a pencil. Whatever misery the SS could inflict was aimed at breaking the human spirit that kept the emaciated body alive. In the language of the *Lager* (shortened from *Konzentrationslager*), the male prisoners who had reached the end of their strength were called "Musselmen." It was easy to recognize their empty stares, their uncoordinated movements, and their inability to pick the lice from their bodies. They cowered, unseeing, silent. Perhaps they resembled Muslims kneeling at prayer; no one knows the derivation of "Musselmen." Waiting for death without impatience, without any visible emotion, they were sure to disappear at the next selection for the gas chamber.

THE HUNGARIAN TRAGEDY

Hungary had been a more or less reluctant ally of the Nazi regime in order to fulfill its own goals of aggrandizement. With Hitler's approval, Hungary had expanded its territory at the expense of Slovakia, Romania, and Yugoslavia. Although Hungarian troops were active on the Russian front, Germany found this ally lacking in commitment to the war. The Hungarian government under the regent Miklos Horthy had resisted Nazi pressure to deliver its approximately 800,000 Jews into German captivity. Although restrictions had been placed on the economic life of the Jews, and forced work battalions had been organized, this ancient and renowned Jewish community believed it had weathered the Holocaust; Germany was losing the war, the Nazi nightmare would soon be over.

The situation, however, changed rapidly and tragically in 1944. Internal turmoil had been instigated by the extreme political right and weakened the Horthy government. The dilemma worsened when Hitler suspected that the regent planned to negotiate a separate peace with the advancing Soviet Union. By kidnapping Horthy's son, the regent was forced to cede power to the pro-Nazi Arrow Cross Fascists, who took their orders from Berlin. For all intents and purposes, Hungary became an occupied nation, and the Jews lost their protection.

Beginning in March of 1944, just 11 months before Budapest was captured by the Russian army, the Jews faced the terror of Eichmann. His experienced and well-oiled organization set up ghettos, appointed *Judenraete,* confiscated "abandoned" properties, and set in motion the machinery to transport the Jews. Eichmann had long hoped to get his hands on this, the largest remnant of European Jewry, and with the eager aid of the

Hungarian Fascist Arrow Cross police, the roundups and deportation began almost at once. The first thousands of victims came from the provinces at the periphery of the nation, and the intent was to deport the Jews of Budapest as soon as these regions were *Judenrein.*

Without a shred of doubt, the Germans had lost the war. But the killing of Jews continued without letup. This belated onslaught did not go unnoticed by the international community. The American and British governments and the Pope at long last raised their voices in protest. There was also the promise by the Allies that the Nazis' crimes against civilians would not go unpunished. But despite these efforts, the process of annihilation did not cease. Hungarian Jews were sent to Auschwitz until Himmler ordered the closing of the camp because Soviet armies were nearly at the gates. The confusion of the final battles between the Allies and Germany made it impossible to get the trains the SS so urgently demanded for the Budapest Jews. Eichmann then organized treks to march them north across Austria. This took place in the winter of 1944–1945, and the loss of life was enormous. Mauthausen concentration camp was made an interim destination, but by the end of the war, Hungarian survivors were found in many German camps. Even when the Russians were in the suburbs of the capital, Eichmann's compulsion to destroy Jews never abated. Gas chambers, starvation, freezing, and illness killed thousands of Hungarian Jews every day. Their death toll, so close to the fall of the Third Reich, was a staggering 500,000. Only in the besieged city of Budapest did some 160,000 Jews survive.

SURVIVING A CONCENTRATION CAMP

Not the prisoners, nor the psychiatrists, and certainly not the historians can unravel the mystery of who would live and who would die in Auschwitz and its counterparts. The obstacles that had to be overcome were vast and varied. When the decision was made at the railroad siding upon arrival at a camp, living or dying was a matter of chance. Were any workers needed from this shipment? Did the woman carry a child? Was she pregnant? Did Dr. Mengele or his fellow doctors dislike a face, a body? Did the commander need a violinist for the camp orchestra? Or an electrician? Did the prisoner look older or younger than approximately 40 years? Were any twins on this trainload? Any dwarfs Mengele could use for his "medical" experiments? For such reasons, or no reason, the arm or the riding crop selected arrivals to go to the right or the fatal left.

But what of the inmates who survived the first and many other selections? Their memories and memoirs fill us with awe. Terrorized, emaciated, exhausted drudges, they endured. The SS expected most of their slave workers to die within three months of "natural causes." And yet some of the prisoners, men and women who never cooperated with the murderers, who never did anything to betray their decency, survived; some for the astounding period of five years.

Why? How? Victor Frankl, himself a prisoner and a psychiatrist, author of *Man's Search for Meaning,* believed that survival was connected to the successful search to find meaning to one's suffering. Physical strength, status of health, and erstwhile occupation, all that meant nothing. If a prisoner could discover a reason to endure his suffering, then his mind and body might resist the welcome relief of death. It did not matter what inspired his resistance as long as it filled him with a passion to live. Perhaps he or she wanted to see the day of Germany's defeat, or take revenge against a tormentor, or bear witness to what happened here, or track down members of his family who might have escaped, or, because just one more time, he wanted to eat enough to feel satisfied. The voices of many survivors point toward the need to live to fulfill some obligation: "I had to take care of my sister"; "I knew God had a purpose for me"; "If we all died, who would believe this ever happened?"

Recent studies indicated that women imprisoned in concentration camps had a better survival rate than men. Reared in the tradition of nurturers, women created artificial families in their barracks. Small groups, perhaps four or five girls who may have come from the same town or spoke the same dialect or arrived on the train together, bonded with one another. They shared what little they had, tried to protect each other, and they talked, always, they talked. Often, an older woman would take on the role of mother; she comforted her girls, advised them, assured them that their menstrual periods would return once they ate properly, and yes, they would have husbands and children someday. Because they were always hungry, food was a prime topic of conversation. How carefully they described each detail of the traditional Passover meals they had prepared in the past. Sometimes, they sang together, even laughed. The Orthodox remembered the dates of Jewish holidays and tried to recall the appropriate prayers. And, of course, they often wept, but not alone. Custom and social conventions expected men to suffer in silence—crying and complaining were unmanly. Thus, most of the men suffered isolation within the crowded camp in addition to the sense of abandonment by the world outside the barbed wire, while many women found comfort in sharing their tears and their humanity in the most inhuman places on earth.

THE DOCTORS

In Auschwitz, medical doctors did not practice the art of healing. There was no treatment for the sick or injured, not even an aspirin for pain and fever. The only surgery performed was related to experiments so diabolical that they dishonored the name of science. In all the slave labor and concentration camps, doctors routinely condemned the men and women to death because they judged who was fit or unfit to work; in the death camps, they were participants in the murder of millions.

The plunge from healer to killer originated in Nazi ideology gone berserk. The doctrine of the Aryan super-German was given official sanction by calling it racial science. Biologists and physicians established criteria for the pure Nordic type: skin tones, bone structure, eye color, height, weight, shape of ears, and so on. A distortion of Darwin's theory on the survival of the fittest was used to justify the "purification" of Germany by eliminating its supposedly mentally and physically flawed population. In the Thousand Year Reich, only those declared able-bodied according to government standards had the right to live. Members of the medical profession accepted murderous assignments and became willing instruments and partners in a program that turned the concept of mercy killing on its head. These victims whose life was deemed not worth living had expressed no wish to end their days. They, nor their custodial caregivers, were never consulted. In the case of the young or severely mentally handicapped, parents were told that their charges would be well cared for, even given new treatments to help them improve their disabilities. Within weeks a package would be delivered, the ashes of your kin, dead of pneumonia.

Because the techniques developed in the "processing" of Germans with physical and/or mental imperfections were later used in the medical experiments and killings during the Shoah, they merit a closer look within the context of this text. The use of lethal gas, sterilization, and medical experimentation began with the "purification of the German race," the euphemism for murdering the chronically ill and/or handicapped.

"Useless Eaters"

As early as 1933, indeed, a few months after Hitler became Chancellor, sterilization was legalized. Nazi scientists advanced the opinion that certain individuals were carriers of congenital conditions and must not be allowed to reproduce. Among these supposedly hereditary illnesses were a number of mental deficiencies, several brain disorders, blindness, deafness, physical malformation, and alcoholism. In the ensuing years, more and more "useless eaters" were catalogued as unfit for parenthood or life. Health courts, consisting of two doctors and one judge, determined whether or not an individual was to be sterilized. Ninety percent of the time, the vote was "yes." An appeals court was appointed to hear pleas for reversals of judgments. Robert Jay Lifton in his acclaimed *The Nazi Doctors* states that none knows just how many Germans were sterilized but quotes reliable estimates to range between 200,000 and 350,000.

Doctors in the Third Reich were instructed that their calling was higher than the care of the ill; the health of the entire Volk was their responsibility, and they must safeguard German racial perfection even if that required the rejection of traditional concepts of healing. Step by step the process of winnowing the desirable from the undesirable German shifted from the health courts to secret rooms in asylums and institutions for the chronically ill and the handicapped.

The doctors who tried to "cleanse" Germany of men, women, and children who did not meet the standards of health set by the government had abandoned the Hippocratic warning to do no harm and were well prepared to work in the camps. Here, their power was unlimited as they controlled the life or death of prisoners, when they stood at the railroad stations; conducted fitness inspection during the *Appells* (roll calls); conducted medical experiments that were certain to kill their subjects; and injected fatal phenol into the hearts of inmates in their hospitals.

The infamous Dr. Mengele enjoyed his role at the railroad siding. Dubbed "the angel of death" at Auschwitz, he was a handsome man, immaculate in his SS uniform, as he pointed with his riding crop to the right or to the left; one line for the gas chambers, the other to labor barracks. Surviving the initial selection, however, guaranteed nothing; selections for death occurred continuously. Every morning, the prisoners stood at attention to be counted and recounted during the dreaded *Appell.* Black-clad SS doctors moved up and down the rows of men or women to supply fodder for the gas chambers. The weak, the ill, and the bruised, the men or women who simply did not please the SS men, were ordered to join the lines leading to the deadly showers.

Medical Experiments

The medical experiments conducted at Auschwitz and several other camps were cruel beyond belief. Ostensibly to advance medical research, these scientists with credentials from German universities used human beings in ways that ordinary language cannot portray nor a rational mind comprehend. They tested various types of male and female sterilization techniques and competed to see how many hundreds of sterilization procedures a single doctor could perform in a day. They sought the limits of human endurance to heat and cold and deprivation of oxygen by using prisoners in deadly experiments. Infections were artificially introduced to discover when the disease would kill the subject. New mothers had their breasts bound to observe how soon they would die of deadly fever. Doctors supervised forms of torture to learn what breaks a man and finally destroys him.

Dr. Mengele's experiments with twins were expected to yield information that would increase the number of multiple births for Aryan women. Few adults or children survived his vivisections of their bodies. He was also fascinated with dwarfs and hunchbacks and kept them in the hospital facilities until his experiments killed them. The Nazi racial and eugenic medical institution in Berlin collected the findings and specimens sent by camp doctors. After all, no other place on earth afforded such unlimited access to experimentation on people whose screams they did not hear. The many rows of surgically removed body parts taken from nameless prisoners and preserved in glass jars presents a quandary to the German government to this day: Should they be made available for research or buried?

Camp hospital facilities doubled as medical killing centers. Some Jewish and non-German doctors were used to assist the Nazis in the camps. Their efforts to do some healing, to help some patients, should be noted, but overall they could not be effective. When it was doubtful that a prisoner could return to work or when the hospital wards were too crowded, the phenol injections were ordered. Patients had no idea what it meant when a doctor or an orderly, needle in hand, told them to cross their arms over their eyes. Only when inmates were sure that their illness or exhaustion made them certain targets for the next selection, did they venture into the hospital. There was always a chance, indeed, a small chance, that they could survive if unnoticed, if allowed a few days' rest and slightly better food. It was a risk taken only as a last resort.

CAMPS IN CENTRAL EUROPE

The death camps were located in Poland, but the concentration camp system spread across Central Europe from the borders of France and Holland into Austria and Czechoslovakia. Some of the sites confined permanent prisoners, others were used as stopovers for the eastward journey. Moving inmates from one camp to another was a common practice; some survivors could recall more than a dozen in their memoirs. The map of Germany was dotted with *Lagers*: some huge, others holding a few hundred slave laborers for a nearby factory. The prison population always included Jews, but they were not necessarily in the majority. After the advance of the Soviet armies impelled the Nazis to march the inmates westward were the German camps deluged with the pathetic, dying remnant from Poland.

During the early years of the Third Reich, Dachau, Buchenwald, and Sachsenhausen were the destinations of political dissenters, trade union leaders, and members of religious organizations who opposed the Nazis. Most were held without trials and served sentences of indeterminate length. When the harshness of German rule over their foreign conquests created opposition, the Gestapo seized hundreds of thousands of accused resistance fighters. It was never clear why the Nazis shot some suspects immediately, while others were shipped to death camps and still others to concentration camps. The arrests of underground resisters required expansion of the number and size of camps. When the Nazis began to force foreign workers and prisoners of war into the German defense industry, many slave labor camps, often indistinguishable from concentration camps, were constructed. In addition, there was an increase of German citizens who ran afoul of the secret

Inmates in their barracks at the Buchenwald concentration camp. (Corbis/Bettmann.)

police for such crimes as grumbling against the war and the nebulous offense of defeatism. Although only estimates are available, the total of prisoners numbered not in the hundreds of thousands, but in the millions. Nor will it ever be known how many died due to starvation, disease, despair, beatings, or shootings.

THERESIENSTADT AND RAVENSBRUECK

Each concentration camp had unique features due to its geography, its administration, its inmates, and/or its work requirements. Two of the *Lagers* were extraordinary and merit particular attention. Theresienstadt (Terezin), located in the Bohemian section of Czechoslovakia, was established by Reinhard Heydrich in 1941. It was organized to resemble a ghetto, with a council of elders and a chairman running the internal affairs of the Jewish community. Originally a military fortress, the site had stables, workshops, and a street of ramshackle houses. Theresienstadt was reputed to be the most humane camp in the constellation of German camps. Well-connected elderly German Jews, decorated Jewish war veterans, prominent scholars, and Jews married to Aryans paid with their life's savings for the opportunity to go there. The Germans had promised that some privileged few could live out their pleasant retirement years in lovely Bohemia. Once the Jews arrived and realized they had been deceived, they were unable to escape their prison/ghetto. The inmates who were permitted to remain had a fair chance of survival, but their numbers were small. It has been suggested that the Nazis considered some of these "residents" to be worth more alive than dead as possible pawns in exchange for German prisoners or for purposes of blackmail.

Theresienstadt had two faces. One looked like an impoverished but viable Jewish community of old people, who sustained themselves by their own work in several cottage industries and through gifts from the Red Cross. Families lived together; the food was poor, but lectures and music nourished the soul. These inmates were not as cut off from the rest of the outside world as were other camp prisoners. The SS dealt with the council rather than with individuals. Almost the entire group of Danish Jews who had not taken part in the great escape from Denmark (see Chapter 10) survived here because of the scrupulous vigilance of the Danish government. When the Nazis were pressured by the International Red Cross to permit an inspection of the camp, they grudgingly gave permission. The inspectors were treated to an elaborate charade. After an intensive cleanup, flowers appeared on the sidewalks, well-dressed people sipped tea in the afternoon, and children played around the well-stocked pushcarts of street vendors. The sham lasted one day. The Red Cross representatives saw nothing of the suffering of the hidden camp and wrote a favorable report on their findings.

Theresienstadt, however, was also a stopover for thousands of Jews on their way to Auschwitz and other camps. While waiting for transport east, they lived in overcrowded misery for weeks or months. There was no fuel to heat their stonewalled rooms, too little food, and the ever-present fear of where the next train would take them. The former Chief Rabbi of Germany, Leo Baeck, was among the prominent Jews imprisoned in Theresienstadt. He knew what "resettlement to the

East" actually meant and resolved not to reveal the truth. One can only guess what that decision must have cost him. Many Jews from Prague, Berlin, and Vienna were routed through Theresienstadt to Auschwitz as well as the dreaded stone quarries at Mauthausen in Austria. Much of the work of organizing the transfers was handled by the Jewish council, which hoped to save a remnant by cooperating with the Nazis.

Ravensbrueck, established in 1939, was a camp for women only. Before the influx of Jewish women sent there at the approach of the Soviet armies, the majority of inmates were Christian. Like so many other concentration camps, it was located in a swampy, unhealthy area. The internal camp administration was largely in the hands of German women convicted of crimes. But its population was international and included female Russian soldiers, nurses, Red Cross workers from everywhere in Europe, and resistance fighters, especially from France and Poland. The latter were subjected to medical experiments involving the transplanting of human bones. Their suffering resonated with all inmates who tried to ease their pain through words and acts of solidarity. The main industry employing the prisoners was grotesque considering the country was under bombardment on three fronts and from the air: the remodeling of the furs expropriated from Nazi victims.

Probably 50,000 women perished in Ravensbrueck. The number would have been greater were it not for a last-minute rescue of 14,000 prisoners in April of 1945. Himmler finally agreed to the entreaties of the Swedish diplomat Count Folke Bernadotte to permit them to be taken to Sweden. Himmler was then entertaining the illusion that he would represent Germany during peace negotiations and believed this gesture of goodwill would be appreciated by the Allies.

THE DEATH MARCHES

The encirclement of Germany was almost complete in the late winter of 1944 and early spring of 1945. Soviet armies rolled across the Polish plains and the Western Allies crossed into Germany from France. The deadly showers were ordered closed in November 1944 during the Nazis' frantic efforts to cover up their crimes. Huge shipments of goods taken from the dead were sent to Germany, gas chambers and crematoria were blown up, and bodies disinterred from mass graves hurriedly burned. Mountains of accumulated paperwork were thrown into the flames, but time was running out. Some of the inmates were able to hide vital Nazi records before the evacuations virtually emptied the death camps.

During the final months of the Thousand Year Reich, the remaining prisoners, many of whom were recent arrivals from Hungary, presented a problem for the SS. The nation was engulfed in last ditch fighting; it was a time of complete confusion, yet most of the concentration camp guards obeyed their final orders to march their prisoners westward. The roads were choked with fleeing Germans, there was no food or shelter, and the SS had no instructions as to how they were expected to reach their first stopover at the Silesian camp of Gross-Rosen. A final tragedy was the inevitable result. The roads on which starved, freezing, barely

The crematoria at Buchenwald. The remains in the oven are of women. (AP Wide World Photos.)

alive survivors were hurried along were littered with the dead and dying. Many were left where they fell; others were shot by the SS. Just a few hours from liberation, from food and medical care, from life itself, they were destroyed by the Shoah. But it must be remembered, the Shoah was not a natural disaster, it was planned and executed by men beyond our understanding, and for some of us, beyond our forgiveness.

CHAPTER 10

Resistance Against All Odds

For decades after the liberation of the Jewish remnant, the image of the Jew during the Nazi *Endloesung* was woefully one-sided. The unfortunate depiction of victims waiting for death like lambs going to their slaughter ignored the fact that some resisted the Nazis, that they fought back and did so under extremely difficult conditions. In the more recent past, books, movies, and television programs have dealt with the topic of opposition more frequently but not always with accuracy. It is fair to state that yes, Jews offered opposition, but it is also correct to say that their participation in the military defeat of the Germans in World War II did not speed the end of the Nazi Reich. Nonetheless, their choice—and it was a choice—to take a stand had great psychological significance. Their heroism lives as a definitive symbol of courage against overwhelming odds.

In the context of Jewish opposition to the Nazis, the term "resistance" requires some definition. Does the word refer only to organized combat, such as military action, or does it include individual assaults against the Germans? Is the use of weapons required or is nonviolent opposition rightfully classified as resistance? Is it appropriate, as has been suggested, that survival itself was a form of resistance because the Nazis sought the death of EVERY Jew? Surely, the Jewish men and women who fought as members of partisan organizations in occupied lands were resisters. How should one characterize the workers in ghettos and in slave labor camps who sabotaged the economic enterprises of the Nazis by producing flawed goods? What of the Jewish writers who risked their lives to publish forbidden newspapers and the teachers who defied the Gestapo when they secretly instructed their students? The illegal smuggling of food delayed the total collapse of ghetto life and was frequently carried out by children. Did they not offer resistance? The historian Emanuel Ringelblum and others collected and preserved information on the fate of ghetto Jews in defiance of orders. Art and music, as well as poetry, expressed opposition to the Nazis in the ghettos and camps. Clearly, resistance had many forms.

Without diminishing the heroism of the many individuals who fought the Nazis in various ways, in this context resistance designates systematic or organized guerrilla-type clashes between Jews and Germans. Many silent acts of heroic opposition will never come to light nor can their effectiveness be measured. The dimensions and results of industrial sabotage are equally difficult to gauge. German industrialists complained frequently about the low productivity of their forced laborers, but it is not possible to know if this was the result of physical or emotional

VOICES

My Mother and the Rosenstrasse Protest

I was born in Berlin in 1941 and, according to Nazi law, was labeled a *Mischling*: my father was Jewish, my mother a so-called Aryan. Only four years old when the war ended, my knowledge of my parents' struggles comes mostly from documents and notebooks meticulously kept by my father throughout his life; some of the events I heard from my brother, eight years older than I, and occasionally, not very often, my father spoke of some specific memory to me.

The Nazi government put a lot of pressure on the Christian partners of mixed marriages to divorce their Jewish spouses. But after the divorce, the Jewish mates were sent to concentration camps. Even without that threat, my mother would never have considered such a step; my parents were totally devoted to one another. Like most people who came through Nazi persecution, Allied bombing, and Russian occupation, my family survived many narrow escapes. I will recall for you two events, both examples of my mother's astounding courage.

The Gestapo arrested my father in 1939 and put him to work as a slave laborer. It was up to my mother to earn and find food for us, to plead with the teacher to allow my brother to go to class, and to keep us safe during the bombings of Berlin. German children were evacuated from the city to the countryside but not the *Mischlinge.* When the air raid sirens sounded, *Mischlinge* were forbidden to go to the air raid shelters, and we hid in a little closet.

When my brother was 12 years old, the Gestapo came for him. My mother, I believe instinctively, ran to the window of the apartment, put one leg over the ledge, and shouted that she would jump into the street if they took her son. The Nazis must have seen that she meant to do exactly that and left—without the boy. But the most remarkable test of her love for her family took place in February and March of 1943. The event is now called the Rosenstrasse Protest, and it is historically significant because it showed that the Nazis feared public demonstrations.

In the spring of 1943, the Gestapo arrested the remaining 6,000 Jews of Berlin. The husbands of "Aryan" women, about 1,800 of them, were separated from the rest—they had no idea why—and housed them in the Jewish community building at 2–4 Rosenstrasse. Word soon got around among the wives where their men were being held, and the women gathered there until their numbers reached 6,000. Of course, my mother was among them. They milled around the Rosenstrasse, chanting "Let Our Men Go" all day and night for two weeks. Goebbels, the *Gauleiter* (the highest Nazi official in Berlin), who had ordered the arrests, now faced something unheard of: an anti-Nazi street demonstration. He ordered soldiers to remove the protesters. There they were, unarmed women with guns pointed at them, but no one left. Whether or not these soldiers would have shot them, I cannot say. But Goebbels didn't want a blood bath on the Rosenstraase, and amazingly, no—miraculously, within two weeks the men, including my father, came home.

By permission courtesy of Katrin Balaban.

exhaustion or subversive action or all three. It is credible, however, to assess the impact of organized Jewish resistance both as members of insurgent units as well as that of ghetto and concentration camp fighters.

The Germans did not consider fugitive Jews to be dangerous to them. Some believed their own propaganda that had marked Jews as cowards. The SS was aware of the practical difficulties Jewish resisters faced, especially in the Polish countryside, where they met nearly insurmountable obstacles, for example: The number of Jews with military training was small; procurement of weapons was almost impossible; animosity between Jews and Poles created great danger for Jews trying to find food, medicine, and clothing and secure hiding places. Added to these practical difficulties was the psychological hurdle of parental teaching; from childhood on Jewish boys had been warned to avoid confrontations with the Gentile world in order to avoid fierce retaliation.

MILITANT JEWS

Some historical events speak so clearly that they need no interpretation; others evolve into controversial expositions. The problem of Jewish militancy belongs to the latter category. Some scholars, notably Raul Hilberg and Hannah Arendt, stated that the Jews were passive, even compliant, and consequently they and the activities of the *Judenraete* rendered valuable aid to the Nazis. The death toll, in their view, would have been smaller without the cooperation of the victims. Opposing this concept are, among others, Yehuda Bauer and Schmuel Krakowski. Their research led them to the conclusion that Jews tried to fight Germans whenever and wherever they could, at some cost to the Nazi war effort.

It is a fact that six million were killed. It is also true that relatively few Jews defied Nazi orders to move toward the deadly ditches or the gassing chambers. Hundreds of thousands of slave workers followed orders because they hoped that work would give them life. Nearly all of the Jewish elders urged compliance out of fear of reprisals against the entire community. A case from the history of the Vilna ghetto makes the point. A group of young Jews had escaped and joined the partisans in the forest. The Germans ordered the execution of the families they left behind. The head of the *Judenrat,* Jacob Gens, called the escapees traitors who endangered all the inhabitants of the ghetto.

Submission, however, does not portray the complete picture. A body of evidence exists that recognizes that Jews fought against the Nazis. Indeed, in some cases, Jewish resistance pre-dated the native anti-Nazi underground organizations in the conquered nations. Jews carried out revolts in several Polish ghettos and death camps; they formed resistance groups in the forests of Poland and western Russia; where accepted, they joined anti-Nazi guerrilla organizations, and where rejected, they formed their own partisan groups.

The hardships they faced were appalling. With few weapons and little training, constantly on the move for fear of denunciation by Nazi collaborators, they had to spend much of their strength in the daily struggle for food. The Germans, on the other hand, were experienced, well-equipped soldiers, with nearly unlimited supplies.

Only in their zeal to kill the enemy did the guerrillas exceed the Nazis. A large number of the Jewish fighters were sole survivors of their families. Hatred and the hope to avenge the death of their loved ones gave them daring and resilience beyond all expectations.

THE WARSAW GHETTO REVOLT

For the past several decades, Jews throughout the world commemorate the anniversary of the Holocaust during the middle of April. They gather for religious and secular observance of Yom Hashoah, the Day of Remembrance. The day was selected because it marks the start of the Warsaw ghetto uprising of 1943. Although this was not the only revolt of Jews against the Nazis, it amazed the world and influenced others to defy the Nazis. A brick wall with an 11-mile circumference had been erected, which enclosed the Warsaw ghetto since the summer of 1940. It was 10 feet high and the cost of construction had to be paid by the prisoners it enclosed, an area of three and a half square miles. As many as 360,000 Jews were confined there. When its 22 gates were sealed that November, a drastic increase in the death toll by starvation followed. Eventually, the daily losses reached 300 to 400 people, and the total death rate due to famine was estimated at 80,000. But these numbers were deemed insufficient after the Nazis had decided that total destruction was the meaning of the Final Solution. On July 22, 1942, deportations to the death camp Treblinka began. Within two months, the ghetto population was reduced by a staggering 300,000. The *Judenrat* was compelled to deliver 6,000 victims daily to the *Umschlagplatz*, where the trains were loaded. It was no longer possible to hide the truth that deportation was equivalent to death. At this point, with just 120,000 Jews remaining, the remnant rejected the authority of the council of elders whose acquiescence to German demands in the hope of saving lives had proven to be a total failure. A new breed of leaders emerged; they were younger, committed to resist, to kill Germans, and, if necessary, to die fighting.

The Ghetto Fighters

Several political organizations had continued to function in the ghetto, and from the ranks of these groups came the ghetto fighters. Most of them had been affiliated with the socialists and the Zionists. Now they set aside their theoretical differences to forge a united front. Six days after the deportations to Treblinka began, they joined to become the ZOB (*Zydowska Organizacja Bojowa* or Jewish Combat Organization), headed by Mordekhai Anielewicz. Their combined strength approximated 700 to 1,000 men and women willing to take up arms. Most of the remaining ghetto population gave them support and cooperation. These young people had no illusions. They knew their choice was not between life and death, but between death in combat or death in Treblinka. Anielewicz combined the attributes of the idealist with the activism of the realist. He came from a working-class family and, as a youth, had been attracted to Zionism. In the ghetto, he published an underground newspaper, *Against the Stream,* which called for Jewish resistance. Other young men and women were drawn to him and his determination to make a stand. During the final months of the ghetto's life, he was its military leader and the virtual chief of its public administration.

The ZOB

The first order of business was the procurement of arms. In this effort, the ZOB was never very successful. Contact with the Polish Home Army, the major underground militia of the Polish people, resulted in a few guns and some explosives. At first the Poles were not convinced that the Jews would actually fight and were reluctant to give up any of their own few and precious weapons. On January 18, 1943, however, it became clear that the ghetto was ready to resist the Nazis. On that day, as a large group of deportees was escorted out of the ghetto, Mordekhai Anielewicz with a small number of his men attacked the Nazi escort. In military parlance, this was merely a skirmish, but it was the first time that the Germans sustained losses at the hands of Jews. While the astounded SS troopers were responding to the assault in the street, a second cadre of the ZOB attacked Nazis inside a building. On that day, the myth of Jewish cowardice was dispelled.

The Polish partisans were impressed and increased their contribution of weapons to the ZOB. By April, when earlier skirmishes had come to resemble battles, the ghetto arsenal included many revolvers, grenades, homemade bombs, and one machine gun. Although pitifully inadequate, by means of resourceful deployment, the small army snatched from the Germans their ability to do whatever they pleased within the ghetto.

It would have been foolhardy for Mordekhai's few hundred, ill-equipped fighters to meet the Germans in any sort of battle formation, where the enemy's superior weaponry would quickly annihilate them. Clearly, the Jews had to attack from entrenched positions, retreat, regroup, and fight from another bunker. By repeating this formula, they gave the impression of much greater firepower than they actually had. With great ingenuity, the people in the ghetto built bunkers, connected houses, and constructed escape routes. Tunnels were dug that led from one cellar to another cellar, a number of hidden routes led to rooftops and attics, and to sewage pipes. At various points, they cached food, water, and ammunition; some of the bunkers were equipped with electricity and radios. The ghetto became a maze of hideouts and combat positions designed to maximize the firepower of a small army that must be able to move from one position to another without exposing its fighters.

Nazi Reaction

While this feverish activity was taking place, the Nazis were unable to bring their quota of victims to the *Umschlagplatz* and the trains. The Jews, no longer deceived by the resettlement fiction, were hiding. Threats of dire consequences had lost their power, and now the SS tried persuasion. They posted notices that there would be no further expulsions from the city, it was safe to come into the streets, and German employers needed workers in their factories. Amnesty would be given to all who would willingly come forward. Most tempting was the promise that bread and jam would be distributed at the *Umschlagplatz*. But the duplicating machines of the ZOB were busy as well. They distributed leaflets that countered the German lies with the truth: Death awaits you if you go on the train; stand firm, do not leave your hiding places, and evade the Germans by any means you can.

The German realized that the destruction of the Jews of Warsaw would require more than orders from the now impotent *Judenrat.* On the first day of Passover, April 19, 1943, they were ready to attack with military force. A new commander, Major-General Juergen Stroop of the *Waffen SS,* had been assigned the task of clearing out the ghetto. He had under his command a force estimated at between 2,000 and 5,000 men, SS, Polish and Baltic auxiliaries, and policemen. They expected to finish their job in three days. Before dawn they surrounded the ghetto to prevent escapes. Then they moved through the gates with their arsenal of hand-held weapons, their armored vehicles and, emphasizing their determination to make this a short campaign, they brought in tanks.

The ghetto fighters responded from their hiding places. The Germans were met with a barrage of bullets, with grenades, and homemade Molotov cocktails. By shooting from parallel attic bunkers, they caught Stroop's men in their cross fire. Because the ZOB fighters rushed from place to place, the Germans misjudged their total strength to be greater than it was. Again and again the Nazis were forced to withdraw to reorganize their attacks. On the third day, they changed their tactics and called in aerial support. Thus began the firebombing of the ghetto. To find the secret bunkers, the Germans used listening devices that could detect life beneath the rubble. But the ghetto continued its resistance. Finally, Stroop was convinced that there was only one way to end this embarrassment to his honor—he decided to raze the entire ghetto, burn it to the ground.

The End of the Warsaw Ghetto

At least 50,000 Jews were still in hiding, Jews that Himmler wanted in Treblinka. They refused to follow German orders to emerge even when SS guns attacked their hiding places. Only flame throwers or gas attacks caused some of the trapped remnant to run into the open. They were killed on the spot or transported to death or concentration camps. German incendiary weapons created a veritable holocaust, a sea of flames. Stroop, with the approval of his superiors, torched the ghetto, house by house, block by block. Six hundred and thirty-one bunkers were destroyed. When the beautiful main synagogue would not go up in flames, it was dynamited.

Day by day the number of defensive positions shrank. On May 7, 18 days after the start of the insurrection, the Nazis found the Anielewicz headquarters on Mila Street. All means of resistance had been exhausted, and just one option was left: How shall we die? The remnant of the Warsaw ghetto fighters used their final bullets to commit suicide or kill each other. That was preferable to falling into the enemy's hands. Among the dead was Mordekhai Anielewicz. He was 24 years old. Seventy-five of the surviving fighters had been able to escape through the sewers that ran beneath the ghetto wall. They continued their resistance with Polish partisans in the forest. Only a handful lived to see the end of the war. The ghetto lay in rubble. Nearly all its inhabitants were dead. On May 10, Stroop informed his superiors that the battle was over. He claimed victory.

RESULTS AND SIGNIFICANCE

But was this a German victory? The ZOB had never considered that defeat of the Germans was an achievable goal, never had that been a realistic prospect. Yes, the Germans had won, they had destroyed the ghetto. But the ZOB fighters accomplished the goal they had set for themselves: to prove that not all Jews were passive victims and that they could and did give battle against overwhelming odds in defense of their honor. Furthermore, their revolt gave other oppressed subjects of the Nazis the incentive to resist. If a few hundred Jews could hold off the mighty Germans for nearly a month, then the power of the Germans was not unassailable. Prisoners in other ghettos, concentration and death camps, partisans in the forests, and underground fighters throughout the Axis world saw events in Warsaw as a model they could emulate. When the final moments of the ghetto were near, Anielewicz sent a stirring message of defiance in the face of death to the world outside the walls. It reached the Polish government in exile in London and was read over the radio. Young Jews in several Polish ghettos paid homage to their dead comrades by their refusal to obey SS orders.

The estimates of German casualties in Warsaw range widely. Stroop admitted to only 16 dead and 85 wounded; the Polish Home Army's assessment was 500 Germans killed. No matter what the true number of casualties, the symbolic importance of the ghetto revolt was never in question. The Warsaw uprising was fought by Jews only. Appeals by the ZOB for assistance from the Polish partisan army had been refused. While the ghetto fought without hope of victory, the Poles decided to delay their armed struggle until there was a chance to defeat the Germans. In the fall of 1944, as the Red Army advanced into Poland, with Soviet encouragement, the Polish underground thought their time had come. It was a tragic irony of fate that the Home Army was left to fight and die alone, without Russian assistance. The Germans crushed the Warsaw uprising of the Poles, and some 200,000 members of Polish partisan battalions died. Only after the Nazis had smashed the Polish insurgents did the Red Army march toward Warsaw. The establishment of a pro-Soviet regime in Poland was facilitated by the losses sustained by the resistance army.

CAMP REVOLTS: AN OVERVIEW

While conditions in the ghettos made armed resistance extremely difficult, organizing a revolt in the camps seemed totally impossible. Only in the death camps and only near the end of the war did prisoners in Treblinka, Sobibor, and Auschwitz–Birkenau attempt to resist their killers. The plotters hoped that an uprising would result in a breakout, and some of the prisoners might escape. Even that limited goal was far-fetched. An abbreviated account of their overwhelming obstacles included the following:

1. The isolation of prisoners in death camps was nearly total. Not only was there no contact with the outside world, but within the camps various work battalions were prevented from communicating with one another. Organizing and

planning any coordinated resistance required ingenious and dangerous circumvention of Nazi surveillance.

2. The prisoners lived under inhumane and debilitating conditions. Everything they had valued in their former lives was gone, and the temptation to let go, to end their suffering, was inescapable. Suicides were common.
3. Newly arriving prisoners required some time to orient themselves to the camp before it was possible to organize a circle of coconspirators. However, the longer an inmate was in the camp, the greater was his/her loss of physical and mental stamina.
4. The opportunity to buy weapons was almost nil. Slave laborers who worked with the property of murdered Jews managed to hoard some valuables, but to exchange jewels for arms was a deadly business. Some members of the Ukrainian and other auxiliary troops were willing to take the risk for the right payment, but such arrangements were infrequent. Most of the arms used by the camp rebels were stolen from German armories or were put together from parts filched from workshops. The number of weapons accumulated was pitifully small; clubs and shovels had to do for most of the resisters.
5. If the miracle of a breakout was accomplished, the escapees faced a second hurdle of awesome proportions. The chances of survival on the other side of the barbed wire were precarious at best. They were dressed in prison stripes, and they had no money and probably no friends in the surrounding area. Helping an escapee was a crime the Nazis punished with execution. The SS camp guards reacted with fierceness to any act of Jewish resistance, and their use of tracking dogs reduced the chances of evasion to nearly zero.

Treblinka

Revolts in three of the death camps confirmed the desperation underlying this unequal struggle. As symbolic actions, these efforts merit respect; as battles to save Jewish lives, they failed. The resistance group at Treblinka revolted in August 1943, two months before the official closing of the camp. There were 700 Jews working in the facility, mainly sorting the goods of dead victims or disposing of corpses. Upon a given signal, a group of conspirators rushed to recover their few hidden guns and grenades. With these they forced open a door into the SS arsenal. Two hundred men helped themselves to firearms; the others used whatever was at hand that could serve as a weapon. The crematoria were set on fire as well as several other buildings. The Germans responded with rage and called in additional troops. Most of the rebels were killed within the compound. Between 150 and 200 men made their escape, but only 12 survived the intensive German manhunt. At the end of the rout, the gas chambers were still functional, and their operation was resumed.

Sobibor

The Sobibor uprising took place in October of 1943. This death factory, located near the Bug River, was enclosed by three circles of barbed wire, a minefield, and a ditch. An adjoining dense forest improved chance for a successful escape. The leader of the resistance was a Jewish Soviet prisoner of war, whose military background contributed to the partial success of the breakout. In Sobibor's workshops, the SS had employed Jews to make items for their personal use. On October 14, the tailors and shoemakers arranged staggered appointments for fittings for their "clients." As individual SS men stepped into the workrooms, they were attacked and killed by prisoners who had been waiting in hiding. By the time the general attack began in the evening, 19 officers, including the camp commander, were dead. The resulting confusion enabled some 400 of the 600 prisoners to escape. Of these, many died when they stepped on mines, some were killed in the manhunt organized by the Germans, and others joined partisan groups in the woods. Only 40 of the men survived to see the end of the war. But they had the satisfaction of knowing that as a result of their attack, the gas chambers at Sobibor were permanently closed down. Himmler ordered the camp to be leveled two days after the uprising.

Auschwitz–Birkenau

At Auschwitz–Birkenau, an international resistance movement had been secretly organized. Although the members of the *Sonderkommando* who worked with the corpses in the death factories were kept apart from other inmates, a tenuous line of communication was established between them and the other inmates. Plans to stage a revolt involving both groups were developed but never completed. The men of the *Sonderkommando* knew their days were numbered when Eichmann's trains with Hungarian victims arrived less frequently. Unable to convince the underground leadership in the main camp to coordinate an uprising, the prisoners working at the crematoria revolted on October 7, 1944.

These men had no weapons, but they had a small store of explosives. Women prisoners who worked in a German factory had smuggled the chemicals to them over a period of months. That they managed to hide forbidden materials beneath the rags they wore to cover their emaciated bodies was in itself a story of heroism. The men killed several SS guards and blew up one of the four crematoria. About 600 of them were able to break out through the barriers, but their freedom was short-lived. Several hundred SS troops went into immediate pursuit, and it is believed that all the prisoners were killed. An investigation by the Gestapo revealed the involvement of Rosa Robota as the leader of the dynamite smugglers. Rosa was tortured but never betrayed the names of her comrades. She and three other girls were publicly hanged.

These events took place even as the war was drawing to its inevitable conclusion. One might have expected the SS to be too preoccupied with the cover-up of their crimes rather than the fate of a few hundred Jews. But orders were orders. On January 18, 1945, those inmates able to walk were marched westward, still guarded by SS men who systematically shot prisoners unable to continue their Death March.

WITH THE PARTISANS

The degree of harshness of Nazi rule differed widely between eastern and western areas of occupation. Nazi racial theories played a major role in their attitude toward the defeated peoples. Also, military necessities and the need for food and oil frustrated the realization of Himmler's Aryan fantasy. The treatment of Frenchmen, Danes, or Norwegians, for example, was quite dissimilar to the conduct of the conquerors toward the Poles and Russians. The great majority of all the subjugated people responded to the German presence with emotions ranging from dislike to hatred, but it must also be acknowledged that every nationality acquired its contingent of collaborators who worked for the Nazis. They carried out administrative duties, served with German auxiliary armies, and joined local police forces, where they assisted in the roundups and murders of the Jews.

Between 1942 and 1943, secret anti-Nazi organizations began to develop in German-occupied nations. Romanticized in many movies and novels, freedom fighters performed daring exploits despite the ever-present Gestapo agents, who routinely terrorized and tortured suspects. The most successful missions were carried out by groups rather than heroic individuals. With the exception of some Yugoslav and Russian underground companies, who had the resources to give battle, they resorted to hit-run-hide guerrilla tactics. They derailed trains, rescued imprisoned comrades, printed counterfeit identity papers, committed theft and robbery to finance their operations, and killed selected enemies. In the western occupied nations, France, the Low Countries, Denmark, and Norway, they attempted, and sometimes succeeded, in saving Jews from arrest and shipment to the death camps. Whether urban cells or forest guerrillas, the objectives were the same: Hasten the day of liberation by fighting the invader. In contrast with the ghetto and death camp fighters, these men and women had reasonable expectations of surviving the war.

The Forest Camps

By 1943, when Polish underground units became effective, the destruction of the Jews was almost completed. As the last ghetto survivors faced death, the elders finally urged their young people to escape into the countryside to join, or create, partisan units. The hour had come to preserve a remnant that might someday rebuild Jewish life. Escape from the ghetto was harrowing because the most fit had to abandon their helpless relatives. Nevertheless, the number of Eastern European Jews who fled was believed to reach tens of thousands. Their survival rate, however, at this point in time was very poor. Many Polish, Ukrainian, and Baltic anti-Semites denounced them to the Germans or killed them for whatever possessions they still had, while others died during the winters, freezing and starving to death. Their best hope lay in acceptance by one of the partisan organizations hidden in the dense forests of the Baltic States, eastern Poland, or the western Soviet Union. As a rule, only Jews who had weapons were admitted to join the Polish Home Army. That meant that very few qualified no matter how eager they were to fight the Germans. In brigades commanded by Russians and/or Polish communists, their chances of acceptance were better. Considering the intensity of hatred that Jews harbored for Nazis, the policy of refusing most of them an opportunity for revenge was self-defeating.

A number of family camps, a mixture of old and young, able-bodied and dependent Jews, were established in the woods. These groups were particularly vulnerable. Unless the local farmers gave or sold them food, they starved. When, in desperation, they tried to steal from the fields, they were hunted like animals. Family camps greatly burdened the partisans who protected them. To find even the most basic staples, potatoes, beets, and bread, was the most pressing problem, but equally difficult was the frequent need to pick up and move to another location at a moment's notice. The care for their noncombatants, children and the elderly in particular, restricted the vital mobility of guerrillas. The fact that several such groups maintained themselves in hiding throughout the war was a tribute to the endurance of its members as well as to the humanity of the Jewish and non-Jewish resistance fighters who provided for their needs.

Brigades that included complements of Jews were most numerous in eastern Poland and western Russia, where some units were organized and commanded by Soviet soldiers, who had been parachuted in for this purpose. These officers (some were Jewish) enrolled all who were willing and able to fight, and several of them accepted the obligation to safeguard family camps. In the forests near Vilna, a Lithuanian Jewish brigade operated; in White Russia and the vicinity of Minsk, Jewish guerrillas formed effective combat battalions. If the estimate of 20,000 Jewish survivors in the eastern wilderness is correct, much of the credit must go to the Soviets.

Underground Organizations

Jews had no difficulty in joining the underground movements of France, the Netherlands, and Belgium. French Jewry, although 1 percent of the population, accounted for 15 to 20 percent in French resistance activity. There was also a Jewish Maquis organization, founded and led by Robert Gamzon, who reputedly killed more than a thousand Nazis and committed many hundreds of acts of sabotage. Other distinctly Jewish battalions smuggled Jewish children into neutral safe havens, such as Spain and Switzerland. In the Balkans and in Greece, young Jewish men and women were active in their national liberation movements. Some 2,000 Jews fought with Tito's Yugoslav army. In Italy, a Jewish unit was formed, later merged with other freedom fighters, which operated in Piedmont and in the Italian Alps. In Slovakia, Jews were among the original organizers of that resistance.

Clearly, history and the many medals for courage awarded to Jewish fighters, often posthumously, contradict the allegation that during the Holocaust all Jews were passive. Where circumstances permitted, they fought with distinction. The military history of Israel could not have been written by a people unwilling or unable to defend itself. In fact, the surviving partisans who made their way to Israel invigorated the Jewish homeland's defense units when the infant nation was attacked by its neighbors in 1948.

It is not possible to approximate the number of Jewish guerrilla fighters active in the last two years of the war. By the very nature of their function, such estimates cannot be based on the sort of documents historians seek. Some of the survivors, for example, the Bielski brothers, who were active in Belarus, told their stories to historical writers (*The Bielski Brothers* by Peter Duffy) and hence allow us a glimpse into one forest camp of 800 to 12,000 Jews, but there were many others. In their isolation, it was inevitable that each leader impress his own personality on his company.

Certainly the Soviet soldier, who had been parachuted into the woods to form and lead a partisan force, commanded his unit differently from that of the ex-school teacher and ghetto survivor from Warsaw. The psychological and physical stamina required of people living under such incomparable conditions is breathtaking. Most Jews were urbanites, who now had to live in primitive shelters; they had been reared with the usual comforts of hearth, home, school, shops, and houses of prayer, but now, these consolations were displaced by fear and hunger. The very sight of a gun had made most Jews uneasy in their former lives, and now they became soldiers. And yet, they fulfilled the mission that had brought them together—they saved Jewish lives.

CHAPTER 11

Rescue: Too Little, Too Late

Very little was done by the world to rescue Jews during the Holocaust. It would be expedient to simply condemn the Allies and neutrals for their lack of compassionate action and claim that anti-Semitism was at the root of this inaction. Such a wide brushstroke, however, discounts the unsung heroes and martyrs who aided Jews at their own peril. It is also important to give credit to the efforts of a number of organizations and the courageous stand taken by the leaders of several governments who resisted German demands to deliver their Jews into Nazi hands.

What causes individuals to act with compassionate courage? Psychologists have been unable to provide definitive answers to this ancient puzzle. Questions regarding genetic predisposition or the influence of religion, family environment, or social pressure—all deserve consideration but none give conclusive answers. The men and women who saved Jewish lives and whose names appear among the designated Righteous at Yad Vashem came from all social classes, every economic status, and diverse educational backgrounds. It appears that neither age, sex, nor national origin played a part in their altruistic decisions. Until we understand the enigma of benevolence, we must be content to merely examine the facts connected to the responses of governments, organizations, and individuals to the plight of the Jews. Specifically, we need to ask: What was known, what was believed, what was done, and what might have been done? Our answers, however, must not be distorted by the improved vision of hindsight. And that means placing events into the context of a period of Western history that was fraught with emotional, political, and economic shocks that influenced decisions at every level.

When the concentration camps were liberated and the Jewish survivors counted, their number approached 40,000. Nearly all were in miserable physical and emotional condition. There is no dearth of rationalization, breast-beating, or excuses to account for the failure of powerful nations and institutions that allowed the Nazis to kill the six million. Several successful rescue efforts, such as in Denmark, in Bulgaria, and belatedly in Hungary, demonstrated that much more might have been done. As the leader of the free world during the war, the burden of inactivity falls heavily upon the United States. Great Britain's policy of restricting immigration to its mandate of Palestine must also share the guilt. No doubt, the failure of the refugee commissions of the League of Nations, the International Red Cross, and the international conferences in Evian and Bermuda, and the silence of the great churches, contributed to the genocide. Would the losses have been smaller if American Jewry had adopted a less diffident stance toward Roosevelt? And how destructive was the prevailing attitude that held only the perpetrators accountable but not the mute bystanders?

VOICES

My Parents—My Heroes

Only after I became a mother did I understand and appreciate the extraordinary courage of my mother and father. It took strength and love for them to put my welfare ahead of their own need to be with me and to send me away to be cared for by people they did not know, in a foreign country—possibly forever.

I was born in Berlin, the only child of assimilated middle-class German Jews. I had my own room, filled with books, toys, and pictures of Shirley Temple. When the Nazi government forbade Jewish children to attend public school, my parents enrolled me in the *Theodor Herzl Schule*, a private Jewish day school. I had many friends and was too young to understand the seriousness of our situation in Hitler's Germany. I felt secure in our apartment, played with my friends, loved ice-skating, and father continued to place a piece of marzipan on my night table when he thought I was asleep.

Then came *Kristallnacht.* My school was burnt down, Jewish businesses were ransacked, and the long-cherished hope that things would improve vanished. Jewish families frantically searched for a place—any place—that would grant us a visa. I believe my folks read about the *Kindertransport* in the *Aufbau*, our Jewish newspaper. This was an attempt by the people of Great Britain to save Jewish children from Germany and Austria. British families volunteered to care for youngsters under the age of 17. I cannot imagine the pain it must have caused my parents to decide that they must let me go.

I was 12 years old. Did I cry when they told me? or protest? Perhaps, but my mind remains blank. I do recall, however, the cold day in January 1939 when we went to the train station. I wore a blue ski suit, carried my favorite doll, and held onto my small suitcase. We met many other families, some with toddlers. I saw older siblings holding younger brothers and sisters in their arms or by the hand. Many children were crying. I was, too. I think we sensed something enormous was taking place without understanding that we were about to be separated from our families.

My parents kissed me and handed me over to one of the counselors who accompanied the *Kindertransport.* I recall looking out the window when the train moved and seeing all those waving handkerchiefs. Of the rest of the journey I remember nothing until I reached Scotland. My new home was in Glasgow. How very lucky I was to be taken in by such a caring family, complete with foster sister and brother. I went to school, and in three months had learned to speak English, with a slight Scottish accent. Although I missed my parents, the war and the Nazis were far away. I stayed in Glasgow for two years until, miraculously, my parents were able to come to England. You can imagine our joy. At that time we did not know how rare such reunions were. Ten thousand children were saved through the *Kindertransport,* but fewer than 10 percent saw their parents again. Now I don't know if I should weep for the parents or for their orphaned children—perhaps both.

By permission courtesy of Anita Frank Payson.

ORDINARY PEOPLE

Who were the people who accepted the dangerous moral challenge to try and save Jewish lives? As a rule, individuals demonstrated greater courage than institutions. Thus, nuns in convents saved Jewish children, while the papacy was silent; consuls representing governments as diverse as Japan and Switzerland defied their official instructions and provided visas for doomed Jews in contravention of their national policies. In the occupied nations, and, yes, in Germany too, gallant men and women from every walk of life ignored the Nazis' dire warnings not to aid the persecuted. They took great risks, and some paid the ultimate price to help people they often did not know. After the war, when Madame Trocme of Le Chambon in France was asked why she and her husband, Pastor Andre Trocmé, endangered their own families and friends in their successful rescue of hundreds of Jews, she replied: "They came to my door, hunted and fleeing; so I said 'come in, come in.' What else could I do?"

The Righteous

In Jerusalem, the Israeli government's Authority of Heroes and Martyrs at Yad Vashem designates rescuers of Jews as The Righteous Among the Nations. The title is bestowed on men and women for "their compassion, courage and morality who risked their lives to save Jews." Men and women from 40 nations are on this honor roll, which reached 5,503 in 2007, while the number of rescued totals 21,758. The Authority of Yad Vashem continues its search for the Righteous and those they protected in order to honor the living and posthumously the dead. A path has been laid in Jerusalem, flanked by commemorative trees, dedicated to individuals, groups, and organizations who met the Authority's qualification to receive this tribute.

It should be noted that the largest number thus distinguished were from Poland, followed by the Netherlands, France, the Ukraine, and Belgium. Denmark might have led the list of the Righteous, but the Danish underground that saved nearly all Danish Jews asked to be represented as a single unit. (The rescue of the Jews of Denmark is discussed in the following sections.)

While most political leaders, whether from Vichy France, the United States, or England, theorized about the difficulties of saving Jews, individuals, alone or in groups, took life-saving action. They came from all levels of society—dock workers, shopkeepers, farmers, and schoolteachers; nuns, priests, businessmen, and professionals; members of the old aristocracy; and day laborers. They protected Jews they knew or had never met; they hid them in attics, in cellars, in barns, and behind false walls; they shared their food rations; and they carried out pails of their waste. Often they were forced to deceive their own families because a slip of the tongue by a child about a stranger in the house might find its way to the Gestapo. Collaborators with the Nazis were a constant danger, whether a "guest" stayed a night, for several weeks, or months, and even years.

Fleeing Jews passed along the names and addresses of safe houses, which in turn increased the danger to the hosts. Whenever possible, the fugitives were spirited across borders into neutral territory such as Spain and Switzerland and helped to escape to Palestine, which was sometimes legal, often illegal. As noted earlier, the

Nazi search for Jews continued even when invasion threatened the German heartland; thus, in Germany, Austria, Poland, and Czechoslovakia, some Jews were hidden and supported for as long as six years. The memoirs of survivors emphasize the physical and emotional strain experienced by both Jews and Gentiles who shared lives of unrelenting anxiety.

QUESTIONS OF OPPORTUNITIES

The feasibility of safeguarding a Jew was largely dependent on the type of control the Germans established in a region. Where Nazi authority reached into every sphere of human activity, such as in Germany and Poland, rescue attempts were most perilous. Where puppet governments had been installed, as in Vichy France and Norway, the possibility for covert defiance of the regime was greater. The level of assimilation of the Jewish population also had an impact. For example, many of Italy's long-integrated Jews could disappear from German eyes by claiming to be Catholic with baptismal papers supplied by willing priests. On the other hand, Latvia's Orthodox Jews, whose mastery of the native language was poor, could not vanish among the local factory or farm workers. Physical appearance also mattered, and blond, blue-eyed Jews had a distinct advantage.

Every nation can point to examples of righteous people among its citizens. The entrepreneur celebrated in the book and movie *Schindler's List* was Sudeten German. Notable among the champions of Christian ethics in action were the villagers of Le Chambon sur Lignon in Vichy France. Under the leadership of their Huguenot pastor, Andre Trocme, they created a safety zone for Jews. Hundreds of members of the pastor's congregation conspired to protect thousands of Jewish children and adults. Many were handed over to the French underground to be escorted to nearby Switzerland, while others remained in the village and surrounding farms until liberation. *The Diary of Anne Frank* is so well known that the compassion, generosity, and courage of some Dutch people need no further amplification. From the Pyrenees to the Urals, in an era when might made right, perhaps 5 percent of the population stayed faithful to their concepts of decency, humanity, and courage and the precepts taught by Jesus Christ.

THE FINAL SOLUTION REVEALED

Within Germany and in the occupied nations, no information of the genocide was permitted to reach the public. Stories about mass murders and death camps were whispered in some circles but lacked verification. The United States and Great Britain were fighting on three continents, and the fate of European Jewry was not central to their efforts. None of the Allied Nations wanted to be accused of fighting the war for the sake of the Jews. Then, in August 1942, indisputable evidence reached the desk of Gerhart Riegner—an observer working for the World Jewish Congress in Switzerland. An unnamed German industrialist contacted Riegner because he had authoritative information concerning the Wannsee Conference's decision. The German was appalled when he learned of the planned annihilation of the Jewish people and hoped to alert Americans through Riegner's contacts. Riegner was stunned but sought confirmation. He did not have to wait long before other sources corroborated the information. In keeping with previously made arrangements, he passed this information to the U.S. State Department to be forwarded to Rabbi Stephen S. Wise, the major spokesman for American Jewry. The State Department, however, sought its own verification before contacting Rabbi Wise. The source they approached for corroboration was the Vatican. But the papacy, despite its international contacts, would not or could not confirm the ongoing massacres. Unable to understand the lack of any American reaction, Riegner alerted the British. Now the U.S. government had no choice but to notify Rabbi Wise. Eleven deadly weeks had passed since the receipt of the first cable.

Though the alarm had been sounded, it did not arouse the Gentile world. With some notable exceptions, the Jews were alone in their distress. The general public and the Roosevelt administration expressed concern, but that was all. On December 17, 1942, the United States joined the other Allies in a general condemnation of German atrocities, but no other action was taken. Some of the rationale for the apathetic response will be discussed later, for now it should be noted that the world outside of Hitler's European fortress was apprised of the fate of the Jews, while the majority of them were still alive.

The fact that a genocide was in progress could no longer be doubted. The Polish government in exile supplied much of the documentation; escaped concentration camp prisoners told their horror stories; and even photographs, taken secretly and at great risk, became available. But the focus of the world was elsewhere, on the war, which strained even the great resources of America. Except in the Jewish press, newspaper reports on events such as the destruction of the Warsaw ghetto were consigned to the inside pages. The war against Germany and Japan touched the whole nation; Hitler's war against the Jews was an aside compared to the main arena. Not until the Wallenberg mission in 1944 (see the following section) did President Roosevelt take an active part in the rescue of the remaining Jews.

DIVERSE CONDITIONS FOR RESCUE

The statistics representing the national percentages of Jews murdered during the Holocaust do not reflect the dissimilarities of the difficulties or possibilities of rescue. As noted earlier, these variables included the degree of Jewish assimilation into the native mainstream, physical appearance, age, and strength and the number of Jews within a locality as well as the duration of German domination. For example, in Germany or Austria, a Gentile might have to look after a hidden Jew for seven years, while in Hungary, the Nazis were in direct control for only one year. Topography, too, mattered. In the flat and almost woodless terrain of Holland, concealment was very difficult, while the mountains and forests of western Russia and eastern Poland could swallow up thousands of refugees. The type and amount of aid dropped by Allied planes or smuggled across borders to support underground fighters also differed considerably from place to place. Difficult to appraise but surely significant was the quality of political and religious leadership. Thus, the Metropolitan Stephan of the Holy Synod of Bulgaria set an example that strengthened the resolve in that country's leaders to withstand German pressure to transfer Jews into Nazi hands. By contrast, Premier Pierre Laval of Vichy France tried to ingratiate himself with the SS by eagerly enacting, even anticipating, anti-Jewish legislation.

Certainly the lack or prevalence of anti-Semitic traditions related directly to the Christians' willingness or reluctance to aid Jews. Some righteous Poles were hesitant to disclose their altruism even after the war had ended because they feared that their neighbors would disapprove of their actions. The Jews of Budapest were saved largely as a result of the work of American Jews, in conjunction with the U.S. government and the intrepid Raul Wallenberg (see the following section). The rescue of Danish Jewry was an entirely Christian effort carried out by their underground fighters.

Within each of the conquered countries, the Germans had no choice but to allow some local autonomy; they simply did not have sufficient manpower to manage every phase of administration themselves. Puppet regimes received anti-Jewish directives, and local police or militia were commonly used to round up Jews for deportation. The native authorities could comply with Nazi instructions or they could try to protect the Jewish population. Until the moment the trains to the death camps were sealed, some choices were still possible for the officials of the occupied areas: Obey and ingratiate yourself with the Nazi masters; disobey and risk loss of your job or worse. The numbers cited below demonstrate the contrasting successes and failures of Jewish survival in Europe.

Approximate Percentages of Surviving Jews:

Country	Pre-Nazi Jews Estimated (Percent) killed	Estimated Survivors
Austria	185,000 (35)	120,000
Belgium	65,700 (45)	36,800
Bohemia/Moravia	118,310 (60)	47,160
Bulgaria	50,000 (0)	50,000
Denmark	7,800 (8)	7,740
Estonia	4,500 (44)	2,500
France	350,000 (22)	272,680
Germany	566,000 (36)	366,000
Greece	77,380 (87)	10,380
Hungary	800,000 (74)	204,000
Italy	44,500 (17)	36,820
Latvia	95,000 (84)	15,000
Lithuania	168,000 (85)	25,000
Netherlands	140,000 (71)	40,000
Norway	1,700 (45)	938
Poland	3,300,000 (91)	300,000
Romania	342,000 (84)	55,000
Slovakia	88,950 (80)	17,950
USSR	3,020,000 (36)	1,920,000
Yugoslavia	78,000 (81)	14,700

DELAY AND OBSTRUCTION IN THE UNITED STATES

More than 65 years have passed since the death of Franklin Delano Roosevelt, but his name and his policies continue to arouse both admiration and scorn. His first inauguration and that of Adolf Hitler took place within a few weeks of each other. Interesting, too, is the fact that both were called upon to solve such critical problems as severe unemployment, disillusionment with government, pressures from the radical right and left to use drastic measures to alleviate problems and disappointments of World War I. During the decades of the 1920s and 1930s, many traditional values and mores were questioned and often rejected by the postwar generation. Social changes were exacerbated by the economic upheavals of the era. On both sides of the Atlantic, the general misery encouraged a search for scapegoats, and Jews and communists were often held responsible for all ills. Surely, the remedies advanced by Roosevelt and Hitler exemplify a noteworthy study of contrast and comparison.

Roosevelt's critics fault him for many of the measures he enacted to ease the national depression. He has also been criticized for his long inaction on behalf of European Jewry. The charge that this was due to anti-Jewish bias, however, cannot be substantiated. In fact, nearly all American Jews admired him, voted for him, and were grateful to him. Religious discrimination was not discernible in his personal relationships or in his political appointments. His directives opened many more civil service jobs to the merit system, and many bright young Jewish college graduates found employment in government service. It must be remembered that in the United States during the 1930s, few hospitals, law firms, banks, universities, or large industrial and manufacturing companies hired Jews regardless of their qualifications. Ours was a nation where many people were deeply, even proudly attached to their prejudices, where drinking fountains in the South were marked For Whites Only, where universities applied quota systems to prevent "them," including Jews, from enrolling in unwanted numbers, and where hotels displayed signs "Jews Not Welcome." When Roosevelt broadened the civil service system and nominated Jews to his cabinet and to the Supreme Court, he never again needed to be concerned about the Jewish vote. It was his for the asking.

When the news of the ongoing genocide reached the United States, Jewish leaders believed that the President would share their deep distress and provide a haven for the persecuted. Perhaps Roosevelt did care, but not to the extent of jeopardizing the delicate balance of party politics. Congress had severely restricted immigration to this country between 1924 and 1929. The quota system was particularly inequitable toward immigrants from Eastern and Southern Europe, but Congress showed no inclination to lift these limitations. The incident involving the ship *Saint Louis* was a tragic case in point. In May of 1939, some 900 German Jews had boarded the ship, confident that their visas to enter Cuba were valid. Upon reaching Havana, the Cuban government refused to accept their documents and did not allow the passengers to land. Urgent appeals to the American government requesting that the passengers be permitted to disembark in Miami were rejected. Florida, so clearly visible from the deck of the ship, remained a forbidden hope even though the American Jewish community was willing to defray all costs. After weeks of failed negotiations, the reluctant German captain was forced to return to Hamburg. The feverish activities of Jewish organizations secured havens for a majority of the passengers in Holland, England, and France at a price of half a million dollars. The unlucky remainder had to disembark in Germany to share the fate of the thousands to whom all exit doors were closed.

After 1942, the Germans no longer permitted Jews to leave; however, there were still possibilities for rescue. One can speculate that if the United States had provided energetic leadership, several of the neutral nations would have done more to provide visas for victims of the Holocaust. Perhaps if Great Britain had been willing to ignore the illegal immigration to Palestine, other non-European nations might have offered refuge to the fleeing Jews. Opportunities to save hundreds of children were frittered away by long bureaucratic delays in the U.S. State Department. Temporary reception centers could have been set up in neutral areas. American bombing missions could easily have inflicted damage on the perimeters of the death camps and the rail lines leading there. Several State Department officials, such as Breckenridge Long who controlled the immigration desk, were actively involved in preventing "these people" from entering the United States. His telegrams to consulates advised "Delay, delay, delay" the issuance of visas. Several Jewish members of Congress pleaded with their colleagues to open the quotas but to no avail.

It must be remembered that during the early 1940s, the United States was going through a national trauma. Most of the fleet had been sunk at Pearl Harbor, the war in the Pacific was going badly, England was hanging by a thread, and Hitler was at the gates of Moscow. This country exerted its supreme and total effort toward winning the war. To the cries for help for Europe's Jews, the administration responded again and again with assurances that winning the war was the first priority; the sooner Germany was defeated, the sooner Hitler's victims would be freed. How few Jews would remain alive to benefit from future assistance was as yet unimagined.

AMERICAN JEWRY

American Jews were not passive in the face of the genocide. They organized rallies, circulated petitions, lobbied members of Congress, and collected money. Even though their voices were joined by some prominent Christians, they never evolved into a resounding chorus. Today, after Martin Luther King, Jr., and others have instructed protesters in the art of civil disobedience, the activities of the Jews seem modest. Clearly, they feared that too much pressure would backfire, first by increasing American anti-Semitism and second, by enraging the Nazis, causing them to commit greater atrocities. The ideological split between Zionists and anti-Zionists further weakened the advocacy for immediate rescue attempts. It seemed to many American Jews that vigorous support for the establishment of a Jewish homeland might be viewed as unpatriotic, likely to create the impression of a divided allegiance. The Jewish conservative establishment was dismayed when the radical Committee for a Jewish Army ran an advertisement: "For Sale, 70,000 Jews; guaranteed to be human beings; at $50.00 a piece," in response to a Romanian initiative to "sell" its Jews.

Belated Action

At the eleventh hour, the administration was finally energized. Secretary of the Treasury Henry Morgenthau provided the impetus. He had become aware of the inertia, even obstructionism, in the State Department. At his behest, a brief was prepared that exposed the tactics of the immigration officials who prevented the entry of Jews, even within the established limits of the quota laws. Morgenthau handed the President this expose, provocatively entitled "On the Acquiescence of the Government of the Murder of the Jews." Roosevelt was shocked. He immediately created the War Refugee Board; its mission was rescue; its partner was the World Jewish Congress.

In January 1944, the greatest number of Jews in immediate danger of annihilation were the 144,000 assembled in Budapest. Eichmann was there, loading trains to Auschwitz. The resettlement myth was no longer believed, and there was no doubt regarding the actual fate of the deported Jews. The Nazis were not without opposition in the destruction of this last of the major Jewish population centers. Within Hungary, rescue efforts had been mounted by the Hungarian Zionist Youth, by the International Red Cross, by the papal nuncio who issued false baptismal papers, and by the Swiss consular staff. Citizens of neutral nations were exempt from the directives of the Nazis that conscripted Hungarian Jews into labor gangs. Several members of neutral legations used this loophole to rescue Jewish people in Budapest. The Swedish consulate was first to issue papers to Jews who had commercial ties to Sweden. To provide for these new "citizens," the Swedes hung their national flag from buildings bought to house them, making them inaccessible to Eichmann. Other countries followed that example, most notably Switzerland. Some 50,000 Hungarian Jews were saved by the efforts of Carl Lutz of the Swiss legation in this manner. He maintained close contact with the Zionists organization in Budapest, whose young members saved thousands from Auschwitz with their cleverly forged passports. Nonetheless, the death trains were filled every day.

This was the state of affairs when the American War Refugee Board, appointed by President Roosevelt, went into action. When the newly appointed Board asked a young Swedish diplomat, Raoul Wallenberg, to undertake the mission to save Jews in Hungary, they made a brilliant choice. Wallenberg was daring, ingenious, and his pockets were filled with American money. His arrival in Budapest marked the beginning of a new intensity in rescue activities. Officially a member of the Swedish legation, he issued passports and safe conduct passes and bought houses in the name of the Swedish government, whose neutral flag afforded safety to thousands. He organized a squad of 400 operatives, young Jews who imitated his bluff and bravado as they pulled prisoners out of transports, claiming they were under Swedish protection. The families he saved required housing, food, medicine, and confidence that they had a future—all supplied by the remarkable Wallenberg. His greatest exploit was executed as the Soviet Army approached the city. The SS commander of Budapest had been ordered to murder all the remaining 70,000 Jews before pulling out of the city. Wallenberg, with a combination of threats and persuasion, convinced the German general not to stain his reputation by ordering such a horrendous massacre of civilians. It is tragic that the righteous Swede disappeared the very day the Russians entered Budapest. Nothing was ever admitted, but it is probable that he was arrested by the Soviets who mistakenly believed him to be an American anti-communist agent. Despite intensive inquiries, the exact nature of his fate remains unknown.

SURVIVAL IN BULGARIA

Not every country within the German sphere became a partner in genocide. There was Finland, an uneasy ally of Germany in the war against the USSR, which simply said "no" to Himmler and kept its Jewish community of 2,000 intact. Franco of Spain, the Fascist dictator who had accepted German aid to attain power, remained neutral during the war. He turned a deaf ear to the complaints of the SS that he was obstructing Hitler's intent to blot out Jewish existence. Franco's policies were responsible for saving 40,000 Jews; most were refugees who made their way across the French border to the Spanish coast to take ships to destinations overseas. Franco reversed history when he declared that Sephardic Jews, whose ancestors had been expelled by Ferdinand and Isabella in 1492, were de facto Spanish citizens, thus entitled to asylum in Spanish embassies. In Italy, even when Mussolini was in power, Jews who had fled from Greece, France, and Yugoslavia found asylum. Only after Germany occupied Italy did the trains begin to roll toward Auschwitz. The majority of Italian Jews lived through that traumatic final year of the war because the Italian people and their institutions were supportive.

Bulgaria, a nation that had joined the Axis in 1941, was home to about 50,000 Jews, 0.8 percent of its population. Most belonged to the middle class, and about half lived in the capital, Sofia. The majority of Bulgarians were Eastern Orthodox Christians, who traditionally accepted their Jewish fellow citizens with tolerance. Until 1941, the government, headed by King Boris III, had remained neutral in the war, but this policy changed when Germany permitted Bulgaria to annex long-desired Greek and Yugoslav border territories. The King joined the Axis powers and to appease their new partners, a reluctant parliament passed a version of Hitler's Nuremberg laws. Bulgarian Jews were now subjected to discrimination and economic exploitation. Much of their property was seized, and they were ordered to wear a yellow star. Many of the younger men were forced to work in road-building gangs. But the German authorities demanded complete compliance with their racial principles; they wanted the Jews delivered into their hands. The Bulgarian government agreed to give the SS free reign only in their recently acquired regions of Thrace and Macedonia. And so, in 1943, SS roundups began. More than 11,000 were shipped to Auschwitz, and of these, nearly 95 percent were killed.

Next, the Nazis began their preparations for an *Aktion* against the Bulgarian Jews. The date was set; in fact, arrests were in progress when the Bulgarian government called for a postponement. Behind the scenes, the leaders of the Jewish community and their Christian friends had worked a miracle. The rumors that "resettlement" meant death had been confirmed, and the majority of Bulgarians did not want their government to be an accessory to mass murder. A public protest and the intervention of the head of the church, the Metropolitan Stefan, won a stay of execution for tens of thousands of Jews. An anti-Nazi resistance movement was organized, whose members equated saving Jews with opposing the Germans.

In 1943, Boris went to see Hitler and returned in the Fuehrer's private plane. Within a few days he died, perhaps a victim of poison. If he was killed to insure the Nazi version of the *Endloesung* of the Jewish question, the plot misfired, and succeeding governments continued to oppose deportation of Bulgarian Jews. Their rescue was due to the combined efforts of the leaders of the Jewish community and the resistance of the parliament to German demands and to the opposition of the Holy Synod. The fact that German victory in the war was no longer a certainty may well have entered into the resolve of the Bulgarians.

THE DANES MOBILIZE FOR RESCUE

No Holocaust history is complete without some detailed reference to Denmark. The number of Jewish survivors in that small German-occupied nation was a remarkable 92 percent. How and why was such an extraordinary rescue achieved? Events resemble a play in three acts: the first sets the scene, the second reveals the plot against the Jews, and the third unveils the rescue operation.

The six and a half million Danes were swept into the German hegemony in a bloodless invasion during the spring of 1940. Danes were considered to be Aryans, and cooperation was deemed to be cheaper than force; therefore, the Germans opted for a lenient occupation policy. King Christian X, the parliament (which included several Jewish members), the cabinet, and even Denmark's small army were left in place. Danish autonomy was, however, restricted in regard to its economic output and its foreign policy. As long as Danish food poured into the Reich, the German military presence under General Hermann von Hannecken and the diplomatic representative, Reich Commissioner Dr. Werner Best, were fairly unobtrusive.

Dr. Best, however, was an ambitious Nazi. What better way to ingratiate himself with his masters in Berlin than to institute anti-Jewish measures in Denmark? When Best approached Prime Minister Scavenius, he was told that the Danish cabinet would resign rather than pass such legislation. The king replied in the same manner, stating that there was no Jewish problem and that all his subjects were equal.

That nearly 8,000 Danish Jews walked freely and unmarked on the streets of Copenhagen stuck like a bone in Werner Best's throat. Other problems were developing as well. The Danes had organized an effective anti-German underground, which sabotaged trains and ships carrying goods to Germany. Soldiers on occupation duty complained that they were treated with disdain; indeed, Danish women crossed the street to avoid them. Best's situation became worrisome when Hitler berated him and warned him to do better. Determined and empowered to teach the Danes the meaning of obedience, Best changed his approach. The executive and legislative branches of the Danish government were dissolved, the king became a virtual prisoner in his palace, and the army was forced to disband. This, predictably, increased the numbers and activities of the anti-German underground. When the Reich Commissionar ordered the seizure of the records of the Jewish community that enabled him to identify nearly all the Jews in the kingdom, the Jewish community grew uneasy. Then Best inquired whether or not the Danish civil service would participate in any anti-Jewish action. He was given a clear "no." Nonetheless, he decided that the time had come to execute a lightning strike against the Jews; surely that would restore him to Hitler's good graces.

The Plot

Best decided to arrest all Danish Jews on October 13, 1943, on the eve of the Jewish New Year, when most of them would be conveniently assembled in synagogues for religious services. To transport the intended prisoners as quickly as possible, he imported SS, German police, and railroad cars. Ships were readied in the harbor to ferry the sealed trains across the sea to Germany. General von Hannecken was opposed to the entire enterprise and had to be persuaded to allow 50 of his men to be made available in case of disturbances. The plan required the expertise of a maritime specialist, and the Reich Commissioner called in a German specialist, a longtime resident of Denmark, Georg F. Duckwitz. When apprised of the scheme, Duckwitz was appalled but did not voice his objections to the Germans. Instead, he decided that he must follow the dictates of his conscience. He called on an old friend, a Dane with connections to the underground, and revealed to him the fate awaiting the Jews of Denmark in just a few days.

A chain reaction was now set into motion. The Danish resistance was notified, and its members decided to do everything in their power to protect the Jews. But where could thousands of men, women, and children be hidden? Certainly not within the confines of Denmark. Duckwitz, who was free to travel with his German passport, accepted the mission to ask the Swedish government for permission to bring the Danish Jews to Sweden. That assurance was given without reservations. While the details of the rescue were planned, it was vital to persuade the Jewish leadership of the imminent danger facing them. Overcoming their initial incredulity, the rabbi and other influential members of the community accepted the fact that Danish Jewry, so secure since the Middle Ages, was on the verge of extinction.

On the eve of the Jewish New Year service, the rabbi stood before his stunned congregation in Copenhagen's main synagogue. He told the assembled crowd what the Germans had planned. Yes, he was certain. No, you cannot return to your homes, you must disappear. Not next week, not tomorrow, but at once. At first there was disbelief but the rabbi persisted—"find someplace to hide for the next few days, we'll contact you somehow and get you out of the country."

Because it had not yet been possible to arrange transport to Sweden, it was necessary to find temporary hiding places for thousands of men, women, and children. And at this point, it seemed that the entire population of Denmark participated in an enormous conspiracy to save their Jews and defy the Nazis.

As word of the immediate danger spread throughout Copenhagen and to other Jewish communities, the intended victims simply vanished. When the SS entered the main synagogue on the morning of Rosh Hashanah, it was empty. Hotels, hospitals, private homes in remote villages, Christian friends, churches, funeral parlors, taxis, ambulances, and even the police became partners in a single objective: Hide the Jews; do not, by a word or a glance, allow the Germans to find a single one. Some Danes went through the telephone books, searched for Jewish names, and called the numbers to sound the alarm. Amazingly, the secret was kept, and the promise that the Jews of Denmark would not be abandoned was fulfilled.

The Escape

A few dozen Jews were caught in the German net. Most were people who refused to believe that they were in danger or did not hear of the planned arrests. Several Polish refugees committed suicide; they could not imagine that Gentiles would risk their lives to save them. The captured Danish Jews were deported to the Theresienstadt concentration camp, where nearly all survived because of the continued vigilance and food packages of the Danish Red Cross. The hidden Jews, meanwhile, had to be whisked out of the country as quickly as possible. Members of the underground found fishermen who were willing to transport Jews to the Swedish shores. Throughout October, there were daily departures. Danish doctors and nurses stood by every night to give injections to keep children asleep during the crossing. German ships patrolled these waters constantly, and a crying child could endanger everyone on board.

The Germans suspected that certain villages along the coast were used as departure points and tried to barricade the roads. In the skirmishes between the resistance fighters and the SS, several Danes were killed. But, unlike the unfulfilled and wasted lives of so many millions, their deaths enabled others to live. The sea did not part on this exodus; instead, Danish fishermen carried the Jews across the waters of the Kattegat to safety.

Until the end of the war, for nearly two years, the hospitality and generosity of the Swedish people and their government sustained the Danish Jews. When they returned home, they found their gardens had been tended by neighbors, their pets had been cared for, and their Torahs had been hidden in churches.

ACCOUNTING FOR THE DANISH ACHIEVEMENT

It is very tempting to use the Danish experience as an example of the possibilities of rescue that other people did not attempt. No doubt, a greater humanitarian commitment could have saved lives, but it is a fallacy to believe that the success of the Danes could easily have been duplicated elsewhere. Every European nation had distinct and unique problems during the Nazi era. Prevailing attitudes toward Jews differed widely, native and occupation administrations varied considerably, and diverse geographic factors affected the possibility of keeping Jews safe.

The Danes saw an opportunity and went into action; that fact is forever to their credit. Their achievement was predicated on some, perhaps all, of the following prerequisites:

1. The Danes had a well-established humanitarian attitude toward their fellow men. Anti-Semitism had been outlawed since 1814!
2. The political leadership, the king and Parliament, set the tone for ethical behavior.
3. The Christian religious leadership was not intimidated, and from their pulpits, ministers urged their parishioners to aid their imperiled countrymen.
4. When the Germans executed Danish saboteurs, they believed the population would be cowed; instead the opposite resulted.

5. The willingness and proximity of neutral Sweden provided a necessary haven for the potential victims.
6. The underground movement was well organized and eager to prove its effectiveness.
7. The Jews were well integrated into Danish society; their numbers were small and the rate of intermarriage with Christians was high.

The men and women who, like Madame Trocmé, opened their door and their hearts to imperiled Jews deserve our admiration, our gratitude, and our respect. Each of us may hope that we would respond with equal courage under similar circumstances. But dangerous circumstances do not lend themselves to simple answers. Do we have the right to condemn the mother whose children are sleeping in the next room, when she tells a fleeing Jew that she cannot endanger her children by allowing him to hide in her house? Indeed, what would you say to the stranger seeking refuge? My answer is, "I do not know."

CHAPTER 12

After the Deluge

We may understand what happened during the Holocaust, but we cannot understand why it happened. Indeed, the more intensive the study of the facts, the more elusive the answer to that question. The explanations of philosophers, theologians, psychiatrists, and historians ring hollow against the fact of babies smashed against a wall. So, there can be no satisfying conclusion to the moral dilemma raised by the Holocaust. As students of history, we must be content to deal with the measurable, definable results of events. Among these are the following themes:

1. Germany after defeat
2. The liberated remnant
3. War criminals on trial
4. Present-day Germans and Jews

POSTWAR GERMANY

When Germany surrendered in May of 1945, much of the nation lay in rubble. A half million German civilians had perished during Allied intensive bombing raids, and many cities were unable to provide even the most basic services required to sustain life. At this point, Germany was a country virtually without able-bodied men. The male population between 16 and 70 years of age had been drafted into one or another of the various military and paramilitary units. As a result, women, children, and old men were left to struggle in a world that lacked electric power, health facilities, government services, food, fuel, water supply, schools, and public transport. Industry was disrupted, paid employment was scarce, and many homes and apartment houses were uninhabitable. To add to the chaos, some 10 million Germans had been expelled from the Prussian provinces east of the Oder–Neisse line. The Soviet Union had ceded this territory to Poland to compensate for Russian annexation of lands in eastern Poland. The newly installed Polish authorities ordered that this region be made *Deutsch-rein*, free of German inhabitants, and, depending on the location, gave them a day, perhaps a week, to leave. These suddenly homeless Germans had to abandon their property and were permitted to take with them nothing more than a few personal possessions. These impoverished evacuees made their way into war-ravished central and western Germany. By and large, they were accepted and aided by the natives who themselves lacked food and housing, yet shared whatever little they had with these destitute strangers. In addition to massive shifts in population, German soldiers who had evaded capture by the Allies were trying to make their way home. Furthermore, waves of trekkers crisscrossed the nation. The Nazis had used approximately seven million workers and slave laborers in German fields and factories. They had come from all parts of the continent, and now large numbers of them were choking the roads, trying to make their way home. Some of these foreign nationals, however, did not want to return to their homelands which had become communist dictatorships. So many millions were on the move, the fortunate ones still in possession of a horse and wagon but the great masses walking with a few possessions on their backs, in baby carriages, in baskets, and sacks, bewildered, angry, and fearful and debilitated by the uncertainty about the fate of loved ones and the uncertainty of their future.

Zones of Occupation

In February of 1945, the Allied leaders had met at Yalta and agreed that upon Hitler's defeat, Germany would be divided into temporary zones of military occupation. During the spring, the Axis powers were vanquished, and beginning that summer, the Yalta decision was implemented. Germany was cut into four zones of occupation. The area west of the Elbe River was shared by American, British, and French forces; the eastern region, except for Berlin, was controlled by the Soviets. Berlin, situated within the Soviet Zone, was partitioned into four districts, which mimicked the division of the Reich itself. An agency, the Allied Control Commission, was set up in order to formulate and enact a joint occupation policy. This compromise was seen as an interim step, to be abrogated when the occupying nations were satisfied that the Germans were ready for self-government. At that point, democratic elections were to be held and gradually the German people would achieve autonomy and admittance into the family of nations.

This plan, however, was dependent on cooperation between the Soviets and the Western Allies. But soon it became clear that Stalin followed his own agenda. He had succeeded in his quest to dominate Eastern and Balkan Europe; wherever Soviet soldiers had marched to liberate the people from Nazi oppression, there they remained until a communist regime had been installed. These subjugated nations became Soviet satellites; their people were denied self-determination. Stalin increasingly refused to collaborate in the decisions of the Control Council, and in 1948, the Soviets walked out. As a result, the military zones hardened into the formation of two German states, East and West. The three western zones were combined in 1949 to form the Federal Republic of Germany with its capital in Bonn; in the East, the German Democratic Republic, surely a misnomer for a communist satellite, was governed from East Berlin. The Cold War had begun.

Governing the devastated zones of occupation required immense material effort and political skill. To aid in the feeding, the reconstruction, the healing was but one challenge, separating innocent Germans from the guilty Nazis, presented great difficulties. The process of reeducation, from kindergarten up, was deemed of great importance. To direct the German people toward democracy and freedom required more than a handbook to guide the occupation forces. The entire structure of Nazi administration had to be dismantled and replaced by new agencies. None of the military commanders had experience or precedents to follow for such nation building. The directives from their home governments, far from the scene, could not envision the complexity of the situation on the ground. Unusual problems called for untried solutions that sometimes worked and sometimes failed. Essentially, great ingenuity was needed to overcome language and cultural barriers in order to provide the Germans with the basis for both practical and ideological renewal.

SURVIVORS IN LIMBO

The suffering of the defeated Germans and the displaced people of various national origins could not be compared with the anguish of the concentration camp survivors. These tens of thousands of men and women and a few hundred children were physically and emotionally on the brink of death. When a stunned General Dwight D. Eisenhower, chief of the European Theater of Operations, saw his first concentration camp, he cabled newspapers in the United States and elsewhere to send reporters to the scene. He feared that without pictures and descriptions, the world simply would not believe the truth about Nazi atrocities. Indeed, it became clear that earlier accounts of the genocide, which had often been characterized as exaggerations, could not approach the horrendous sights and indescribable smells of the dead and half-dead inmates.

At the end of the death marches, whether at Neuengamme, Ravensbrueck, Sachsenhausen, Bergen-Belsen, Flossenbuerg, Dachau, Mauthausen, or Buchenwald, the survivors had been dumped behind barbed wire fences. The SS guards disappeared, leaving the prisoners in worse conditions than they had ever experienced. The camps were overcrowded and lacked any sanitation facilities; there was no food or water, and no one to care for the sick or bury the dead. The stunned liberators were not prepared for the enormity of the task they faced. Their initial hope was to save many of the starving Jews by providing them with nourishing food; this turned into a medical disaster. The months or years during which their bodies had been deprived had robbed their intestinal systems of normal digestive abilities. There simply was no medical knowledge on how to deal with such emaciation, and thousands died because they ravenously filled their stomachs. The resulting diarrhea sapped their strength at the moment of their possible rebirth.

How many Jews survived the Holocaust? The answer is subject to definition as well as point of view. Who should be counted as a survivor? Only those who had been in concentration camps? What of the hidden Jews, the partisan fighters, and the quarter million Polish Jews who fled to Russia ahead of the German armies? What about those who passed as Gentiles? Or the half Jews, offspring of mixed marriages?

Clearly, the numbers are subject to interpretation. In the chaos of the weeks, months, and even years following the end of the war, no agency was in a position to gather accurate records.

Experts at the U.S. Holocaust Memorial Museum in Washington indicate that in 1945, the number of Jews in Displaced Persons (DP) Camps was 69,098. A year later it had risen to 173,592, and in 1947 reached 182,000. The continuing increase was probably the result of the longing of most of the survivors to live among their fellow Jews. They streamed into the DP camps after they gave up their initial search for surviving members of their families. Only about 20–30 percent of Jewish DPs lived among the German population in towns and cities. Of the total number of survivors, more than three-fourths were Polish nationals, the rest mainly Hungarian and Czech.

It is estimated that approximately 50,000 Jews were liberated from the concentration camps. Because thousands died within days after liberation, even this number cannot be cited with accuracy. What can be said without fear of contradiction concerns the condition of the survivors. Many were near death, often numbed by emotional and physical exhaustion. They greeted their liberators with disbelief, with tears of joy, and with stunned silence. But after the momentary euphoria of liberation, the survivors had to face the reality of their position. And that reality was bleak.

No Place to Go

They found themselves on German soil, because the occupation authorities did not know what else to do with their DPs; they were gathered into camps, usually guarded by soldiers. Suspected Nazis and their collaborators were often confined in the same facilities. The overwhelmed military authorities had designated all the homeless as displaced persons, including former prisoners of war, slave laborers, concentration camp survivors, and even criminals. The shortage of housing in Germany was acute, and several concentration camps were used as holding facilities. Jewish survivors constituted about one-fourth of the total number of DPs. For weeks, in some cases months, they were identified and billeted according to their national origin; that meant German Jews were housed with Nazis, Polish Jews with anti-Semites, and so on. Obviously, this arrangement caused great tensions.

The Jews were liberated, but were they free? The guards outside the barbed wire were no longer the black-shirted SS, but they were soldiers nonetheless who had orders to prevent them from roaming the countryside. For medical aid they had to rely on German doctors whom they had learned to fear. Because so many of the homeless and stateless people wanted to be in the American zone of occupation, U.S. camps were particularly overcrowded. The original number of Jewish survivors in the American zone, estimated at 30,000, grew by a third when 10,000 Polish Jews made their way west. These were survivors who had retraced their steps back to their hometowns to search for members of their families. Some had hoped to reestablish themselves on familiar soil. What they found instead was devastating beyond all expectations. No relatives came to welcome them, and often the Poles who had moved into their houses greeted them with open hostility. Clearly, Jewish life could not be renewed in Poland, and so they tramped westward toward the DP camps.

A further, even larger, increase resulted from the arrival of tens of thousands of Polish Jews who had fled to the Soviet Union during the war and did not want to live under a communist regime. Prominent among these were partisan fighters and Zionists hoping to get to Palestine.

Many survivors had difficulties in facing and adjusting to the realities of their losses, to their half-free, dependent existence, to communal kitchens, and to the continued lack of privacy. Their physical and emotional problems required care which was not available in the DP camps. In their later recollections, survivors gratefully commended the heroic efforts of individuals who tried to help them. Some Jewish and non-Jewish soldiers and especially the army chaplains worked indefatigably in their behalf. With little or no training, they tried to meet the psychological and physical needs of their charges, instituted improvements in living conditions, and listened sympathetically to their doleful histories. In tandem with American Jewish organizations, these men played an important role in changing U.S. policies. President Truman was made aware of the urgency of the needs of Nazi survivors, and he appointed Earl G. Harrison to conduct an official investigation. The report, completed in August 1945, was sharply critical. As a result, many of the worst problems were alleviated.

Among the many issues facing the liberated remnant, two questions arose invariably: Am I the only one left in my entire family? Where can I go to start rebuilding my life? Jewish and non-Jewish organizations assembled and distributed lists of names of survivors, which facilitated the search for relatives. Reunions were rare indeed and were celebrated with joy and envy. For many victims, the realization that their parents, children, wives, or husbands were dead caused psychological disorders from which some patients never recovered completely.

The aim of Allied DP policy was repatriation. Most of the non-Jewish workers, whether free or enslaved, were urged and aided to return to their homes. Willingly or reluctantly, they were pushed out of the military zones. But what was to be done about the eastern European Jews? It was no secret that survivors who had returned to Poland had encountered rabid anti-Semitism and that some of the returnees were murdered when they tried to reclaim their possessions. Clearly, repatriation was not an option for this group. To remain in Germany was equally and understandably out of the question. Hopes of the survivors revolved mainly around two destinations: The majority wanted to emigrate to Palestine; naturally, the Holocaust had greatly encouraged the growth of Zionism and intensified the longing for a Jewish national homeland. The second choice of survivors was the United States. But the path to either haven, Palestine or the United States, was blocked by many obstacles. So they remained in their camps, waiting for the English and American governments to admit them.

The revelations of the Harrison report resulted in improvements in camp conditions. Jewish DPs were placed into separate housing and, where feasible, were permitted to manage their own affairs. The survivors held elections, organized associations according to religious or political preferences, negotiated with the Allied authorities, established recreational and educational facilities, and conducted religious services. As health was improved or restored, many survivors wanted to establish families of their own. Marriages were celebrated, and newborns, often named after murdered relatives, were greeted with joy. Meanwhile, they prepared for their future by learning trades and studying English and Hebrew. Jewish organizations from the United States and Palestine and the United Nations' Relief and Rehabilitation Administration (UNRRA) provided financial and emotional support. American Jews engaged in intense lobbying to ease U.S. and British immigration restrictions because the search for a home, for a place to resume a normal life, remained the most urgent, the all-consuming quest.

SEEKING A REFUGE: THE UNITED STATES

Although the international press had feasted on the pictures and stories of the Nazi atrocities for months, notoriety did not translate into offers of asylum. These survivors were, of course, dirt-poor. Many had aged prematurely, while some suffered from permanent physical and emotional infirmities. They had no political or economic power. Politicians in the United States as well as in Great Britain were preoccupied with helping their citizenry and their economies to switch from wartime to peacetime requirements. Meanwhile, American immigration restrictions remained in force. The British government, ruling Palestine as her mandate for the League of Nations, permitted a mere trickle of Jewish settlers to enter the region.

Since 1929, the immigration policy of the United States was based on the national origin's law, the Johnson–Reed Act. The law established a quota system that favored Northern and Western Europeans, and severely limited immigration from Eastern and Southern Europe. This bias was rationalized by the theory that the preferred groups would assimilate more easily to American life than, for example, Poles, Italians, Greeks, or Russians. Most of the DPs, both Jewish and non-Jewish, were born in nations whose American quota was very small. As the months of waiting turned into years and the camps still teemed with DPs, the hopes of many turned into despair. Congress, under the pressure of public opinion and a sympathetic President Harry Truman was finally moved to change the immigration policy. The remedy, called the Displaced Persons Act of 1948, opened the door a mere crack. The law did not set aside the quota system but permitted DPs to "borrow" against future quotas of up to 205,000 persons in two years. But few of the applicants for visas were able to obtain them because restrictions still discriminated against Jews and Catholics. Finally, in 1950, that is *five* years after liberation, an amendment to the legislation provided some additional relief: 415,000 men, women, and children were permitted to enter within a four-year period. Finally, it was possible for some 80,000 survivors to make this country their home and become a grateful and valuable component of our citizenry.

SEEKING A REFUGE: PALESTINE

British reaction to the longing of the survivors to settle in Palestine was weighted down with Arab opposition. In trying to balance Arab and Jewish claims to the land, the Jewish minority was at a distinct disadvantage. The half-million Palestinian Jews, approximately 30 percent of the regional population, were eager to welcome the

European remnant of their people. But the British Labor Government under Ernest Bevin was unwilling to keep Prime Minister Arthur Balfour's 1917 promise to support Zionist aspiration. In 1939, the British government had issued its so-called White Paper, which stipulated that during the following five years Jewish immigration to Palestine could not exceed 75,000. These restrictions were precisely, even cruelly, enforced. Throughout the war, the British fleet turned back the ships of fleeing Jews, many in crowded vessels that were barely or not at all seaworthy. The same strict guidelines were applied to the postwar Nazi survivors. The British navy patrolled the Palestinian harbors, impounded refugee ships, and diverted them to the island of Cyprus. There once again, the exiles, some 12,000 of them, were consigned to concentration camps. Certificates of entry to Palestine were actually held below the promised 75,000 until the drowning of refugees in the Mediterranean aroused such a storm of criticism that the government permitted the quota to be filled.

But even the determined hostility of the British government could not stop a continuous, though small, stream of survivors from reaching the destination of their hopes. They came via several illegal escape routes. These schemes were conceived, funded, organized, and run by Jews. Among the most active members of this group were veterans of the Jewish Brigade, soldiers who had fought as an independent unit in the British army. They were combat-experienced, and at the end of the war, many decided to use their training to aid the Holocaust survivors. The appearance of Jewish soldiers, young, strong, in uniforms with a star on their shoulders, created a sensation in the DP camps. Their optimism was infectious, and their escape plans seemed workable. With the help of money from American contributors, members of the Brigade leased ships and secretly escorted survivors across borders to reach holy land harbors. Most of their vessels were intercepted by the English fleet, and the Jews were interned on Cyprus, to await the final completion of their journey after the creation of the state of Israel.

But what of the bulk of the survivors still lingering in Germany? Despite the worldwide recognition of the continued plight of concentration camp survivors, English policy remained unchanged. Unchanged, that is, until the virtual civil war in Palestine became too costly, in men, material, and reputation. In 1947, the British had had enough; they ceded their mandatory authority to the United Nations. The vote of that body to partition Palestine established the State of Israel in 1948; and hundred of thousands came home at last.

JUSTICE FOR THE MURDERERS?

Among the many problems facing the victorious Allies in their aim to decentralize, democratize, and demilitarize their respective zones of occupation, two have direct impact on Holocaust history: First was the demand for punishment of the Nazis who had turned so much of Europe into a cemetery and second was the need to root out Nazi ideology and its supporters. Both efforts were undertaken to prepare the German people for eventual democratic independence.

The Allies, after many discussions and delays, agreed to create an international tribunal that would try the most infamous Nazis. The court was empowered to collect evidence, present the charges against Nazi criminals in public hearings, permit legal council for the defendants and arrive at and carry out the verdicts.

To rid Germany of the advocates of Nazism was a complicated and perplexing task for the occupying Allies. Reeducation and de-Nazification were the twin objectives. Of course, the German people lived amid the most obvious inducement to renounce Nazism: Millions dead and millions missing; Nazi savagery broadcast to a shuddering world; their own cities in desolation. To reenforce such graphic lessons, the Allied occupation forces instituted sweeping changes in the school curricula and tried to purge ex-Nazis from positions of authority. But often it was not easy to replace former Nazi Party members with "good Germans." As might be expected, nearly all Germans claimed that they were never "true" Nazis; yes, they pretended to follow Hitler, but that was done for one reason or another. And certainly, they were not anti-Semitic—did they not try to help this or that Jewish friend?

THE NUREMBERG TRIALS: 1945–1946

The Bavarian city of Nuremberg had been a favorite showpiece of Nazi pomp and ceremony. From here the anti-Jewish racial laws of 1935 had been issued. To conduct the trial of 22 leaders of the Third Reich against this background seemed eminently appropriate. That such a prosecution took place at all was a victory for humanity. It implied acceptance of the concept that international law may supersede national law when heinous criminal acts are committed regardless of national boundaries.

The topic of punishment for the Nazis was first raised at the 1943 Teheran Conference of Allied chiefs of state. Among the suggestions offered was Stalin's idea to liquidate the entire German General Staff. In the United States, Secretary of the Treasury Henry Morgenthau urged that Germany be reduced to an agricultural country without its own industry. At the Potsdam meeting in 1945, the various draconian proposals were rejected in favor of convening an international extraordinary court of justice. Specifically, high-ranking Nazis were to be tried on charges of crimes against peace, humanity, and defenseless minorities. The original objections of some jurists and some members of the public concerning the lack of legal precedents were muted as the full testimony of Nazi terror was unveiled.

The presiding justice of the Tribunal was British Lord Chief Justice Geoffrey Lawrence. The United States was represented by Attorney General Frances Biddle; France sent an expert on international law, Henri Donnedieu de Vabres; and the Soviet judge was Major-General LT. Nikitchenko. Each of the four participating Allies also sent several prosecutors to Nuremberg. Robert Jackson, an Associate Justice of the Supreme Court, led the U.S. team. The accused were permitted German defense attorneys, and procedures were fixed according to extant legal principles. The defendants, accustomed to Nazi justice, were surprised that the trial was not a sham but was conducted with careful attention to their rights.

The Defendants

Since Hitler, Himmler, and Goebbels had committed suicide, Hermann Goering emerged as the highest ranking of the Nazis. Among the indicted were men who held high positions in the military, the foreign office, and the economic and propaganda ministries. Holocaust survivors noted with satisfaction the indictments of several Holocaust implementers, among them Hans Frank, Governor-General of much of occupied Poland; Ernst Kaltenbrunner, who had succeeded Reinhard Heydrich as head of the security and other police organizations; Julius Streicher, publisher of anti-Semitic hate material; and Alfred Rosenberg, proponent of the Nordic superiority theory and Reich Minister of the eastern territories. The tribunal also condemned several organizations, such as the *Fuehrerkorps,* composed of the upper echelons of the Nazi Party, the Gestapo, the SS, and the SD. Officials of these organizations could expect to be arrested, and simple membership was equated with commission of a criminal act. It should be noted that, in the long run, prosecution of all members of these associations was not feasible.

The Verdicts

The amount of evidence collected for the Nuremberg Tribunal filled 42 volumes. Bushels of documents, many signed by the defendants, attested to their guilt. Their letters, directives, orders, and speeches, and the testimony of witnesses whose recollections reduced listeners to tears, collectively condemned all but three of the 22 defendants. Sentenced to death by hanging were Hermann Goering, *Reichsmarschall* and head of the air force; General Wilhelm Keitel, Chief of the High Command of the Armed Forces; Joachim von Ribbentrop, Foreign Minister; Wilhelm Frick, Minister of the Interior and Nazi Party (NSDAP) leader; Fritz Sauckel, Minister of Labor; General Alfred Jodl, Chief of Armed Forces Operational Staff; Artur Seyss-Inquart, Reich Commissioner for the occupied Netherlands and the aforementioned Kaltenbrunner, Frank, Rosenberg, and Streicher. Prison sentences were pronounced on Rudolf Hess, Hitler's early deputy; Walther Funk, president of the national banking system; Admiral Karl Doenitz, Hitler's last naval commander; Admiral Erich Raeder, earlier chief of the German navy; Baldur van Schirach, leader of the Hitler Youth organizations; Albert Speer, Minister of Armaments; and Constantin von Neurath, who had governed occupied Bohemia and Moravia. Hjalmar Schacht, head of the economic sector until 1939, was acquitted, as were Franz van Papen of the foreign service, and Hans Frizsche, who had headed Goebbels' radio division. Martin Bormann, who had not been found, was sentenced to death in *absentia.* In a last-minute act of defiance, Goering escaped the hangman by means of a long-hidden cyanide capsule.

FURTHER TRIALS

The Nuremberg Tribunal laid down the parameters for many other trials. Some were conducted during the Allied military occupation, such as the SS doctors, but as soon as the Germans organized their own courts, they brought Nazis to justice. The penalties they handed down were generally more severe than those of the International Court. As the nationals who had suffered under German domination reestablished their judiciaries, they indicted and tried the men who had committed crimes in their countries. The same was true of native collaborators with the Nazis. For example, the infamous commandant of the Auschwitz camps, Rudolf Hoess, was sentenced to death by a Polish court, and Hitler's puppet in Norway, Vidkun Quisling, was tried and shot in Oslo. Soviet Union judges handed down numerous death sentences against Nazi criminals within their jurisdiction. The most notorious Nazi to stand before the bar was Adolf Eichmann. He had been one of the major criminals to carry out the Final Solution and had escaped to South America in 1945. After years of pursuit, he was located by Israeli agents who smuggled him out of Argentina. At the conclusion of his spectacular trial, an Israeli court condemned him to death in 1960.

THE WESTERN MILITARY ZONES

It was relatively simple to outlaw the NSDAP and its accessory organizations and to arrest their leaders. Men who had volunteered for the SS, Gestapo, and SD, or held high office in the Third Reich, were identified, removed from their positions, and charged with crimes if the evidence warranted. But to fill positions that required public confidence with men and women who had not been Nazis was extremely difficult. Precisely what was the definition of a Nazi? Many organizations had been incorporated into the Party without consent of its members. Employment in numerous occupations had required Party membership. Advancement in business, industry, and the civil service usually had required the telltale swastika pin in one's lapel. Hitler Youth enrollment had been virtually coerced; artists, writers, and musicians had found it nearly impossible to obtain work without NSDAP affiliation; and the list goes on and on. If de-Nazification were to be enforced in the broadest definition, then who would be left to restore civic and economic life in Germany? A distinction needed to be made between nominal and active Nazis.

In October of 1946, the Allied Control Council tried to solve the dilemma by establishing categories of Nazis that ranged from major offender, offender, lesser offender, and follower to the exonerated. Adults in the Western zones were ordered to register and complete a lengthy questionnaire, the *Fragebogen.* The responses to 131 questions, as well as other documents, were used as criteria for positions of public trust and/or possible indictment. German courts, conducted by known anti-Nazis, aided in the processing of millions of people. It was fortunate that Hitler ruled Germany for only 12 years, and some retired jurists were available to participate in the cleanup. According to a 1950 report by the U.S. High Commissioner for Germany, General Lucius D. Clay, in the American zone 27 percent of the adult population, more then 13 million people, were registered as a prelude to further investigation. That number was reduced by amnesties for the very young, the very poor, for returning prisoners of war, and several other categories. But nearly a million ex-Nazis were tried, often accused by people from their own communities. Sentences were imposed, which ranged from execution to the payment of fines. The commanders of the French and English zones followed their own, but similar methods to eliminate Nazis from responsible positions and conducted trials as warranted. According to the conclusions of historians in the field, the most thorough de-Nazification was completed in the Soviet zone.

It is not possible to know just how many Nazi criminals escaped their punishment. Even the German Federal Republic, which pursued the guilty with great diligence, could not prevent the infiltration of prominent ex-Nazis into the ranks of its government. Even now the files on the prosecution of leading Nazis are still open, but of course, old age and death are fast overtaking justice.

GERMANY AND THE JEWS TODAY

It would be absurd to claim that the punishments meted out compensated for, or even fit, the crime of genocide. Perhaps we can take some solace from the fact that it appears that the German people have turned their backs on totalitarianism. Germany, made *Judenrein* in 1945, today has a vibrant Jewish presence. Hebrew prayers rise from synagogues, and Jewish day schools echo with young voices. And some people say that history is a rational study. . . .

As we noted, Germany under occupation had drifted into two states, East and West. As the Cold War underwent a thaw, the reunification of East and West Germany was accomplished on October 3, 1990. The Berlin Wall, which had separated the political as well the physical parts of Berlin, had been the symbol of the gulf between the two Germanys. When in 1989, people on both sides tore it down, literally stone by stone, and embraced one another, it heralded *die Wende,* the turning point.

The government of the present-day German republic is democratic, and we may infer that its leaders carry out the wishes of the majority of its citizens. Their newfound autonomy presented them with a choice in dealing with their Nazi past: Blame the Nazi crimes on "a few madmen" and allow the ordinary citizen to deny culpability, or accept the fact that nearly all Germans must bear some blame for the horrors inflicted by the regime. Put in a different context the question was this: Shall we whitewash our past or shall we accept the guilt? The notion that "all but a few of us were also victims of the Nazis" had obvious appeal, but in its official voice, the Germans refused to take that road. The members of the government decided to use unvarnished history, indeed, the truth, as a lesson for the future.

What evidence can be presented to confirm such an assessment? Actually, a great deal. Most convincing is the revival of Jewish life in Germany. At this time about 200,000 Jews live in Germany; most came as immigrants from parts of the former Soviet Union. This group constitutes the fastest-growing minority population in Europe. They have recreated a vibrant Jewish life in places that Hitler had pronounced to be *Judenrein.* Synagogues have been rebuilt at government expense, Jewish day schools receive government support, or the children may attend public schools. A new generation of Jews the majority of whom emigrated from the Soviet Union, calls Germany its homeland. If they are unhappy there, they need not stay, Israel would gladly bid them welcome.

Facing the Past

German children learn early and often about their country's Nazi crimes. The lessons are presented with an honesty that must make their grandparents cringe. Academic studies of the Holocaust are reenforced with field trips to the sites of mass murder. One cannot visit Dachau or Auschwitz without meeting classes of German children and their teachers. The success of these educational programs can be measured by the fact that several top universities now offer doctoral degrees in Judaic Studies.

Even the vaunted army has not been spared its share of disgrace. For decades after the end of the war, most Germans believed that their military forces had played no part in the murder of civilians. But that illusion was shattered by an exhibit of photographs called *Crimes of the Wehrmacht.* Graphic pictures proved that members of the regular army had participated in the roundups and in the shooting of civilians. The success of the exposition amazed its curators as nearly a million Germans filed through the gallery and viewed the pictures in shocked silence.

German municipalities have erected and maintain many Holocaust memorials. Every city has a plaque or a museum or a sculpture to recall its own lost Jews. Large communities may have dozens of reminders; in Berlin, huge tablets stand in the streets with the inscription: LEST WE FORGET, followed by the names of concentration camps. Many synagogues that had been destroyed during *Kristallnacht* have been repaired and serve as educational centers and/or houses of worship. The magnificent dome of Berlin's once grand *Neue Synagoge* has been restored, and since 1995, the facility is used as a research center. The site of the Wannsee Conference has been turned into an archive of shame. More recently, a remarkable museum has opened in the center of the German capital. This rather strange-looking building, with its slanting walls and uneven floors, expresses in steel and cement the sense of loss caused by the Nazi tragedy and seeks to balance that grief with the remembrance of German Jewish achievements in the more distant past. This, the Jewish Museum of Berlin, designed by the architect Daniel Libeskind, opened its doors in September of 2001. Its major focus is educational; Germans are reminded that the Holocaust is one but not the only connecting link between German Jews and Christians.

Anti-Nazi Laws

The German legislature has enacted persuasive evidence that it is the will of the people to reverse their xenophobic past. It is illegal to deny the Holocaust, to publish anti-Semitic books or articles, or to exhibit Nazi paraphernalia in public. Anti-Jewish remarks by politicians are punished by expulsion from their party. Financial restitution continues to be paid to Holocaust survivors and the state of Israel. While no one claims that money can atone for past crimes, these reparations continue to aid the Israeli economy and many aging survivors.

The governments of Germany and Israel have entered into a special relationship of support and friendship. Aside from the United States, the next largest contingent of visitors to the Jewish State is from Germany, and treaties of cooperation and

Berlin street scene. The words above the names of the concentration camp warn: PLACES OF HORROR WHICH WE MUST NEVER FORGET.
(Leonard Botwinick.)

trade have been concluded. As early as 1951 the President of Germany, Richard von Weizaecker, set the tone when he said:

> The Federal Government and with it the majority of the German people are aware of the immeasurable suffering that was brought upon Jews in Germany and in the occupied territories. . . . Unspeakable crimes have been committed in the name of the German people calling for moral and material indemnity.

In the same year Chancellor Konrad Adenauer stated that Germany could not become a respected member in the family of nations until it had recognized and proven its will to make amends.

For a fitting voice to conclude this text, we turn once more to Richard von Weizaecker. On the occasion of the first visit to Germany by a President of Israel, Chaim Herzog, in 1987, he made these comments:

> The fact that you are the first president of the State of Israel to visit our country makes this a most outstanding event in the history of our two peoples. . . . Official intergovernmental contacts are normal and rest on firm foundations. Practical cooperation is broad ranging and is borne by a spirit of mutual trust. But besides the intergovernmental relations there are human beings with feelings. We cannot simply put them on the same level. No Israeli can meet a German without recalling the suffering of the Jews under National Socialism. . . . There can be no forgetting the Holocaust. . . . We must be honest with one another and that means first of all being honest in our recollection of the past. Only in this way can a credible and lasting relationship grow between the generations who at that time had not been born and who, today and tomorrow, will have to live and get along with one another in this one world.

Glossary and Abbreviations

Abwehr: German military counterintelligence.

Allied Control Commission: Organization of senior administrators of the military zones of postwar Germany.

Appell: Roll call, often lasting hours, used in concentration camps.

Aktion: Nazi operation involving the deportation and/or killing of Jews.

Anschluss: German annexation of Austria, March 1938.

Aryanization: Nazis force Jewish businessmen to sell to Aryans at bargain prices.

Bermuda Conference: Anglo–U.S. conference, which failed to solve the refugee problem, April 1943.

Boycott: Nazi discourage German public to stop all economic dealings with Jews, April 1933.

Bund: Anti-Zionist Jewish socialist party, originated in Poland.

CV: *Centralverein deutscher Staatsbuerger juedisches Glaubens,* Union of Jewish citizens of Germany.

De-Nazification: Removal of Nazis from important positions by the Allies at the end of the war.

Der Stuermer: *The Attacker;* Julius Streicher's violently anti-Jewish weekly newspaper.

Displaced Persons (DPs): Europeans made homeless by the Nazis or as a result of World War II.

Displaced Persons' Camp: Facilities, often former concentration camps, used to house displaced persons in the military zones.

Einsatzgruppen: Mobile killing units of SS and SD members used mainly in Poland and Russia.

Endloesung: See Final Solution.

Evian Conference: International conference held in 1938, which failed to alleviate the refugee problem.

Final Solution: Nazi plan to solve Jewish problem by annihilation.

Fuehrerprinzip: Leadership principle; Nazi concept that all power is in the hands of the totalitarian leader.

Gauleiter: Nazi administrative leader in a *Gau,* or district.

General Government: Western Polish territory conquered by Germany and administered by Hans Frank.

Genocide: The partial or total destruction of a racial, religious, or national group.

Gestapo: *Geheime Staatspolizei,* Nazis' secret state police.

Gleichschaltung: Consolidation of all political activities and nonpolitical organizations under Nazi dictatorship.

Judenrat: Jewish council of elders, used by Germans in ghetto administration.

Judenrein: Cleansed of Jews; Nazi policy of removal of Jews.

Kapo: Prisoner in a concentration camp who was in charge of other inmates.

Kristallnacht: Night of broken glass, pogrom carried out between November 9–10, 1938, in Greater Germany.

Lager: Camp, as in concentration or death camp.

Lebensborn: Himmler's program of increasing Aryan population.

Lebensraum: Room to live, euphemism for German policy of expansion.

Madagascar Plan: Briefly considered notion by Germany to ship four million Jews to the island of Madagascar.

Maquis: French anti-Nazi guerrilla fighting organization during World War II.

Mischlinge: Nazi classification for people of Jewish–Christian parentage.

Mein Kampf: *My Struggle,* book by Adolf Hitler, which outlined his program.

Munich Agreement: Appeasement policy of England and France, which permitted Hitler to take part of Czechoslovakia.

Musselman: Term denoting a concentration camp prisoner who had given up the struggle to stay alive.

NSDAP: *Nationalsozialistische Deutsche Arbeiterpartei,* National Socialist German Workers' Party, the Nazi Party.

Nuremberg Laws: German legislation, which deprived Jews of citizenship rights, passed in 1938.

Nuremberg Trials: An international military tribunal that tried 22 Nazi leaders, 19 were found guilty of war crimes.

Pogrom: Organized violence directed against Jews.

Protocols of the Elders of Zion: Anti-Semitic book, a forgery claiming existence of an international plot by Jews to attain world domination.

Putsch: Attempted coup d'état.

Righteous of the Nations or Righteous Gentiles: Non-Jews who saved Jewish lives during the Holocaust.

RSHA: *Reichssicherheitshauptamt,* Central German Security Department under the Nazis.

SA: *Sturmabteilung,* the Brownshirts; Nazi political storm troopers.

SS: *Schutzstaffel,* the Blackshirts; elite of Nazi storm troopers.

Shtetl: Eastern European town or village with large Jewish population.

Third Reich: Germany under the Nazis.

Umschlagplatz: Assembly place for deportees, usually at rail junctions.

Wannsee Conference: Meeting of Nazi leaders in 1942, which confirmed the implementation of the Final Solution.
War Refugee Board: U.S. government special agency to rescue and aid victims of Nazi persecution.
Wehrmacht: German armed forces.
World Jewish Congress: A voluntary association of major Jewish organizations.
Yad Vashem: Israeli authority of commemoration and research on the Holocaust.
ZOB: *Zydowska Organizacja Bojowa,* Jewish fighting organization in Poland, active in Warsaw ghetto uprising.

Time Line

1920	Hitler announced NSDAP program in Munich
1921	SA organized
1923	Failure of the Hitler/Ludendorff Beer Hall Putsch
1924	Nazi Party won 6.4 percent of votes in Reichstag elections
1925	*Mein Kampf* published
1928	Nazi Party won 2.5 percent of votes in Reichstag elections
1929	Joseph Goebbels made chief of propaganda for NSDAP
1930	Nazi Party won 18 percent of votes in Reichstag elections
1931	Hitler lost presidential election to Paul von Hindenburg
1932	Hitler granted German citizenship
1933	Hitler appointed Chancellor by Hindenburg
	The Reichstag fire and subsequent emergency powers given to Hitler
	Dachau concentration camp opened; SS organized
	Adoption of Enabling Act gave Hitler totalitarian power
	Boycott of Jewish businesses and professionals
	Gleichschaltung consolidated political, social, and economic institutions
	Gestapo organized
	Jews ousted from government position
	Books deemed undesirable or dangerous burnt
	Concordat between papacy and Germany signed
1934	Germany and Poland signed 10-year nonaggression pact
	Heinrich Himmler appointed acting chief of the Gestapo
	Blood purge (Night of the Long Knives) carried out
	Death of Hindenburg; Hitler assumed title of Fuehrer

	Plebiscite confirms Hitler's new role; nearly 90 percent voted yes
1935	Military conscription enacted; Jews barred from military
	Nuremberg Laws deprived Jews of rights of citizenship
	Definition of who is a Jew or *Mischling*
1936	Rome–Berlin Axis formed
	Jewish doctors forbidden to practice
	Sachsenhausen concentration camp opened
1937	Buchenwald concentration camp opened
	Hitler nullified Treaty of Versailles
1938	Austrian *Anschluss* accomplished
	Jews must register ownership of all property
	Munich Appeasement by France and Great Britain
	Deportation of Polish Jews from Germany
	Hershel Grynzpan killed vom Rath in Paris followed by Crystal Night pogrom; Jews fined one billion marks
	Aryanization of Jewish businesses
	Jewish children expelled from German schools
1939	Molotov–Ribbentrop nonagression pact signed
	German invasion of Poland; start of the Second World War
	Poland defeated
	Establishment of Polish ghettos begun; Polish Jews must wear identifying stars
	Jews expelled from Vienna
1940	Germans conquered Norway, Denmark, the Netherlands, Belgium, and France
	The Battle of Britain began
	Japan joined Axis powers
	Italy invaded Greece and required Germans to come to her aid
	The Warsaw ghetto was sealed off
1941	The war spreads to the Balkans
	Deputy Fuehrer Rudolf Hess landed in Scotland; Martin Borman named his successor
	Germany attacked the USSR
	Himmler opened Maidanek, Sobibor, and Auschwitz camps
	German Jews sent to Eastern concentration and death camps
	Pearl Harbor attacked by Japan; Germany declared war on United States
1942	Wannsee Conference confirmed Final Solution to the Jewish question

	First use of gas in Auschwitz, Belzec, and Sobibor
	French, Belgian, Dutch, Croatian, Greek, Norwegian, and German Jews sent to Polish ghettos and death camps
	Battle of Stalingrad ended German advance into USSR
	Jewish resistance organizations formed
1943	Warsaw Ghetto revolt
	Italy surrendered to Allies
	Revolt of Auschwitz prisoners
	Rescue of Danish Jews
1944	D-Day landings of Allied armies established a second front in Europe
	Attempt to assassinate Hitler failed
	Nazis began deportation of Hungarian Jews
	Death marches of remaining concentration camp survivors
	Allies defeated German troops in Eastern and Western offensives
1945	Russian and Western Allies' armies joined near Berlin
	Hitler, Goebbels, and Himmler commit suicide
	Concentration camp inmates freed by Allied soldiers
	VE Day proclaimed on May 8
	VJ Day marked end of war in Pacific theater on August 14
	DP camps established in Germany
1946	International War Crimes Tribunal, Nuremberg

Bibliography and Selected Readings

The amount of material on the Holocaust is massive, and the following books represent a small selection. The rationale for including a book while excluding hundreds of other excellent works was based on these factors: (1) most students read English only, thus the research published in other languages is not useful; (2) most books on Holocaust history contain further bibliographies; a long list here is likely to be redundant; and (3) the books catalogued in the following sections are based on recommendations by students and the author of this text.

PRIMARY READINGS

Aly, Goetz, *Final Solution: Nazi Population Policy and the Murder of European Jews.* Trans. from German by Allison Brown. London: Arnold, 1999.

Anger, Per, *With Raoul Wallenberg in Budapest.* Trans. by David Mel Paul and Margarita Paul. New York: Holocaust Library, 1981.

Arad, Yitzhak, Yisrael Gutman, Abraham Margialot, eds., *Documents on the Holocaust.* Jerusalem: Yad Vashem, 1981.

Botwinick, Rita Steinhardt, ed., *A Holocaust Reader From Ideology to Annihilation.* Upper Saddle River, NJ: Prentice Hall, 1997.

Botwinick, Rita, *Winzig, Germany* 1933–1946. *The History of a Town Under the Third Reich.* Westport, CT: Praeger, 1992.

Brostoff, Anita, ed., *Flares of Memory: Stories of Childhood during the Holocaust.* Oxford, N.Y.: Oxford University Press, 2001.

Browning, Christopher R., *Ordinary Men: Reserve Battalion 101 and the Final Solution in Poland.* New York: Harper Perennial, 1998.

Engelmann, Bert, *In Hitler's Germany: Daily Life in the Third Reich.* Trans. by Krishna Winston. New York: Pantheon Books, 1986.

Gay, Peter, *Growing Up in Nazi Berlin.* New Haven, CT: Yale University Press, 1998.

Hallie, Philip, *Lest Innocent Blood Be Shed: The Story of Le Chambon and How Goodness Happened There.* New York: Harper Torchbooks, 1979.

Heck, Alphons, *A Child of Hitler.* Fredrick CO: Renaissance House, 1985.

Hitler, Adolf, *Mein Kampf.* Trans. by Ralph Manheim. Boston: Houghton Mifflin, 1943.

Korczak, Janus, *Ghetto Diary.* New York: Holocaust Library, 1978.

Laska, Vera, *Women in the Resistance and in the Holocaust, The Voices of Eyewitnesses.* Westport, CT: Greenwood Press, 1983.

Levi, Primo, *Survival in Auschwitz: The Nazi Assault on Humanity.* Trans. by Stuart Woolf. New York: Collier, 1966.

Mayer, Bernard, *Entombed My True Story: How Forty-Five Jews Lived Underground and Survived the Holocaust.* Ojus, FL: Aleric Press, 1994.

Meed, Vladka, *On Both Sides of the Wall.* New York: Summit Books, 1986.

Mosse, George L., ed., *Nazi Culture.* New York: Schocken Books, 1981.

Noakes, J. and G. Pridham, eds., *Nazism: A History in Documents and Eyewitness Accounts.* Vols. 1–2. New York: Schocken Books, 1990.

Remack, Joachim, ed., *The Nazi Years: A Documentary History.* Prospect Heights, IL: Wavelength Press, Inc., 1990.

Ritter, Carol, and Sondra Myers, *The Courage to Care, Rescuers of Jews During the Holocaust.* New York: New York University, 1986.

Rubinstein, Erna E., *The Survivor in Us All: Four Young Sisters in the Holocaust.* Hamden CT: The Shoe String Press, 1983.

Salvaged Pages: Young Writers' Dairies of the Holocaust. Collected and edited by Alexandra Zapruder. New Haven: Yale University Press, 2002.

Tec, Nechama, *When Light Pierced the Darkness: Christian Rescue of Jews in Poland.* New York: Oxford University Press, 1986.

Wiesel, Eli, *Night.* Trans. by S. Rodway. New York: Bantam Books, 1960.

SECONDARY READINGS

Ainsztein, Ruben, *The Warsaw Ghetto Revolt.* New York: Holocaust Library, 1979.

Allport, Gordon W., *The Nature of Prejudice.* Reading, MA: Addison Publication Co., 1986.

Astor, Gerald, *The Last Nazi: The Life and Times of Dr. Joseph Mengele.* New York: Donald I. Fine, Inc., 1985.

Borowski, Tadeus, *This Way for the Gas, Ladies and Gentlemen.* Trans. by Barbara Vedder. New York: Penguin Books, 1959.

Breitman, Richard, *The Architect of Genocide. Himmler and the Final Solution.* New York: Alfred A. Knopf, 1991.

Donat, Alexander, *The Holocaust Kingdom.* New York: Holocaust Library, 1978.

Eyck, Eric, *A History of the Weimar Republic.* Vols 1 and 2. Trans. by H. P. Hanson and R. G. L. Waite. New York: Antheneum, 1970.

Fest, Joachim, *Inside Hitler's Bunker: The Last Days of the Third Reich.* New York: Farrar, Straus, and Giroux, 2004.

Friedlander, Albert H., ed., *Out of the Whirlwind.* New York: Schocken Books, 1976.

Furet, François, *Unanswered Questions: Nazi Germany and the Genocide of the Jews.* New York: Schocken Books, 1989.

Gilbert, Martin, *Auschwitz and the Allies.* New York: Henry Holt and Company, 1981.

Gross, Leonard, *The Last Jews of Berlin.* New York: Simon and Schuster, 1982.

Gutman, Ysrael, *The Jews of Warsaw.* Bloomington, IN: Indiana University Press, 1982.

Herf, Jeffrey, *Divided Memory: The Nazi Past in Two Germanys.* Cambridge and London: Harvard University Press, 1997.

Hoehne, Heinz, *The Order of the Death's Head.* Trans. by Martin Seeker & Warburg Limited. Hamburg: Verlag der Spiegel, 1966.

Katz, Jacob, *From Prejudice to Destruction, Anti-Semitism, 1700–1933.* Cambridge, MA: Harvard University Press, 1980.

Lipstadt, Deborah, *Denying The Holocaust: The Growing Assault On Truth and Memory.* New York, N.Y.: Plume, 1994.

Lifton, Robert, Jay, *The Nazi Doctors, Medical Killings and the Psychology of Genocide.* Scranton, PA: Harper Collins Publishers, 1986.

Marrus, Michael, and Robert O. Paxton, "The Nazis and the Jews in Western Occupied Europe 1940–1944." *Journal of Modem History*, 54, New York: Basic Books, 1981.

Mueller, Ingo, *The Courts of the Third Reich.* Trans. by Deborah Lucas Schneider. Cambridge: Harvard University Press, 1993.

Novitch, Miriam, *Sobibor, Martyrdom and Revolt.* New York: Waldon Press, 1980

Patai, Raphael, *The Vanished World of Jewry.* New York: Macmillan Publishing Co. Inc., 1980.

Roth, John K., and Michael Berenbaum, eds., *Holocaust: Religious and Philosophical Implications.* New York: Paragon House, 1989.

Stoltzfus, Nathan, *Resistance of the Heart, Intermarriage and the Rosenstrasse Protest in Nazi Germany.* New Brunswick, NJ: Rutgers University Press, 1996.

Tusa, Ann, and John Tusa, *The Nuremberg Trial.* New York: Antheneum, 1986.

Vincent, Isabel, *Hitler's Silent Partners.* New York: William Horrow and Company, 1997.

Waite, Robert L., *The Psychopathic God: Adolf Hitler.* New York: Basic Books, 1977.

Wyman, David S., *The Abandonment of the Jews: America and the Holocaust, 1941–1945.* New York: Random House, 1984.

Zuccotti, Susan, *The Italians and The Holocaust.* New York: Basic Books, 1987.

SELECTED WEBSITES

BBC's History on the Holocaust
http://www.st.-edmunds.cam.ac.uk

German Website on the Shoah
http://www.st.-edmunds.cam.ac.uk

The Imperial War Museum Holocaust Exhibition
http://www.1wm.org/lameth/holoc-ex1.htm

Jewish Museum in Berlin
http://www.jmberlin.de

PBS Holocaust Website
http://www.pbs.org/holocaust

Simon Wiesenthal Museum of Tolerance
http://motlc.wiesenthal.com

The Women of the Holocaust
http://www.interlog.com/~mighty

United States Holocaust Museum
http://www.usamm.org

Index

F

G